Ego Psychology and Communication

The Author

NORMAN A. POLANSKY is Professor of Social Work and Sociology at the University of Georgia. He received his A.B. from Harvard, his M.S. from Case Western Reserve University, and his Ph.D. in social psychology from the University of Michigan. Dr. Polansky's career has included teaching, research, and clinical work as an individual therapist, group therapist, caseworker, and supervisor. Well known in his field, Dr. Polansky is the editor of *Social Work Research* and the Director of the University of Georgia's Child Research Field Station, which studies low-income families in rural southern Appalachia. He has been Chairman of the Research Station and a member of the board of directors of the National Association of Social Workers and a director of the American Orthopsychiatric Association. Dr. Polansky's contributions to scholarly publications include some fifty papers in the areas of social work research, group dynamics, group therapy, and processes of communication in the treatment situation.

Ego Psychology and Communication

Theory for the Interview

Norman A. Polansky

ATHERTON PRESS
New York · 1971

To the Carbondale Polanskys

Celia K.
Joseph J.
Adele L.
G. R. Vaughn
Jonathan R.
Nancy F.

Address all inquiries to:
Atherton Press, Inc.
70 Fifth Avenue
New York 10011

Library of Congress Catalog Card Number: 74-116533
FIRST EDITION
Manufactured in the United States of America

Preface

My intention has been to bring together what seem to me to be the most important ideas and phenomena relevant to verbal communication by patients in clinical interviews. I found that in order to discuss communication meaningfully it was first necessary to provide the reader with basic elements of modern ego psychology. Therefore, this is a book about ego psychology and communication or, better, verbal communication in the light of ego psychology.

The sources for such a book are many, as befits any project attempting a selection out of a wide and diverse subject matter. I have drawn on what I was taught and, of course, on what I have continued to read, and on the shrewd observations of friends and colleagues which they have shared with me. Most important, however, I have tried to write of principles whose relevance to helping clients and patients through talking treatment has passed the test of my own direct experience as a researcher and a clinician. We are beyond the point at which it is enough that an idea be fascinating and have potential. There is, by now, a lot of solid information about why people behave as they do. The needs of our clients and patients are too urgent to permit dithering with doctrine. We need theory that works.

We also need theory that reduces rather than compounds the complexity in nature. It has seemed to me for some time that major simplicities are finally emerging out of the welter of ideas which burgeoned in the last four decades of behavioral science, and that these should be placed before our students early in their training. While trying not to overestimate the degree to which parsimonious formulations are yet possible, I have tried to represent here syntheses among concepts and principles which I have found useful. Some of these bridge fields usually treated independently in the literature. It is my hope that the connections I have traced will provide the student a context in which to grasp more of the whole.

I have been advised that a writer is wise to have a particular audience in mind as he writes, and I believe it. The group—or groups—for whom this was written are: students of social work, particularly those in the first year of graduate work or the senior undergraduate year; advanced undergraduate and first-year graduate students in psychology, sociology, educational counseling and guidance, psychiatric nursing; and professional colleagues in social work, psychology, and psychiatry who may be generally familiar with the area covered here, but who may be interested in a new view and an overview of how theory has advanced since their own formal training.

The book will serve as an introduction to ego psychology. It assumes practically no background to begin with, and advances gradually in difficulty in the later chapters. Ego psychology, however, is an area of enormous boundaries; it cannot be encompassed in one volume. Therefore, I have deliberately limited the discussion to those aspects of ego psychology of most direct relevance to appraising verbal communication, especially in the casework interview, the therapy hour, the counseling session, and group treatment situations. Although I have tried to avoid "the textbook style" of exposition, this is, in fact, intended as a text. It offers those elements of theory I believe basic for those who seek to understand and treat the human personality through speech. The book is my synthesis of the theory underlying skilled clinical interviewing.

It is my hope that the student will be encouraged to go forward in acquiring a more elaborate understanding of what is here written about, and for this the References for each chapter will serve as a guide to original sources for further reading. It has also been my hope that while the student will still have much to learn after finishing this book, not much of what I have given him will have to be unlearned. The rest, of course, is up to him, and to his teacher.

It is pleasant, now, to thank some of those who were influential teachers in my own life, whether or not each would accept responsibility for what I have written: the late Gordon Allport, scholar and truly Christian gentleman and my lifelong role-model for psychology; the late, great Kurt Lewin; Fritz Redl, whose obstinate unstuffiness extended also to the psychoanalytic movement; Ronald Lippitt, teacher, good friend, dauntless in research attack on the sloppy, meaningful problems of our time. Sidney Berkowitz taught me casework in the beginning, and John D. Patton was a supportive and able supervisor of psychotherapy. I have benefited from working on the same staffs with such others as Benjamin Lyndon, Jacob Kounin, Selma Fraiberg, David Rapaport, Erik Erikson, Leon Festinger, James Mann, Esther Clemence, Alfred Khan— I wish I could list all the distinguished friends and colleagues of a lifetime of good luck in acquaintanceship in the fields of psychology, social work, and psychiatry. Many of my gifted students' names appear in the various References in this volume, often in publication of work undertaken jointly. They will recognize their contributions to my thinking, I am sure.

My friend, Howard Parad, has acted as the publisher's editorial consultant for this book and has, as always, done what needed to be done with intelligence, conscientiousness, and humor. I am grateful to Marlene Mandel, and the Atherton Press, for support in bringing this book into being. My old and dear friends Donald and Laura Boone have helped in numerous ways; Elizabeth Harkins delightedly gave permission for me to use our joint paper on psychodrama as Chapter 11; Margaret Jewett has typed and retyped the various drafts, correcting my grammar as she did so; Charles Gershenson and the Children's Bureau have provided research support which partly made time available, as have Charles Stewart of the School of Social Work, and the Office of General Research, of the University of Georgia; Ernest Witten, M.D., has seen to keeping me fit to work. And without my wife, Nancy Finley Polansky, I should neither be, nor wish to be, undertaking major projects toward the future.

Chapters 8–11 have been revised and adapted from previously published papers. Acknowledgment is gratefully made to the following publishers and individuals for permission to include these papers. *Smith College Studies in Social Work,* "The Concept of Verbal Accessibility," vol. 36, pp. 1–48, 1965. *American Journal of Orthopsychiatry,* "On Duplicity in the Interview," "Verbal Accessibility and Fusion Fantasy in a Mountain County" (with Sara Q. Brown), vol. 37, pp. 568–579, 652–654, 1967; copyright, the American Orthopsychiatric Association, Inc. *Psychiatry,* "Psychodrama as an Element in Hospital Treatment" (with Elizabeth B. Harkins), vol. 32, pp. 74–87, 1969. To Grace Ganter and Margaret Yeakel and the Child Welfare League of America for permission to draw from our monograph, *Retrieval from Limbo,* 1957. To Faber & Faber and Harcourt, Brace & World, Inc., for permission to reprint lines from "The Love Song of J. Alfred Prufrock" and "Whispers of Immortality," *Collected Poems 1909–1962* by T. S. Eliot, copyright 1936, by Harcourt, Brace & World, Inc.; copyright © 1963, 1964, by T. S. Eliot.

Contents

Chapter 1

Scientific Method and Ego Psychology

IT IS PRESUMED THROUGHOUT THE FOLLOWING PAGES THAT a theory about why people act and feel as they do is worth learning. It is worth learning because it can be used to bring about important changes in the lives of patients and clients, in their all-too-real worlds. In my experience, not too many students in the helping professions really believe that the learning of concepts and laws is worthwhile. One could accuse them of being too concrete-minded to take in such subject matter, but usually this is not the reason for their reluctance. Rather, they have been rendered sensitive and then allergic by undergraduate courses of the wrong sort.

In too many courses, psychological theories are treated as pawns with which academicians play mental chess. Their students are required to learn the rules in order to know when to applaud—and how to pass examinations. Some young people prove gifted at weaving concepts into peculiarly provocative incantations of turgid prose; they are encouraged to go on into fields dedicated to training more

1

undergraduates to pass more examinations. People who want to make things happen in the real world are not typically that fascinated with their own thought processes, as such. They enter such fields as social work or clinical psychology with the thought of trying to do some good in their own lifetimes. And here we await them, once again urging them to take an interest in "theory." Is there more than one way to go about the building of theory in psychology? If there is, what criteria do *we* use in selecting theories for practice?

The Role of Theory

To answer these questions, let us begin with the aim of the game. *The aim of theory in the helping professions is to improve our ability to control events.* I will assume that anyone who involves himself in a clinical profession has a desire to ease the lot of others and to make them happier. This is one reason we should like to be able to exercise control. There is another reason, which becomes the more pressing as one matures in the field, and it has to do with pride of workmanship. We, too, would like to construct bridges in the lives of our clients and remark with satisfaction their ability to bear weight. Unless we are unlucky, our ability to do so gradually increases with experience in the work, with or without a formal knowledge of theory. The effect of a really good theory, however, is to put succinctly at the student's disposal much of what generations preceding his have been able to glean. There is no substitute for experience in the development of a first-rate practitioner; there is also no reason the student should not avail himself of all the knowledge he can get from the experience of others.

Theory that markedly increases our ability to make things happen has certain characteristics. First, it helps us to predict. Second, it simplifies our lives. After a quarter century in the field, I find this a most pleasant sentence to be able to write. Once again, however, I doubt it is believable. The student usually finds himself foundering under a mass of precepts, injunctions, formulations, half-digested facts, not to mention agency policies and regulations. It is hard to image that this is about to simplify his life. Before he entered graduate school, the student used to have conversations with people, and he enjoyed them. Indeed, he was not lying when he said on his application that he wanted to be in social work, for example, because he liked people. Now that he is conducting *interviews,* however, he feels uncertain; he is tongue-tied, he makes furtive notes (written and mental), he watches the client like an Indian snake charmer. He cannot wait for the end of the hour, and neither can the client. To the weight of responsibility which he already carries, all he needs to add is some "theory."

Yet we know that an interview is a conversation with a purpose, and this makes a crucial difference. It is not forbidden that client and worker enjoy their conversation, but immediate enjoyment is not enough. Something useful is supposed to come of it (not that it always will, no matter how long you work in our field!). The practitioner's task is to make something happen merely by talking. He must know on which conversational keys to play, which to let alone. Above all, he has to know what to attend to in watching the client and in listening to him. There are myriad facts, after all, from the client's age, to her hair color, to her mother's depression at age forty-one. Which facts matter? More precisely, which matter the most if one wishes to help her? We need a precise basis for judging relevance. Let us face it: raw reality is simply chaotic. Therefore, a cardinal aim of a good theory must be *to reduce the chaos of raw experience.*

The sequence by which clarification occurs is straightforward. A good theory consists of a series of statements that are actually dependable predictions. If A happens, B will follow—if not always, at least usually; if not immediately, eventually; if not at all, for good reason. Let us call A the *cause,* and B the *effect.* A clinician who needs to produce a given effect will be alert to see whether he can introduce its cause. This is all we mean by a *planned interven-*

tion. Planned intervention requires *dynamic* theory—ultimately simply a network of highly dependable predictions.

Not all theories have this dynamic quality. For centuries people thought a scholar had nicely reduced the chaos of raw experience if he found a way to arrange ideas (usually), objects (often), and events (infrequently) into neat and mutually exclusive pigeonholes. I recall as an undergraduate being taught that there were three types of itinerants: the tramp, the hobo, and the migratory worker. Each type had his own characteristics, and I dutifully memorized the textbook definitions. Subsequently, I had some experiences which I doubt the writer of our textbook had ever had. I spent more than two years as a caseworker in civilian and military prisons; I interviewed "Veterans Administration bums" (inadequate personalities created by act of Congress); I worked in family agencies. Never did I find any use for the distinctions I had learned to help me with these men. Not one had taken a course in social pathology! In this way, I learned to distrust theory that is purely classificatory in its intent. While it may put to rest the obsessiveness within the textbook author, it does not ease the mind of the social worker confronted by a situation that demands action.

A *concept* is a term or symbol for a class of objects or events having something in common. Unfortunately, it is not at all difficult to invent concepts. Select two objects at random in the room and demonstrate to yourself that you too can think of an abstraction which will subsume both of them. It is similarly easy to erect systems of terminology which permit you to categorize types of people, expression, or behavior. We have all listened to the man who has managed to acquire age without wisdom as he says, "Basically, my friend, I find there are two kinds of people. . . ." (After seventy-five years, he still cannot count to three?)

Setting up idea systems for classifying is not hard. What is hard is to find a system for classifying that reflects regularities of occurrences in our world. For it is this dynamic theory that enhances our ability to predict and therefore to control the real world.

The Rule of Parsimony

A theory that will simplify rather than clutter our professional lives should be *parsimonious*. The rule of parsimony is meant to guide those who work at trying to adapt or create theory. It can briefly be summed up: the ideal is to encompass a maximal range of phenomena within a minimal number of statements.

During the Middle Ages, if one asked why water runs downhill, he would be answered in terms of the "essence" or the "idea" of water. He was told, in effect, "It is in the nature of water to run downhill." If Newton asked why an apple falls from a tree, he might be told also that it was in the nature of the apple to fall from trees. We owe it to the genius of Galileo and Newton that these many droppings were compressed into one principle, the Law of Gravity. At its more general level, the law covers not only falling bodies but also more universal phenomena. It states that there is an attraction between any two bodies, and that the attraction is inversely proportionate to the distance between the bodies, but directly proportionate to their masses. This is hardly a thought that, under ordinary circumstances, makes one wake up and shout with glee in the morning. But if you are in the business of making objects move through space—which seems to be one of mankind's morbid preoccupations—it is a convenient law to have. Certainly, it is simpler than memorizing a long list of objects, each of which has it "in his essence to run downhill."

A principle in psychology that has shown a rewarding capacity for reducing the chaos of nature is: *the organism will seek to re-establish internal equilibrium.* This principle is closely related to one found in physiology, Cannon's principle of *homeostasis.* Using the notion that the body seeks to re-establish the equilibrium it had before some insult or injury occurred to it, Cannon was able to explain a number of symptoms by offering a reason for their occurrence. Similar processes seem at work, by the way, in group psychology. What happens, for example, if you have a group of people closely bound to each other, and one is seized with an idea at variance with an attitude important to the others in the group? The first effort the group will make will be to pressure this individual to change his attitude and to think as the rest of the group. Should this fail, the group will eventually eject the person. In effect, they establish a group with little internal tension by redrawing their boundaries to contain only like-minded persons. Occasionally the majority will move its attitudes to resemble that of the deviant, but he must be *very* important to them for this to happen.

When we refer to individual reactions, we talk about *drive reduction* and *tension reduction*. These notions are but shorthand for saying the individual does what he does in order to achieve an equilibrium with minimal tension. More interesting, perhaps, is the manner in which psychological symptoms follow the same principles. A psychological symptom may seem extremely painful, but it too is dedicated to keeping the organism in a state of equilibrium which seems better with it than without it. Obviously, we have here a statement about human reactions which is extremely powerful in its ability to organize and simplify a broad range of things that happen. Would that we had many more of like potency!

The formulation of each new guiding principle in psychology seems to reflect an act of genius, and how it is done by a particular individual still remains something of a mystery. Something is known, however, about the approach a science should follow in order to lay the foundations for any major breakthrough. The rule of parsimony is generally accepted to be an essential part of the approach.

From the rule of parsimony we derive that one should never introduce a new hypothesis without examining whether an established one will not cover the case in point. We constantly hope to add generalizations, of course, if science is to cover more and more of the world about us, but the mood is to give ground stingily. When a new explanation is offered to fit one new instance, it is called an *ad hoc* hypothesis. Often it is just as it sounds—a notion volunteered on the spur of the moment to cover an unanticipated research finding.

While *ad hoc* hypotheses are particularly common in chapters of Conclusions in masters' theses, they are not unknown among scholars whose ideas are greeted more seriously. There was a psychologist named McDougall, for example, who was strongly convinced that all behavior is purposive—a notion now generally well accepted. He was also fascinated with the notion of instincts and when specific explanations of some behavior were called for, he was likely to offer an "instinct" as the explanation. It is from him and his confreres that we have such concepts as the maternal instinct, the paternal instinct, the filial instinct which still survive in literary psychology. Obviously, it does not greatly simplify life if, whenever we are faced with a pattern of human behavior, we ascribe it to a newly-coined "instinct." Freud, too, used the idea of basic instincts, but rather than proliferate them, he sought to determine the smallest number he had to postulate in order to explain all behavior. Eventually he settled on two: pleasure seeking or *libido,* and *aggression.* These are still widely accepted and used in analytic circles. Freud, however, seems to many of us to have speculated too far beyond his data when he offered the notions of *Eros* (life force) as opposed to *Thanatos* (the death instinct). One still occasionally sees references to "death wishes" in clinical as well as popular writings, but the general view of these conceptions is that they represent an instance in which the attempt to reach a high level of abstraction in order to synthesize theory did not succeed.

Scientists are Human

Science is a social undertaking. The systematic growth of knowledge is the most impressive monument to man we have thus far been able to erect. A contribution to this growth is considered by most scientists to be one of the few ways to defeat mortality. The task is inspiring, but it is given to men. Where there are many ambitious scientists, each struggling with an admixture of dedication and vanity, self-discipline and group discipline are absolutely essential. Only in this way can work be coordinated and grand simplicities emerge from buzzing confusion. The desire to discover a new principle that will be identified with one's name is enormous. It is countered by the rule of parsimony.

Much has been made about the historical splits, the secessions and ejections from the Orthodox Freudian movement. Left out, finally, were Adlerians, Jungians, Rankians, followers of Karen Horney, and others. Because the ideas represented by many of these great figures often foreshadowed what we now call ego psychology, a word is in order about this facet of psychoanalysis.

I have heard the events involved described as though Freud, the old bull of the herd, simply could not tolerate competition from the men about him. Whether or not this is true, there is more at stake, just as there is more to each of us than his toilet-training. Freud was rather insistent that the development of ego psychology not take precedence over the analysis of the id. By id, we refer in a general way to the great unconscious strivings, the primeval sources of energy and emotion of the personality. It was as if he feared that by tackling parts of the personality closer to the surface, frequently conscious, related to the current culture, psychoanalysis might shirk its more basic, more difficult task. Freud's insights were not at all popular, and there is always the danger a group of scientists will too readily re-repress the hard-won insights into the unconscious, because they are unpleasant.

Adler, for example, proposed as a major explanatory principle his notion of overcompensation for felt inferiority. Of this and kindred insights, Freud is said to have remarked, "There will always have to be a psychology for the Hausfrau, and Adler has created it." Indeed, the idea that a boy who puts on superior airs may be covering up deep feelings of inferiority is not unfamiliar to high school youngsters. It should not be necessary to travel to graduate school in order to learn a psychology which simply accords with common sense. For the truth is that common-sense psychology does not stand the test of parsimony; worse, common-sense psychology can usually contain only those explanations that the conscious mind can readily tolerate. It becomes my duty to record at this point, therefore, that the simplicity inherent in an elegant theory is a great convenience to the busy or even the slothful; but it does not open many doors to the simple-minded. So, one concern we must have about a system of theory is whether it offers the illusion of simplicity at the cost of failing to illuminate anything at all obscure.

No Adlerian analysts I have ever met impressed me as simple-minded, so I believe there was a more profound reason for their being read out of the analytic movement, one having to do more with how a science develops. In the early phases of building a theory, all is in flux—concepts to be employed, their definitions, basic assumptions, and so forth. From time to time, however, it becomes desirable that things be encouraged to settle down, at least temporarily. One has to say, "Let us agree to define the 'ego' as such-and-such for the next few years, and see where that leads us in our attempts to build theory."

The greatest difficulty the various schisms presented to the mainstream of psychoanalysis was that basic assumptions were constantly reopened to question, familiar terms were used with new nuances, new terms were being introduced seemingly *ad libidem*. For a newly emerging theory, the danger is always that the chaos within the science will come to match that within its subject matter. When that happens, one can say there has been absolutely no progress. Freud felt that a number of the schismatics were, in effect, pushing ideas that would make it unlikely for a parsimonious theory to emerge. Moreover, there had to be agreement on the terms to be employed.

No one man is able to do enough work in his lifetime to advance each of our sciences very far through his unassisted efforts. Even the prima donnas, and there are many, grant the need for cooperative effort. But, in order to cooperate, scientists must be able to agree on the meanings of the terms they are using. Only in this way can they communicate readily, and share their discoveries with one another. It is for this reason that we assess the *inter-observer reliability* of any instrument we use in research.

Inter-observer reliability represents the degree to which two or more observers, using the same method of observing, come up with similar pictures of the persons or groups they are studying. If agreement is great, inter-observer reliability is said to be high; if they disagree much of the time, it is said to be low or poor. This is no casual issue, for without reasonably high inter-observer reliability communication of results among colleagues becomes impossible. By the same token, it becomes impossible to add new results to the total of knowledge in the field.

We make this small digression into the logic of science in part to explain why the Freudian schismatics presented such a problem. After all, as we have remarked, they contributed mightily to what we now term ego psychology. Communicability is also at issue in the most strenuous criticisms leveled at psychoanalysis by followers of other theories. Once I even had an elder colleague challenge me, "What is this *anxiety* you practitioners prattle about?" Certainly, he would not know how to observe it, because he had never experienced any. Since he was, indeed, a rigidly well-defended man in poor physical condition, I saw no mercy in demonstrating anxiety for him, on the spot. But, if *he* does not find anxiety a sufficiently objective and observable phenomenon to be worth thinking about, is it necessary that we be able to communicate our results to him?

One of the requirements in beginning college biology was that we spy on various asexual organisms through the compound microscope. Alas, never did I catch sight of what the book said I should—nor amoeba, nor paramecium, nor anybody. Oh, I did see some pretty cloud formations and light-speckled water. Once, I still believe, I examined my own reflected retina. But never a paramecium. From my own experience, I should conclude that the compound microscope is really a fraud. Studies made with it are incapable of replication by other scientists, nor can they be communicated about.

The other possibility is that the test of communicability is not so gross. Perhaps we should conclude that it is not necessary for every yokel who wanders down the pike to be able to repeat our results. Our requirement is somewhat different. Results are to be communicable to suitably trained co-workers; they are expected to be replicable by persons adequately initiated into the methods involved. I would rather not limit our theory at this time to data readily grasped by those to whom Mencken referred as the "Booboisie." The poor in spirit have we always with us, in science, and I would rather not prematurely chain a Freud, a Kurt Lewin, nor you and me.

Our predecessors in psychiatry and social casework eagerly grasped psychoanalysis in the 1920s because it made sense of what was wrong with our clients and patients. It went far beyond the theory then in vogue, which relied simply on "persuasion" to get people to change. Still, this book is not about the version of psychoanalytic theory taught several decades ago. I would ask that it be taken seriously for the same reason we originally grasped id psychology. Modern ego psychology provides a system of ideas even more parsimonious and efficient for helping our clients; it goes beyond common sense; it integrates wide areas of discourse into manageable units.

Functions of the Ego

One aspect of the psychoanalytic literature is delightful, even though it presents a problem. This is the teaching of profound ideas through rich figures of speech, through the paradox and the parable. More than Middle-European *gemütlichkeit* is involved, although it certainly played a part. In the United States, we are accustomed to having ideas conveyed rapidly as high order abstractions, in the unrelieved and deadly style of some professional journals. It is doubtful, however, whether presenting the ideas so concisely does not rob them of associations which would contribute much to grasping their meanings on unconscious levels. Hence, the literary style not only is more vivid and varied but it may also do better at presenting the ideas involved.

A figure of speech employed in discussing the parts of the personality is reification. Terms with highly abstract connotations are made real, given life, even human properties. Thus, a colorful writer like David Wineman might say, "The super-ego made a deal with the id, and was seduced." A concrete example may be found in certain fundamentalistic religious beliefs. Most Americans do not applaud having more children than they can properly care for, financially and emotionally, but still there are people who believe no effort should be made to control family size. So long as a man is able to convince himself that he can earn his way into heaven by thrashing about in the marital bed, he has a pretty unbeatable combination. Id and superego have, indeed, made a deal. The image you have is of two persons bargaining, one knave, one sanctimonious hypocrite. It is a bit of a jolt to be reminded that neither Mr. Id nor his confederate are real persons after all, nor even identifiable bits of the personality. Each is, in fact, an *abstraction* which labels a range of mental processes and operations. These we may term "functions."

If the ego, then, is not something you can reach out and grab, we may list a number of other things ego psychology is not. Ego psychology is not a refuge for the simple-minded. It is not a return to common-sense psychology. Neither does it represent a reversion to the days when academic psychologists presumed that, having taken thought, they were aware of all the content in the mind. Ego psychology is not phenomenology, although some of the ego is, indeed, quite conscious. But most of the processes we will discuss as ego psychology are unconscious. It is not the intent of ego psychology to assist our culture to re-repress its few, hard-won insights into the unconscious.

A powerful factor in the development of ego psychology has undoubtedly been the desire to relate Freudian insights to those that have emerged in the social sciences in a parallel-but-independent fashion. But in social work, for instance, this process of "putting the 'social' back into social work" must be viewed warily. The intent is not now to renounce our knowledge of man's instincts and their vicissitudes in favor of social-economic interpretations, role-theory, or Marxist obtuseness. Ego psychology is intended to *add* to our working body of knowledge, while still striving for parsimonious formulations.

Finally, within the corpus of Freudian theory itself, ego psychology is to be distinguished from id psychology, as we have noted. The latter has to do with the drives, instincts, emotions, the energy which impels the personality. Ego psychology continues to deal with the part of the personality which *mediates* between the id, the superego, and the demands of external reality. But if the id covers a multitude of sins, what is the role of the ego? Here are some of the adaptive functions of personality, commonly referred to as ego psychology, which seem to me of greatest importance for a young clinician to absorb.

1. *Defense mechanisms and the formation of symptoms.* Nearly all students, even if they come from an undergraduate department scrupulously anti-Freudian in orientation, have some acquaintance with the mechanisms of defense. This is partly because the mechanisms have passed from their original auspices into the general knowledge of all educated persons in our culture. Terms like rationalization, repression, and reaction-formation are listed and defined by most writers of textbooks. A knowledge of the logic of the defenses against anxiety is useful and supportive to anyone undertaking to help others through interviews. More for pedagogical reasons than any other, therefore, we will begin our examination of ego psychology in Chapter 2 by discussing defense and its relationship to symptom formation.

2. *Object relations.* The theory of object relations contains many of the most exciting advances associated with the formulations we term ego psychology. It is in respect to this line of theory that this generation starts its work far better equipped. What is the theory of object relations? Well, "objects" in the present context never refers to objects. By objects we typically mean people. This is a nice reversal of the general trend in the culture. Under object relations, then, we study the attitudes clients have toward others, and how these influence facets of their living beyond those we term, sometimes euphemistically, "human relations."

3. *Characterology.* In common speech, the term *character* has value connotations. Someone is a "man of character," or he "has character." This implies that he is a good person, on whom one can rely. In its analytic usage, however, character is a term which is value-free. It refers to the aspects of the personality that are pervasive and color the whole. Character, then, refers to structured patterns in the personality that appear to hold steady over time and in varying situations. Bigots and narcissists, after all, can be relied on to behave in certain ways, but whether the things they are so consistent about are "good" is another question.

4. *Adaptive apparatuses.* There are a number of personality functions which constitute traditional fields of interest to all psychologists, including the non-Freudian. These include the perception of external reality; perception of the self, including one's own motivations and patterns; intellectual and cognitive functions such as learning, remembering, and thinking; processes of adapting to external reality, including the social environment. Although this listing seems to constitute a large chunk of all psychology, it was not examined traditionally by the Freudians. They were, after all, concerned primarily with pathology and treatment. In my observation, the average medically trained psychoanalyst knew no other psychology than the Freudian. Thus his attention would be focused on "blocks" to learning, with only limited understanding of the varieties of physiological con-

ditions and the like which also contribute to poor learning ability. Similarly, when one considered memory, it was in terms of its invasion by *conflict* which had produced repression. Normal forgetting out of disuse, or such processes as retroactive inhibition (which are readily demonstrable experimentally) were not considered. More recently, a group of distinguished Freudian writers has argued the relevance of knowing more about such "normal" processes, and what they term the "conflict-free" spheres of the personality, out of a concern to extend their theory to patients and populations not formerly much served, such as the psychotic and the underprivileged. The result has been a legitimation of psychological content not previously thought proper for analytic consumption, and a number of extensions in Freudian theory itself.

5. *Synthetic function.* Just as it must already be apparent that the headings listed are not mutually exclusive, but simply convenient handles by which to grasp an interdependent network of ideas, so the "synthetic function of the ego" is involved in many of the other processes. By the *synthetic function* we refer to the tendency within the person to try to bring his thoughts, his motives, and—in the final analysis—his life into some harmonious whole. The student may have encountered the "tendency toward closure" in studies of Gestalt principles of perception, by which a nearly completed circle on quick glance will still be seen as a circle. It is also implicated in Festinger's (1964) well-known principle of cognitive dissonance in social psychology, which also has its roots in the Wertheim tradition. At a grander level, we have the synthetic function involved in Erikson's (1950) polarity of Identity vs. Identity-diffusion. The principle is easily stated, but its applications are manifold. Further, not *all* clients reveal the synthetic function in the same degree, and indeed some appear to have developed very little of it. As we shall see, this affects their treatability, or at least their treatability through certain traditional casework approaches.

General Plan of the Book

This book emerged from the conviction that there is, by now, a body of theory that can be brought together in reasonably concise and readable fashion to help a beginning counselor, social worker, or therapist learn his job. Some of this theory represents, of course, my observations in research, treatment, and teaching. Most is a synthesis and reformulation of ideas I have learned from others. I set it down not because it is a final word, but because I have been reassured on a number of occasions that the way I look at these things makes them more readily assimilable by someone who knows less about the field than I do. To be complimented for simplicity is not necessarily flattering, but I am glad if it makes me the sort of teacher after whom the student can go on to learn from more complex, if less articulate, minds. Even I, however, could probably write a more complete and complex book than I plan to set down here. This is frankly presented as an introduction, but for a scholar no longer at the elementary stage. The book will have done its job, therefore, if it permits the student to elaborate his knowledge of theory from this point on, but he does not find it necessary to make any *major* retreats from the basic framework from which this will start him.

Later in the book are some chapters drawn from my own work. These are concerned, really, with two areas at issue to therapists and social workers: *verbal communication in the interview, and the relationship of individual treatment to group phenomena.* I think they are of use, and therefore I hope they will be of interest, also, although they go beyond theory generally accepted in the field. I regard them simply as extensions of ego psychology into new arenas of work, fascinating links with social psychological studies of the theory of social communication. From these connections comes the title of the book, *Ego Psychology and Communication.*

References

Erikson, Erik H. *Childhood and Society.* New York: W. W. Norton, 1950.

Festinger, Leon. *Conflict, Decision and Dissonance.* Stanford, California: Stanford University Press, 1964.

Hartmann, Heinz, Ernst Kris, and Rudolf Loewenstein. "Comments on the Formation of Psychic Structure," in *The Psychoanalytic Study of the Child.* Vol. 2, New York: International Universities Press, 1946.

Rapaport, David. "An Historical Survey of Psychoanalytic Ego Psychology," in E. H. Erikson, *Identity and the Life Cycle.* Monograph 1, Psychological Issues. New York: International Universities Press, 1959.

Stamm, Isabel L. "Ego Psychology in the Emerging Theoretical Base of Casework," in Alfred J. Kahn, ed. *Issues in American Social Work.* New York: Columbia University Press, 1959.

Chapter 2

Symptom
and Defense

I FREQUENTLY FIND MYSELF DEFENSIVE OF THE FREUDIAN movement. Whether it deserves defending is arguable, but that it has needed defending at times in the past is not. Especially against some of its adherents.

Many of the psychoanalysts who formerly would take the time to teach those in other professions were like family physicians in medicine. They were not the investigators and scholars who created theory; they were the technicians who applied it. Most of us were rather uncritical in adopting the fragmented version of analytic psychology that pervaded the social casework practice of twenty-five years ago. Most of them were not very profound in explaining the theory to us, either.

One result of this mutual naivete was that what should have been taught as a science was purveyed as a religion. With no real grasp of the issues involved in theory construction, our teachers nevertheless demanded respectfulness and reverence. The disciples of a charismatic rebel like Freud always busy themselves in establishing a new orthodoxy, in his name. But the disciples of disciples are the most sectarian generation of all, and it was with these men we were in contact.

It is typical of such ideological movements that the area

of strictness also shifts from substance to form. Because many of our teachers did not fully understand analytic theory (indeed, does anyone, yet?), they were likely to be most rigorous about details of clinical practice. The classical technique was then in vogue. For the benefit of those who came in late, this is the method usually associated with psychoanalysis. The patient lay on a couch in a quiet, darkened room, with his analyst seated in a chair at the head of the couch, outside his realm of vision. The patient was then instructed to follow "the basic rule," saying aloud everything that came into his mind. This is a ridiculous injunction. Often two or three thoughts enter one's mind at once, some of what enters is in the form of images that are not verbally communicable anyhow, and so forth. But the *attempt* at free association had led to a number of profound inferences about human behavior. The analyst typically remained relatively silent, even noncommunicative, except to encourage the flow of speech from the patient. From time to time, however, he might make an "interpretation" of what the patient seemed to be unfolding. The idea was that if one could consciously understand his motives and emotions better, he would gradually be cured. The material provided by the patient was grist for the analyst's inferential mill. If the analyst—having examined his thoughts, the last few articles he had read, and his own intuition—made an interpretation, the patient was supposed to accept it as a revelation of his unconscious. If he did not accept it, he was said to be "resisting," and the reasons for his resistance must then be analyzed. Obviously, at fifteen dollars per hour, which was a large sum of money to a caseworker earning sixty-five dollars per week, it was important to try not to resist, but to hurry up and get better. Even the private mythology of dream interpretations, custom-crafted at tedious expense, was to be accepted gratefully.

There is a lot that is right about the classical technique, and few who used it were fools or charlatans. But, in my judgment, and that of many others of my generation, it cannot be regarded as a form of treatment that yielded substantial results for our friends or ourselves. There is now grave doubt whether it was appropriate for many to whom it was so slavishly applied. Some of our famous social workers, who did much to bring the fruits of their own experience of psychoanalysis into our field, and whose work is part of its history, continued to be unpleasant, narcissistic, and downright odd even as they questioned whether anyone should be trusted to do social casework who had not had the benefits of a personal analysis! But the rigidity of the Freudians was at least better than the absences of any standards at all, which pervaded so much of American psychiatry in those days. Patients were financially drained; female patients seduced their psychiatrists; psychiatrists involved wealthy dependent patients and ex-patients in joint business ventures; therapists and patients moved from professional to buddy relationships; patients became cheap institutional labor or disciples of the "great doctor." All these things went on, and continue to go on, of course. They also went on among the Freudians. But there was less of it.

The worst by-product was an inability to discriminate between intellectual curiosity, or scientific skepticism, and resistance. I still recall my experience in the first (and only) Freudian seminar it has been my privilege to attend. Our teacher was the senior, distinguished analyst in town who was a member of Freud's original Viennese circle. He had a sophisticated passion for making money, so we did not pay our fees to a local Institute, but directly to him. Although he was Gentile and married to a baroness (who also practiced lucratively), his teaching style recalled methods employed in the rabbinical seminaries of Europe. To learn theory, one person would read aloud from Freud's famous Seventh Chapter in the *Interpretation of Dreams,* where he sums up his theory. Then the meaning of the section was propounded, sentence by sentence. The room was crowded, the chairs uncomfortable (if you did not end on the floor), and for me the whole thing was a conflict. On the one hand, I was unable to stay away because it was supposed to be a great privilege to be allowed to attend, if one were not a medically trained therapist. On the other, it was tedious, confused, and a strain to maintain the aura of sanctimony. Torn between my narcissism and my stinginess, I used to recall Lord Chesterfield's advice to his son, "As for carnal relations, the pleasure is momentary, the expense is out of all proportion, and the position is ridiculous."

One evening we came across a section in which, in terms of my recent doctoral training, it seemed evident to me that Freud had declared a serious error in logic. Rousing from my fear of being revealed as the tyro I was, I piped up, and said so. Dr. X destroyed me utterly. After all, I had now been *analyzed,* a state of grace otherwise reserved for those whose grandfathers also attended Harvard, or the holy men who wash in the Ganges. Dr. X stared at me through his prominent spectacles and in cold dismissal remarked, "Well, if you do not accept this statement, then you do not accept any of it." The class then adverted to a written report on the forthcoming night's reading from one of its bright boys who had summarized Freud into 1.7 times his original length. I broke into a cold sweat, and my "transference cure" was never again the same.

I do not now think it is good for patients, or for anyone, to accept on faith statements made by therapists. A patient should understand what he is able to with *all* his faculties, including his critical ability and his adult suspiciousness, if he is to grow up and become more integrated. It is especially dangerous for a practitioner to accept a theory of treatment on the basis of the prestige of its author or its current popularity in his field.

As we now embark on what may be the most important set of propositions a caseworker can learn from the Freudians, I want to make one point even excessively clear: these are not ideas to be accepted on faith. Neither is one expected to skip over gaps in logic by appealing to intuition. Once the premises underlying a theory are accepted as plausible, or at least conceivably true, the rest is expected to follow openly, clearly, and logically. Freud was not a new messiah, but simply a scientist having unusual difficulties in gaining acceptance because of the propinquity of his unpleasant discoveries to thought itself. The fact that their observations were unwelcome lent a conspiratorial air to the deliberations of the earlier Freudians which some of them must have enjoyed, because long after their theory had swept the field in psychiatry they continued to regard themselves as a beleaguered band of revolutionaries. But these social processes should have no consequences for the student social worker's learning what he can of the intellectual outcome of the movement.

The Function of Defense

Once I knew a woman whose life was tragic in its outcome, but it became so through a drama that might have been amusing. Very simply, her feet hurt. She was not currently hard at work as a saleswoman, nor running up and down hospital corridors, not even shopping for a bag to match her new red shoes. It was difficult to offer an immediate explanation of her discomfort. An extensive series of medical studies was no more enlightening. All physical findings were negative, but the pain persisted.

Eventually the patient met a man who offered to do what no previous doctor had suggested—operate. It was never clear to me whether he believed he would find diseased tissue in the balls of her feet. Perhaps he was following an idea formerly quite popular among the medical primitives of this country. The notion was that if a female patient continued to complain about abdominal pain one could relieve her mind, at least, by surgically removing something or other not essential to life. The surgeon was paid, and he also retaliated against a patient whom he regarded as something of a nuisance. So one might say the medical decision in the case was *overdetermined*—a term we apply to signify that a given act has been used psychologically to serve more than one purpose. This interaction between well-to-do patient and physician-surgeon was sufficiently widespread that, at one time, it was rare to find a long-term, hospitalizable neurotic who had not had various parts of her reproductive apparatus excised before she finally saw a psychiatrist. We have no way of knowing whether this particular doctor was following such suggestive therapy, but he did claim to have found something wrong and to have rectified it.

The patient's reaction is not one that always occurs, but it was not surprising either. After surgery, her pain increased from bothersome and annoying to excruciating. She became embittered toward the surgeon, and threatened suit. She became extremely anxious to the point that her need for psychiatric treatment was obvious, and she was hospitalized with a serious breakdown. Now there is reason to doubt whether there was anything organically wrong in this case. Even so, the removal of the physical disease could easily lead her to become more upset in other ways. But why?

As a beginning approximation to an answer, we might say that the physical complaint, uncomfortable as it is, must be fulfilling a need. When the complaint is removed, or one threatens to remove it, the patient may seek to have this need met in another way. This may lead to exacerbated pain, as occurred here; it may lead to an outbreak in another sphere, which also occurred here. Because of this rough but credible reasoning, plastic surgeons, for instance, have learned to be chary of the patient who is extremely insistent on his need for a rhinoplasty. If the patient is living on the fantasy that by shortening his nose he will escape his life problems, he may end more despairing than before.

Let us move to a somewhat more precise way of formulating our answer. We will call the psychological support the patient was getting from her physical symptoms a *defense*. But what do we mean by defense? We will define defense simply as any maneuver a person may undertake to keep him from being aware of something he cannot bear to see. In other words, the purpose of a defense is to keep out of *consciousness* that which we need to keep *unconscious*. It is like averting our eyes, or shutting them, or perhaps even fainting at the sight of something that fills us with horror.

The generic term for the process of keeping unconscious that which we cannot bear to have conscious is *repression*. There are many actions or twists of thinking one can go through to *maintain repression;* we might also say they are *in the service of repression*. If it sounds as if I am relating all the defenses to repression, this is my intent. The prototype of all defensive maneuvers is the person's keeping his eyes shut tight, as if in reflex.

But why the effort to keep from looking? If one were to look, what he sees would make him extremely *anxious*. Hence, we may say that the energy motivating any defense is the desire to avoid feeling *anxiety*. The nature of anxiety is something we will discuss later; for now, note that anxiety (which most students have experienced at least moderately in the form of "butterflies" in the pit of the stomach) is perhaps the most unpleasant of human emotions. This is especially true when it comes in the large economy-sized package, as it does for most psychiatric inpatients. It is understandable, therefore, that they might bitterly resist the removal of a defense which is doing its job of reducing their anxiety level; it is equally understandable that, should a defense be penetrated or even, as we say, *threatened,* there will be an automatic response to try either to strengthen it or to substitute another. Should all fail, and the dreaded images with their attached dosage of anxiety come to consciousness, then the patient may be overwhelmed by anxiety, and even become psychotic.

The logic just stated is familiar to most students. Perhaps all I have done is pull it together, and begin to specify the way in which these terms are generally used in the field, and how they are related to one another. There are also some implications of this logic. First, we assume that what happens in the client's mind and emotions is *strictly determined*—that is, all psychic events follow rules that either are known or eventually will be known to professionals in our field. Second, we assume that whatever the client does, whatever he feels, whatever he *thinks* serves some psychological purpose for him. The aim is not always to maintain defense, of course. Often it is to experience pleasure. But the possibility that any psychic process is in the service of defense is a hypothesis we must always keep in mind.

Our little theorizing brings us to another point also generally applicable. You will recall we said the aim of the defense was to keep certain mental *ideas* or *images* from coming into consciousness. The whole psychoanalytic system of psychology is built around such ideas or images, not around *reality* as some outsider might view it. It is assumed that the image in a patient's mind is "real" in the sense that it will have effects. But it is not assumed that the image the patient has conforms identically with the external reality— whatever *that* is. Indeed, the odds are that it does not.

As a rough indication of the chain of events, we assume that any image enters the mind through the sensory organs, through a process which is physiological before it becomes psychological. The image first enters the unconscious. Then, will it come to consciousness and, if so, in what version? What is consciously perceived may in fact be different from all the client has in his unconscious. It is very common, therefore, to find that what we are told as facts about a patient's life may alter as he gets better. Even the way in which a woman describes people in her current environment may change. The husband shifts from beast, to hero, to middle-aged slob, in her descriptions. Since the "reality" around which so much Freudian theory is consistently built is an inner reality, it is extremely hard to link this theory in rigorous fashion to sociological, anthropological, and economic interpretations of events, which deal with an "external reality."

Finally, and more to our present point, a defense represents a *conflict*. We have to ask what the woman with the aching feet was so afraid of recognizing in herself that she had to shield it in this way, and why she shielded it. Actually, we can infer something about the dynamics involved from a knowledge of her life circumstances. She was extremely angry at her husband. He had undergone financial reverses which not only altered their style of life but also made it necessary for her to assist him in his work. This she did not want to do, but neither, I think, could she stand to see herself as a mother too pouty and selfish to help out and lend a hand in providing the money for their daughter's education. Under the circumstances, a physical complaint which rendered her helpless to work and cost her husband even more money was a reasonable compromise of her conflicting emotions. Of course it would not be "reasonable" to the adult side of her, nor would the pain involved seem to have been worth it, but there are parts of the personality, largely unconscious, to which this seemed the only way out. It becomes the task of therapy to decipher such solutions which serve only to make things worse, and then to bring them under the scrutiny of the mature and conscious parts of the personality.

The Mechanisms of Defense

The expression *mechanisms of defense* has become known to practitioners through Anna Freud's book *The Ego and the Mechanisms of Defense* (1946). Miss Freud followed her father in making the treatment of emotional disorders her life work. The story is told that once, when she was delivering a paper at an august gathering of psychoanalysts, one elder of the movement leaned over and whispered to another, "Yonder sits Sigmund Freud, discoverer of the libido and of man's instinctual life. And there stands his daughter prattling of the mechanisms of defense." I repeat this malicious little story for its mnemonic value. It does scant justice to Miss Freud's contributions in her own right, nor her straightforward style in discussing the treatment of children. In any event, the defenses are by no means lacking in color.

In addition to knowing the basic logic of defense, one must also become well-acquainted with the specific ways in which people go about defending themselves. The myriad ways patients have found for maintaining or achieving repression have been classified and named. In this book, as in others, repression is taken to be the prototype and aim of all the defenses. It is to be distinguished, by the way, from *suppression*. In suppression we are making a deliberate effort to rid our minds, and certainly our communication, of a thought that has come to consciousness. In repression, strictly speaking, the whole procedure is unconscious. You may of course be aware of the steps you are taking, which constitute the defense mechanism, but you are unaware of their true purpose. Often the defensive maneuver is itself totally unconscious. Thus, according to the *Psychiatric Glossary*, defense mechanisms are: "Specific intrapsychic defensive processes, operating unconsciously, which are employed to seek relief from emotional conflict and freedom from anxiety. Conscious efforts are frequently made for the same reasons, but true defense mechanisms are out of awareness (unconscious)" (1969, p. 27).

Although it sharpens one's perceptions in the quickness of interviewing to know as many mechanisms as possible, there is no definitive listing of all those thus far traced out. Anna Freud enumerated "Nine methods of defense, which are very familiar in the practice and have been exhaustively described in the theoretical writings of psycho-analysis (regression, repression, reaction-formation, isolation, undoing, projection, introjection, turning against the self, and reversal.)" To these, "We must add a tenth, which pertains rather to the study of the normal than to that of neurosis: sublimation, or displacement of instinctual aims" (1946, p. 47). The *Glossary* mentions eighteen as "common," including: "compensation, conversion, denial, displacement, dissociation, idealization, identification, incorporation, introjection, projection, rationalization, reaction formation, regression, repression [sic!], sublimation, substitution, symbolization, undoing" (1969, p. 27).

It is not necessary to interrupt the flow of this exposition to describe and illustrate each of these maneuvers. Excellent definitions are readily available to the reader in other places, including the two sources cited (cf. Fenichel, 1945). Moreover, our concern here is with ego psychology and communication, to which some operations are more germane than are others. A number of defensive gyrations, therefore, will be spotlighted later, but only in a relevant context—in relation to distortions of communication, and especially in respect to personality structures that make for characteristic distortions. Let me, therefore, offer a few general observations at this point.

The defenses, like all psychic activity, involve thinking, feeling, and acting. When a person preoccupies his mind with one worry in order not to think about something else which is more painful to contemplate, we say he is having *obsessive ideas* or is *obsessional.* All literate members of this generation are familiar with *rationalization,* a method whereby we explain our motives to ourselves in such a manner that we come out well. Recently, for instance, I read, in a paid advertisement favoring the death penalty, that good Christians really have no right *not* to send posthaste to God the soul of the murderer who obviously was meant to be sent there! *Denial* is prominent in the thought of primitive minds: they are able simply to refuse to recognize as real or true anything they do not wish to be real or true.

In the area of *feeling,* we find *substitution* of one affect for another, so that hatred may be hidden behind a false overconcern, for example, or rage is used to cover fear—in line with the folklore that if one can just get mad, he will feel better in the face of threat (it works!). The *phobic defense,* by the way, is especially engaging. The fear that something untoward will happen sometimes masks the hope that it will—the wish is father to the fear. Thus the fear of high places, *acrophobia,* may be most pronounced in men who experience an urge to jump.

The defenses consisting mostly of doing must be further subdivided. There is the act itself, used as a defense. This is found in *reaction formation,* where we try to guarantee that we will not do the forbidden by scrupulously undertaking its opposite. But, there are more elaborate ways of *acting* in support of a defense which are hardly suggested by Anna

Freud's basic list. There are the people who *create whole life situations* for themselves, in the service of defense—for example, the lady in the hospital who repeatedly became involved in compromising situations with male patients. Each time this occurred, there would be a week or more in which she would self-righteously deny anything had occurred, while the staff was under administrative pressure to find out what had been going on. Eventually they noticed that such escapades occurred regularly whenever treatment began to impinge on the lonely and abandoned years of her preadolescence. Rather than deal with this, she would stir up a hornets' nest in her living situation.

Finally, there is a defensive "action" involving the body, in which psychic pain is given a location, as it were, in some bodily part and we speak of *conversion*.

Obviously, in any defensive maneuver it is not possible neatly to separate out its thinking from its feeling from its acting elements. Most mechanisms involve combinations. In real life, too, two or three or more of the mechanisms quoted may well be simultaneously implicated in a single operation a patient is carrying on, which is one reason it is hard to isolate and name the mechanisms in the first place. What I hope to do in this book is impart a way of looking at patients' behavior so that maneuvering in the service of repression is the more likely to be recognized by the reader, whether or not he knows the technical name for the mechanism involved. I cannot help but add that the reader will also find described here a number of patterns not mentioned in the typical course in personality theory or abnormal psychology.

When Is a Symptom?

In our example of the woman with the painful feet we became aware that this form of *conversion* distracted her from a major life problem while simultaneously letting her compromise with it. It was the presence of a conflict that made this defense necessary. After all, had she simply been selfish, without being critical of such feelings in herself, there would have been no need to blind herself to her own anger. We might have thought her an unlikable, dreadful person, but she would not have developed symptoms. It was the fact that besides having childish rage she was also a decent human being that made the elaborate set of defenses necessary. Still, the compromise she worked out was extremely costly. It may have warded off some of her anxiety, but only at great discomfort to herself and burden to her family, and we think of her as having a series of *symptoms.*

Not all defensive maneuvers result in symptoms, physical or psychological. Each of us is constantly at work warding off anxiety; it would be unwise to regard all our solutions as containing symptoms. When, then, is a defensive action thought of as a symptom?

I once worked in a mental hospital catering to "the carriage trade." A large proportion of our patients were adolescent and postadolescent. Many of them came from wealthy and talented families, and it was not surprising to find a high proficiency in the arts. Musical ability seemed especially prevalent. In fact, the number of good piano players struck me as noteworthy. Why did one find so many good pianists with serious emotional difficulties?

To a violinist, the first impulse would be to say that this is what we had always thought of piano players. But examination of the histories indicated that, for many, here was a talent that was actually exercised. At some point in the life of each patient, he had practiced assiduously—compulsively —for three, four, or more hours a day. It became evident that in many instances what appeared to be a devotion to the instrument was heavily reinforced by its convenience as a defense. Here was one sphere in which the already unhappy and phobic adolescent could achieve the same sense of mastery others were seeking on the ball field, and without requiring much contact with other human beings. Practicing —which for so many of us was an unpleasant, duty-laden task—became for these children an outlet for healthy motivations, but within a situation which did not make them anxious or threaten their defensive withdrawal.

Let us return to the key question. Was the practicing "a symptom"? Obviously this is very hard to decide. The net outcome was that they were able to master an instrument for pleasure and, in a few cases, for profit. When the young Mozart practiced, was this a symptom? Schubert while dying in poverty and malnutrition wrote melody after melody on scraps of paper, as songs crowded his mind. Was this behavior disturbed, or an expression of his genius? Or both?

Obviously that which we term a symptom cannot be defined on the basis of the specific behavior. If the behavior serves in part a defensive function, this does not necessarily make it a symptom, either. It must be faced that what we choose to call a symptom is determined by criteria more inclusive than the question of motivation for the behavior, criteria involving value judgments. Any symptom is likely to be in the service of defense, but by no means all defenses are regarded as symptoms.

We regard behavior as "symptomatic" when its other cost to the person clearly outweighs the value derived from keeping his anxiety reduced. The youngster who has locked himself up with his instrument because he has not matured sufficiently to get along in an adolescent group may, with treatment, be *both* a comfortable teenager *and* a proficient musician. After all, the skills learned in the service of his neurosis need not disappear as the neurosis subsides. On the other hand, if all he can do all day is sit and twiddle his piano, rambling through vague and discordant sequences while otherwise living as a recluse, one might well question whether what he is learning about disharmony is worth it. In the case of the woman whose feet ached so badly, the judgment is even easier to make. The extent to which she was crippled and her life spoiled because she was petulant with her husband was not helped by developing the pain.

Indeed, as is not at all uncommon, she was much worse off.

One thing we can usually count on with the human organism is its attempting self-healing. If we cut our finger, we need try only to prevent infection. Otherwise, we leave it to the skin itself to undertake self-cure. It is the same with psychic insults. The ego attempts to heal itself and, in most cases, it succeeds. Otherwise, all of us would have serious and crippling emotional illnesses.

A defense, therefore, is a kind of home remedy which the person applies to his own psychic wounds. As with all such prescribing, the treatment may be ill-advised. Indeed, it often happens that the cure is worse than the disease. It is as if a person had a laceration on his leg which he permitted to heal itself. A scab would form, which would stem the flow of blood, and shut out chances of further infection from the outside. Then we would see the emergence of scar tissue. But if the scar tissue became bulky, disfiguring and drawn, the leg might well end with less mobility than it had while the wound was still open.

There are other examples that help to give us a sense of what we mean by an unhealthy or crippling defense. One I have from a wise elder analyst, who commented, "The child puts on a suit of armor to ward off the immediate danger, and it works. But he is unable to guess that years later, when his friends are running and leaping ahead, he will be dragging along in the rear, still weighted down by the same old armor."

Because all behavior is purposeful, we do not say that a symptom serves no useful purpose. It does serve to ward off anxiety by keeping ideas unconscious. However, the issues are: whether the price is worth the freedom from anxiety; whether the person would still be made as anxious facing the same ideas as he was when he first assumed the defense; and whether he could not find a more efficient way of handling the original conflict if only he could reopen the matter and review it with the help of a professional, and in the light of his present maturity and general competence.

Implications of the Conception of Defense

It is immediately evident that a symptom, indeed any defense, is an outcome of a process which underlies it. Therefore, if one wants to bring about permanent cessation of the symptom, the most efficient thing he can do is to improve its underlying causes. This does not mean that what is termed *symptomatic improvement* is to be scoffed at. Often, we are very grateful if we can get an alcoholic simply to stop drinking, even though we know full well this is only a surface manifestation of what is wrong with him. For a symptom like alcoholism, which is of course an *effect* of one or more underlying causes, stirs up sufficient difficulties that it, in its turn, may become the cause of further symptoms, including death. But the most *efficient* intervention— that is, the way to get maximum benefit for the same input of energy—is to attack the cause rather than the symptom.

Because the defense does serve to *bind* anxiety, as we say, so long as the underlying conflict producing the anxiety is present, the client will not willingly give up the defense. Similarly, he will cling to those maneuvers he carries out which are in the service of defense. The image to bear in mind as we try to follow the gyrations in a case is, to repeat, that the client does not wish to open his eyes and look at something he cannot yet stand to face. This unreadiness to deal with ideas that have been repressed is called *resistance.* Originally, the term was applied more or less specifically to the refusal of a patient to accept an interpretation made in the classical analytic situation. In social work and elsewhere, resistance is now used more generically to refer to all efforts to evade an unpleasant insight. Bear in mind that when we speak of resistance we are not referring simply to a mulish, stubborn unwillingness of the client to be influenced for his own good. This may in fact be present, too, but we are referring more precisely to his need to maintain repression.

A natural question is whether people can deliberately

stop a mode of thinking, behaving, or feeling which they are carrying on defensively. Obviously, it would be silly to regard them as having complete control over behavior that is motivated by anxiety. But, lest clinical compassion be enlisted purely on the side of excusing anything the patient wants to do, it is necessary to point out now that the obverse is also true. Most neurotics have at least *some* ability to counter impulses that occur in the service of the defense; so do most clients with more serious diagnoses. The question of free will—the extent to which the client can exercise conscious control over his symptomatic behavior—cannot be answered in a universal way. As the client becomes better able to stop symptomatic behavior (such as drinking, outbursts of hostility or the like), it would seem reasonable to conclude that either his underlying conflicts were gradually being resolved or he was getting stronger in other parts of his personality and now wanted to stop. Perhaps both processes are occurring simultaneously.

There is a possibility that the client *could* give up some of his more self-destructive symptoms, even at the cost of momentary anxiety, so we sometimes have to ask ourselves whether any part of him really wants to do so. Perhaps what we see as a symptom, he regards as the way people should live. The story is told of an old lady whose family finally got her to agree to see a psychiatrist because they were concerned about actions which implied she was becoming senile. The young psychiatrist talked with her for forty minutes, but had trouble eliciting enough verbal response from her to be able to assess her thought processes. At long last, however, he discovered she did have an interest in cooking, and they found they both liked potato pancakes. Then the patient brightened up. "You must come visit me at my house," she remarked, "I have drawers and drawers full of potato pancakes."

Another example is to be found in the intellectual life of the university. I have often observed that a colleague, at a certain stage in a research, will find his work impinges on an area that is foreign to him. This can happen, for instance, to a sociologist who has been working on the concept of power and now wants to state its relationship to prestige and prestige influence. At this point he has ventured into a theoretical realm that is primarily psychological. He may not be sufficiently expert in psychological theory to proceed with his analysis. If he is not, he can "psychologize," which is a slang term we use to refer to an amateurish attempt by a sociologist to buttress his ideas with half-baked psychological theorizing. He can learn more about the theory of personality than he yet knows, even though he already has a doctorate to his credit. Or, and this is very common, he can baldly state that his aim is to solve the theoretical problem in "purely sociological" terms. In order to be adequately pure as a sociologist, he says, it is *necessary* to remain ignorant as a psychologist. The nice thing about the latter line of thinking is that it helps this otherwise mature man escape the crunch of trying to learn something he does not already know. Instead of admitting a deficit in his equipment for the present task, he erects it into a virtue. We shall advert again to this maneuver, whereby the ego manages to convert a liability into an asset.

Symptoms may occur in the form of a way of acting, a style of thinking, a feeling held in order to avoid another less acceptable one. They may also occur in the form of physiological reactions—such as ulcers, sweating palms, and other disturbances of the autonomic system. A client may have a pattern which we would regard as noxious, even dangerous to him, but he may not regard it that way at all. When the symptom is acceptable to the person who has it, we say it is *ego-syntonic,* implying that it seems to fit comfortably into attitudes of at least the conscious ego. A symptom or pattern the client feels is inappropriate, distasteful, and of which he would like to rid himself, we term *ego-dystonic.* Although this sounds like a dichotomy among symptoms, it is actually a question of quantitative differences. Most symptoms are more or less ego-syntonic.

Part of the skill of the mature caseworker lies in his ability to "start with the client where he is," as we say, accepting noncommittally that part of his self-destructive behavior which is ego-syntonic. Gradually in the course of the casework, the symptom may move in the direction of becoming ego-dystonic. Far from rebuffing help or evading it, the client may actively seek it out and willingly pay for it. At that point, we might say he is very motivated for treatment.

Most private therapists and many agencies require evidence of motivation to change before involving themselves with a client. It is important to note that the *capacity for self-observation* is itself an index of emotional health. If the client is sufficiently healthy he may, following our earlier analogy to self-healing, go all the way and cure himself. Hence, an overweening demand that the client immediately regard as ego-dystonic all those facets of his personality which the caseworker can see as crippling, and be motivated to change them, may well have the same effect as putting the cart before the horse. It would be like an orthopedist's refusing to treat a man for a broken leg because he would not bring himself to the office. We see, then, that the requirement that a person be "adequately motivated" for treatment is not something to be used to escape responsibility for our job. The lack of motivation is itself usually a part of what is amiss with the client. Infantile people, for example, usually do not recognize there is anything wrong with their personalities. Finding some way to arouse sufficient motivation to keep the client in treatment becomes a technical issue— one that we may or may not be able to solve. If we fail to solve it, it is our responsibility, since we, not the client, are supposedly the experts in treatment. It is *our* failure. But it may well be his life-tragedy. On occasion I have found it useful to spell out this line of logic to a defiant or argumentative client mostly bent on challenging me. It usually has a sobering effect.

The notion that the way out of their difficulties is to change themselves is not one that seems to come naturally to many persons when they first seek help. They seek, instead, what we call *alloplastic* solutions, meaning, literally, "change the other." A readiness to see the need for an *auto-plastic* way out (i.e., changing one's self) is more character-istic of mature, intelligent clients—and then they will usu-ally find one trait they believe they can most comfortably do without—like the man who barges past the secretary, bangs his hand on the table, and announces he is tired of being a Milquetoast.

Let's face it, most people come for help because they are hurting. They can be persuaded of the desirability of chang-ing themselves only if they can grasp that this is the best assurance they have that in the future they will not hurt in the same way. Many, perhaps most, of the clients a social worker or counselor sees will be quite cheerful about ending casework treatment at the point they no longer hurt. This raises another classical problem. Is it good to try to stop the hurting as rapidly as possible? In the present context, the obvious answer would be no, but this is not accurate either. After all, we are in the business of alleviating misery, and if we are not motivated to stop pain, we do not belong in the helping professions. It would be easy, of course, to dismiss efforts to make the client feel better on the grounds that this is only symptomatic relief. But, unfortunately, the situation is more complex. A symptom and its psychological cause are really in an interdependent relationship, so that a change in one is accompanied by a change in the other. It *is* more efficient to work on the "cause," but there is good reason to believe that efforts to affect the symptom will usually affect its cause as well.

The trouble is that if we do not fully understand what we are doing, the effect we bring about may be the reverse of what we have in mind. The woman who appears week after week to complain about her husband raises the obvious question, "Why don't you leave him?" This overlooks the possibility that so long as she is complaining against him, it nicely distracts her from what she is worried about in her-self. She can point accusingly at him, saying, in effect, "I'm not evil, you are." Many people are in balance only when they have an enemy. The lady whose feet hurt may be said to have needed foot surgery like the plague. She substituted one set of symptoms for another. She needed a defense, and she found one.

Finally, we cannot leave this general realm of discourse without a word on the effects of *penetrating* or *uncovering* a defense. Especially in inpatient work, caseworkers are subject to becoming targets of aggression. For instance, we may be dealing with a very compulsive man in group therapy who needs always to sit in a certain chair, placed at a fixed angle. Suppose the therapist deliberately occupies the chair himself, before the patient arrives. He is likely to be greeted by either a pouting silence or pained acquiescence or obvious and outspoken annoyance. His reaction, in the latter instance, might be, "I made him angry." But this is not really true. The odds are good that this man is chronically angry. By living a highly controlled, circumscribed pattern, he manages to keep his anger from bursting forth. The effect of interfering with his routine, then, was not to *create* anger. Rather, the worker unleashed it. It is as if he lifted a manhole cover and gases which had been contained beneath now rushed into the atmosphere.

Interfering with a compulsive ritual is a graphic way to describe what is meant by penetrating a defense. Obviously there are other ways, including direct interpretation, refusing to go along with a way of relating which the client uses defensively, encouraging him to try a new way of thinking about people important in his life. In each instance, one has to distinguish between annoyance that hits one because he *is* annoying, and annoyance that comes from uncovering a feeling that was being defended against. How one makes this distinction is something we can only touch on in this introductory book.

Layers of Defense

We have been alluding to processes for penetrating defenses. Let us move next to a related concept having to do with the fact that defenses customarily exist in depth. This is referred to by a term with considerable relevance to practice: the notion of *layers of defense.*

Mr. Z begins his contact with the clinician by letting him know how important are the people with whom he is accustomed to associate. While dropping a name here and there in the interview (sometimes with a bit of a thud), he also acts in a gracious but subtly condescending manner toward the worker. Should the latter proffer a comment, Mr. Z considers it judiciously, accepting it or disregarding it with easy casualness. He may or may not "have time" for his next appointment. The counselor soon learns that he maintains this air of studied superiority in many of his human contacts, to a point where it seriously interferes with his earning a living.

It is not necessary to have a master's degree from a school of social work to draw the deep conclusion that this fellow seems to be trying to protect something about himself—he is "overcompensating for a feeling of inferiority." Adler, who was one of the earliest students of ego psychology, made a fuss about this defense mechanism, and threatened to make it the keystone of a general system of psychology (Adler, 1917). But, it is not exactly news around the ninth grade, either.

The attitude of superiority is a kind of *reaction formation,* if you will, a term we use to refer to doing the opposite of an impulse in order to keep it well hidden from view. Mr. Z is really acting superior in order to keep from showing how inferior he feels. Least of all, of course, does he want to reveal it to himself. This attitude of superiority, of which Mr. Z is more or less conscious, has consequences for his life of which he is at best only dimly aware, if at all. In his contacts with others he sees them as beings whose primary usefulness to him is to confirm his defense—to bolster his feeling of superiority. At the same time, they can be a major threat to him, because anyone who does not acknowledge how important or "special" he is automatically undermines his defense and makes him anxious. Mr. Z *is* aware he has few friends, but he does not know why people do not take to him more comfortably. A major reason is that he is stuffy. For instance, he is extremely careful not to give offense (a characteristic of which he prides himself) because in his youth he learned that if one attacks another person, that person is likely to retaliate. Whereas other boys could easily tolerate the give-and-take of teasing, Mr. Z could not. In his case, the stakes were too high, because any criticism, even a joshing one, was followed by a deep sense of degradation. So he speaks carefully, even pedantically, and his attempts at humor are elephantine. One might say that the need to feel superior, which is immediately visible, gives rise to a series of *further* defenses, such as avoiding free give-and-take with his associates. He prefers to spend his time with folks whom he regards as his obvious inferiors, like servants or even clients of his professional practice. In these limited and stabilized relationships, he is safe, and can even unbend slightly.

One might think that in order to give Mr. Z some substantial help it would be necessary only to get at the core of his problem, his sense of inferiority. Once one could get him to look at this, he would undoubtedly feel better. After all, he is, in fact, quite a capable and attractive man, with a good record of achievement. Whatever *childish remnant* is pursuing him should dissolve in the light of full conscious attention and adult reasonableness. So the worker sets to work with this in view. Eventually, Mr. Z does realize that he thinks of himself as low on the totem pole and is constantly dogged by a sense of failure.

The caseworker, fortunately, is shrewd and experienced. He does not settle for these generalizations. Instead, he asks for specific details, and he gets them. Mr. Z, it turns out, is dogged by a sense of inferiority because he ranked only third in his college class. He used to claim to be frightened that he could not pass exams, but this was not true. What really bothered him was concern whether he would get Honors. In short, the self-degradation, far from being the ultimate source of Mr. Z's difficulties, is itself found to be a defense. It would embarrass him (which is to say it would make him look less than perfect in his own eyes) were he to admit that unlike other students his real concern was whether he would be outstanding. So he claims the acceptably humble worry about passing. We see, then, that his feeling of inferiority is itself invoked with reference to his perfectionistic standards. And we end with a sandwich of defensive switches, if you will. Superiority covers inferiority which, in turn, covers an underlying need to be superior. Garnishing the sandwich, incidentally, are the various complicated and sometimes exhausting maneuvers he has to go through to protect his act of defensive superiority.

There are complications here that the student should already have recognized. When Mr. Z converts the interview from a serious effort to help him live better with his wife into a duel with the worker, on what shall we blame it? Is it because of the superiority at the top of the sandwich, or is the underlying need to be special still peeking through from underneath? And against what is that a defense? These are reasonable and relevant questions, but this is not the place in which they can be answered. For the moment, then, let us firmly grasp the basic notion.

Defenses typically exist in depth. They exist in layers because many defenses solve a problem only to raise another one which must then be defended against. Furthermore, a defense usually involves at least some unreality. Consequently, to buttress it against the raw light of reality requires additional efforts in the service of the defense.

All these statements, by the way, hold true primarily for relatively normal people of normal intelligence. It is not hard to imagine that some childlike folks could be satisfied, if that is the word, with a *rationalization* that would *not* fit the more intelligent person. There would be no conflict and less need to erect layerings of defense. From this one might presume that simple people should present fewer emotional problems, but such is not the case. They in fact have less rather than more protection against raw anxiety. Put another way, when their limited set of defenses slips, everything goes at once.

The notion that defenses are likely to exist in strata should make more vivid to the reader what we mean when we refer, in the theory of treatment, to "uncovering techniques" as opposed to "bolstering defenses." For those of us who have been through a classical analysis, it also makes more graphic the once-popular simile—that of "unpeeling the onion" in search of the *core conflict* (or complex, as it used to be called). Indeed, our worry was whether, once the onion was unpeeled, the analogy would still hold, and we would find that in the middle there was nobody at all. Fortunately, most of us did not end our analyses with this disheartening discovery, although it is possible to find people who see nothing but emptiness and nothingness inside themselves.

References

Adler, Alfred. *A Study of Organ Inferiority and its Psychical Compensation.* New York: Nervous and Mental Disease Monograph Series, No. 24, 1917.

American Psychiatric Association. *A Psychiatric Glossary.* Washington, D.C.: The Association, 1969.

Fenichel, Otto. *The Psychoanalytic Theory of Neurosis.* New York: W. W. Norton, 1945.

Freud, Anna. *The Ego and the Mechanisms of Defense.* New York: International Universities Press, 1946.

Chapter 3

Resilience and Energy in the Personality

WE HAVE BEEN DISCUSSING CONFLICT, DEFENSE, AND THE occasional morbid resolution of a conflict into a symptom. We shall now look at the side of the ego that faces toward health. While the formation of a symptom is an attempt at self-healing which proved ill-advised, most such efforts have better outcomes.

The original view of the ego was as an agglomeration of *adaptive* apparatus (Hartmann, 1939). This still holds. Indeed, it is hard to find a psychologically induced symptom that would be cause for alarm if it were to occur in a smaller amount. To be inadequately clean is to be a slob. But when you find a patient scrubbing his water closet with a toothbrush (and there continue to be such unfortunate souls outside the Army), you wonder what TV commercial he has been watching. A symptom, then, is often a normally useful mode of adaptation which is overworked and exaggerated.

The Case of the Rejected Suitor

There are many pithy comments on the subject of marriage. We have Shaw's remark that marriage is a successful institution because it combines a maximum of temptation with a maximum of opportunity. There is the French saying that a bachelor may live like a king, but he dies like a dog; a married man lives like a dog, but he dies like a king. Such wisdom is not usually in the mind of a young man enamored of his girl. He knows only that he loves her, a state still not adequately described in ego psychology or any other. I commence the study of resilience in the ego with a series of examples drawn from a vicissitude that is all too frequent: falling out of love.

The situation: A young man was attracted to a young lady. After some pursuit, they were in agreement on the desired outcome, and became engaged to be married. Fate, however, willed that they could not marry immediately. The young man had to be away for a number of months on "government business," as we used to say in the Army.

While he was gone, his ladylove found that living without current and pressing attentions was hard to bear. At first she was "seen socially," then she was "seen often," and finally she really was not seen so much as she was with another young man. In the end, she decided to marry this handy alternative. When her fiancé returned, expecting warm greetings and eternal bliss, she let him have the news —tenderly but with a sobriety befitting her condition. She handled her share of this interview well, considering the circumstance that it was not a lovely situation to be handling.

This was not one instance, but several, for rejection is something that happens in this world. So we turn our attention to the reactions of four disappointed lovers, each of whom has suffered an irretrievable *object loss*.

Tom "took his medicine" like a man. He said little, gulped, and left. Then he went home, wrote an oblique but gentlemanly note, and shot himself.

Dick was also a gentleman, bred and born. He, too, commented with a wry grin that he "understood." He made a caustic remark or two about the idiocy of building one's future on a woman but said nothing really offensive. Then he joined the Foreign Legion, where he spent a number of years riding camels.

Harry was quite a different sort. His reaction was to become insulted and to threaten both his ex-fiancée and her new lover with great bodily harm. He made a number of dreadful statements about his ex-lady's morals, and he was not above demanding the return not only of his ring but also of a coat or two she had naturally assumed he would not be needing during the forthcoming cold spell. He left and went to visit his drinking companions, where he continued to make vile comments about his erstwhile girl friend. It is not known whether he remained depressed beyond the second week of this encounter, for he left town to accept a good position with a construction firm. Later, he married and reared three children, one of whom wore braces on her teeth.

George had still a different reaction. He became extremely quiet and pale during the meeting, but made one or two blundering attempts to talk his ex-fiancée into returning to him. Then he left her house, went to a neighboring bar where, fortunately, he found several college friends, and became so drunk he had to be taken home by a friendly patrol car. Although he wept for a time while in his cups, he never did tell his friends what was bothering him. Subsequently, he dated other girls, off and on. George became an alcoholic who never married. His mother, who provides him with money and occasional haphazard courses of psychiatric treatment, blames his lifetime of troubles on his having been so coarsely jilted.

These are of course quite varied responses to the same life crisis. Which is to be seen as the healthiest? There are, as a matter of fact, cultures in which the only appropriate reaction to such loss of face would be suicide, or murder, although it is hard to image that destroying oneself might be taken for psychic health, much less destroying someone else. But one thing does stand out. Regardless of the specific dynamics, we have the impression that some personalities are better able to roll with life's punches than are others. The ego is said to be the arena for such adaptations, so it must be in the ego that one absorbs, or fails to absorb, the punishment which life inevitably deals to all except the most lucky. We practitioners, who spend so much of our lives helping others cope with stress and loss, need a set of concepts to describe the over-all ability of the person to rally from disaster.

Ego Strength and Psychic Energy

Modern casework practice utilizes what we call a *psychosocial diagnosis*. This is an attempt to pin down what is causing distress, both within the person and in his total life situation. In making the diagnosis, it is now common to appraise strengths and weaknesses. Similarly, in discussing the functioning of the personality, it has become habitual to talk about clients who have *strong egos* or *weak egos*. These terms are not used with much pretension to precision. They mean simply that the personality is more or less efficient in adapting to the environment. Strength may come from being born with a highly salable talent, or from having some way to profit from one's disasters and vicissitudes. Some comedians do this expertly. Fritz Redl used to say, "It 'ain't' your neurosis, it's how you use it. "

Perhaps the best way to lend precision to the term ego strength is to bring in the concept of *psychic energy*. In a general way, we assume there is in each person a relatively constant amount of such energy. Predicting the functioning of the personality involves, among other things, estimating how much psychic energy is *free* and available for solving life problems. Persons with *strong egos,* let us say, are able to pay attention to what is going on around them; indeed, they probably get a fair amount of pleasure out of being involved in day-to-day happenings. They can concentrate without becoming distracted by internal preoccupations, and therefore they think more effectively and creatively. Beyond that, they have reserve supplies of psychic energy. Struck by a sudden crisis, they are able to deal with the situation. Given events requiring extraordinary decisions, they can think logically for a long period until able to find the means to solutions. All of us experience impulses to panic or withdraw when struck by the unexpected, but those with a sufficient amount of free energy are able to put forth the effort needed to control such urges and to act in spite of them. For all such reasons, it seems reasonable to accept that the availability of free energy is to be seen as a major index of the health and strength of the ego.

A question that has plagued theoreticians concerns the source of the energy at the ego's disposal. A view that was widely offered during my student days saw the ego as a weak jockey borne at the whim of the willful id, who was the horse. This still begged the question of whether the ego, if it were even to guide the horse around holes in the path, did not have force of its own. By now, it is generally agreed that the ego does, for all practical purposes, have energy "at its own disposal." This energy derives ultimately from the great instinctual drives which, at a most abstract level, can be dichotomized into sex and aggression. However, as the energy in these drives becomes *neutralized* and *sublimated* it is channeled into adaptation and is available as part of ego functioning.

It is now being accepted that another source of energy is available to the ego. This derives ultimately from the parts of the brain and body involved in sensation—the so-called *perceptual apparatus.* Certainly, there is now evidence that in the absence of stimulation to the sensory organs we develop a yearning for it, which has been called, appropriately enough, *stimulus hunger.* But these are abstruse questions, beyond the scope of the present book. Meanwhile, we shall deal with a simpler issue: Given that there is a quantum of psychic energy, how is it depleted?

The Loss of Psychic Energy
in Conflict and Defense

Individual psychology had been studied for half a century or so before serious and detailed efforts were made to
probe the dynamics of groups. As a result of comparative
ignorance, it was common to talk about groups as if they
fitted individual dynamics. People even went so far as to
discuss the birth of a group, its adolescence, and its se-
nescence. It was not always clear whether such writers were
indulging in elaborate figures of speech or whether they
thought they were indeed describing a living organism. I
have worked on problems of both individual and group
dynamics, and my experience runs in the reverse direction.
Certain individual processes and dynamics can often be
better understood and illustrated by looking at what happens in groups. In so doing, however, we realize that we
are only making the processes more vivid for the reader.
These are examples only, not direct reflections of reality.

In the last chapter, we talked about conflicts which the
person experiences. As I write this, I am aware of a group
conflict involving our neighborhood. We live on a long,
meandering street which has homes bordering, on their
rear, a large tract owned by a local operator. The developer
wishes to build a shopping center, and has used his considerable local influence to have the zoning commission
and the city council rezone his land from "residential" to
"roadside trading." In the course of this change, bowing
to anguished yelps from the voters on our street, they did
compose an ordinance that he would leave a fifty-foot buffer
zone undisturbed. Now the developer is encroaching on the
zone, cutting the trees, and those affected are naturally upset. There is nothing unusual about this situation. It is as
American as apple pie and the greed of wealthy men.
Equally American is the urge to protect oneself. An organization within our neighborhood existed, and the members
met to hire a lawyer. The next step was to request a volun-

tary assessment from each affected family for a "retainer" for the lawyer. Immediately, two schools of thought arose. One felt that the fee asked was expectable; the other preferred to wait and see what this lawyer would do before making an investment in him.

One advantage the developer has over the neighborhood is that he can make decisions rapidly, while ours must be filtered through a group process. If there is disagreement in the group, then the whole decision process may be stymied. At a minimum, energy that might properly be spent combating "the enemy" becomes dissipated in debating strategy and in dealing with vague suspicions about the intentions of those who have accepted leadership. Such dissension can become so bitter that it leaves neither strength nor money with which to protect ourselves.

The process is similar within a person. By analogous dynamics, we may note that while he struggles within himself and against himself, nothing is left with which to try to manipulate his environment. A prime example is the person who is immobilized by obsessive indecision. T. S. Eliot presents J. Alfred Prufrock:

> "I grow old . . . I grow old . . .
> I shall wear the bottoms of my trousers rolled.
> Shall I part my hair behind? Do I dare to eat a peach?
> I shall wear white flannel trousers, and walk upon
>   the beach.
> I have heard the mermaids singing, each to each.
> "I do not think that they will sing to me."
> And elsewhere,
> "I have measured out my life with coffee spoons. . ."

We shall have ample opportunity later to examine at more leisure some of the mechanisms of the obsessive-compulsive personality. For the moment, however, our point is simply to illustrate the manner in which psychic energy can be exhausted in the inability to resolve conflict.

Psychic energy is also consumed in great amounts in the *effort it takes to sustain a defense.* To review, a defense is any maneuver—an action, an idea, a way of thinking—which we use to keep from seeing something we do not wish to see. Many defenses waste energy, of course, but the waste is nowhere more visible than in compulsive actions. In their efforts to maintain a sense of safety in starting the day, some compulsive people develop morning rituals of the toilet which use up several hours. I once had a patient whose eating rituals required two hours for a frugal hospital lunch. As with many such patients, he tried to conceal his compulsions from me, sensing rightly that sharing them with his therapist would be the first step in giving up those particular defensive maneuvers. The nurses noticed that, as he came down the hall in front of the nursing station, there was a particular black spot in the tile pattern which he had to touch with his foot before turning off toward his room. This created a number of problems for my youngster. Sometimes he had to wangle his way through a group of fellow patients who were standing about, managing unobtrusively to touch the black tile in some way so he could continue his walk. At other times, there might even be someone standing on his black tile, and he had no alternative but to hover around hoping that person would soon wander off, so he could get access to his safety spot.

We discussed this operation in an interview. I had no luck in discovering *why* he had the need to touch his personal home base, but (as too often happens with such patients) he immediately decided he had been doing evil, and should give up the pattern. He did. My next report from the nursing station concerned an oddity in the patient's gait before their desk. Now, as he approached the spot in question, he would make a detour to avoid the offending tile. As he was a scrupulous person, this often took him as much as three feet out of his way. He had replaced his *compulsion* with something I could only describe as anti-compulsion compulsion. He had not resolved the original problem; rather, he ended by multiplying his expenditure of energy to pretend to himself that the problem no longer existed. The device he was using in this pretense we term a *reaction formation.* Had we truly succeeded in removing the conflict involved, it would not of course have mattered to him whether he stepped on the tile or missed it. Thus, we see one way in which a defense can waste energy, in the first place; we also note how the effort to keep a defense, while appearing to give it up, may increase rather than decrease the net input.

This entire procedure was open to view. Usually, the workings of defense are submerged; they are in the "silent service" of the ego. It takes psychological SONAR to locate them, because the whole process is kept hidden from the patient's consciousness.

A student who has conflicts about sex, for example, may encounter a variety of unanticipated effects on his studies. Let us suppose that this conflict "began" with his hearing, as a child, that his mother did something dirty with his father in order for him to be born. Because he loved his mother very much, he was shaken and dismayed by such news. (Of course, there must already have been the germ of a problem, or he would have managed to shrug off the shock, as most children do.) He did not want to know about such things; he *repressed* the information, "forgot" about it. Next, we find him as a fifteen-year-old, studying biology in high school. He has done well in the course, but finally the text discusses the reproduction process. Whenever he reads about it, he finds himself unaccountably restless and bored. Were he in treatment, he would complain about *difficulty in concentration.* Although he can do mathematics quite well, the simplest logic concerning the entry of the sperm into the ova is hard for him to follow. He must read it and reread it. He complains that he is stupid, and cannot learn "anything." His caseworker would notice that this was not true. The worker might justifiably conclude that he preferred to term himself "stupid" in general rather than search out how and why he is stupid in this particular. In any case, our youngster does manage to pass biology, but only after expending much more energy trying to make the information sink in than he has to with most other such courses. And he is unable to know why this happened to him.

You might say that he cannot learn because he does not want to know, but this would not be true. The fact is that he already knows! But what he knows is something he does not want to have stirred up and made conscious. As fast as he learns something about sex, it becomes associated with his childish reaction of shock and dismay and it is dragged beneath the surface and kept unconscious, joining the imagery from his childhood.

It is as if all new information enters the mind first through the organs of perception—the eyes, the ears, and so forth. The working of these organs is of course unconscious. Therefore, the question is whether the new information will come rapidly through the *unconscious*, into consciousness. *Preventing* information from coming to consciousness takes energy; it is quite different from not caring enough to attend to it. We may allow our eyelids to droop while watching a fisherman because we are drowsy, and nothing worth watching seems to be happening. This is quite different from sitting with eyelids clenched tightly shut because we are afraid he will hook something and we feel sorry for the fish. It is because true information is constantly reaching the unconscious from the outside world that energy must be expended to keep delusions and distortions alive.

Many a neurotic, if he is completely honest, will confess to real nostalgia over the loss of the magic that went with his illusions (Fraiberg, 1959). I have occasionally had to say, "You are giving up the thrills of your exciting daydreams; but at least you are also dropping the horrors of your nightmares." Marriage has also been described as giving up the excitements of the chaise lounge for the comfort of the double bed. There is no use in asking more out of life than there is. This, too, wastes energy.

All these are examples of the manner in which ego strength may be depleted through the loss of energy in conflict and defense. There are other ways efficiency may be impaired.

The Invasion of Ego Functions by Neurosis

We have just read an example of difficulty in learning new material because of its relationship to something that we do not wish to recall. Such inability to bring to mind an event that is actually still alive in memory is termed *repression,* in the strict meaning of the term. Freudians took no interest in the processes of memory except as they involved repression. Indeed, naive young men like me—and we were many—became so impressed with the amount of detail that came to us while free associating on the couch that we acquired a distorted picture of the nature of memory, in general. I recalled, for example, coteries of classmates from the third grade and names of teachers long forgotten. I had the fantasy that everything that had ever happened or that I had ever learned was somewhere stored within my brain on an endless reel, waiting only the release from repression to be brought to light.

This of course is simply not true. Not everything to which we have been exposed actually impinges firmly enough to be "remembered." The laws of memory that Ebbinghaus worked out in the nineteenth century before Freud was prominent still are accepted in a general way. We know, for example, that if we are memorizing a long poem, and repeat it over and over, the parts that we first remember are the end and the beginning. We accept, too, that spaced learning is more efficient than concentrated study. Reading the poem aloud once each day for three weeks will embed it more firmly than reading it twenty-one times at a single session. In short, there is more to repression than memory; and there is more to memory than questions of repression.

Memory, then, is an ego function useful in adapting to one's social environment. Under some conditions, it can be made to work more effectively. Similarly, some of us are blessed with a greater ability than are others to absorb information rapidly and to recall it quickly. There is reason to believe that at least some of the variation among people is due to native endowment. How, then, does repression relate to memory? Repression is present when the person is unable to recall information which, given the normal laws of memory, one would expect him to recall—e.g., his own name, to take an extreme example. We may say that the function of memory has been "invaded" or contaminated by an opposing process of defense. It is in this sense, then, that it is meaningful to talk about the *invasion of ego functions by neurosis.*

Memory serves as a significant and readily understandable instance of such a process whereby the ego is weakened and psychic energy can be utilized less effectively. Perception may also be attacked. A man may look three times on his shelf for a book his wife picks out immediately, a book with which he is familiar. One of my commanding officers in the army went to see our psychiatrist when he found himself repeatedly driving ten miles down the road past the entrance to the post before realizing he had missed the turnoff. Needless to say, the CO over *our* CO was really something!

The ego may be weakened, we have noted, through the *leaking away of psychic energy* into conflict and defense. We now see another form of difficulty. Functions that make up part of what the ego has to offer, when they are operating reasonably smoothly, may become relatively less effective when they are *invaded by conflict.* It is rare, by the way, that a psychological function will be totally eviscerated by such a process. Nearly all psychotic persons I have known were quite clear about how to put on their pants, however strongly they felt that we were holding them hostage. There is scarcely ever a complete loss of reality testing, and this keeps the psychotic busy in squaring his delusions with facts that keep coming to his attention. A woman may be completely illogical about her husband's unfaithfulness but shrewd in calculating the minimum rent she should get for the house after she divorces him. Still, such impairment of an ego function seldom remains confined to the content in which it first appears; it tends to spread. As the impairment becomes more general, the ego becomes weaker—thus it is important not to delay treatment of a neurosis.

When a function like memory is operating reasonably free from the sort of invasions we have been describing, we say that it is a *conflict-free ego sphere*. The more the adaptive functions of the personality have escaped such invasion, the less the person has been crippled by neurosis, the stronger the ego. It is evident, therefore, what one of the main goals of therapy must be. It is to free as wide an area of the ego as possible for conflict-free functioning. In this sense psychoanalytically oriented therapy holds out the same promise as do all those commercialized books about how to exploit your own "hidden reserves of talent and power." I hope this is the only sense in which the two movements are the same. But psychoanalysis ought not be held responsible for the claims made for it by some of its consumers.

The Synthetic Function of the Ego

We have been discussing the manner in which the ego may dissipate its energies through such dynamic interferences as defense and indecisiveness. We cited J. Alfred Prufrock who must be forever held forth as exemplar of the trivialization of life. While "playing it safe," he loses all. Actually, many people have trouble coming to decisions because, to put it bluntly, they are greedy. Most important life decisions require that in order to have A, you must decide not to have B. There is a definition that states: A pessimist is a person who, given a choice between two evils, chooses both. One reason many people are indecisive is that they are trying to devise some way they can have the apple pie, for dessert, and the chocolate cream pie, too.

One of the functions ascribed to the personality is the capacity to resolve such tremendous issues and to live with the outcome. Something must be able to convince the greedy child within us that having the chocolate pie is worth giving up the apple; or that we can have the apple pie the next time; or—and this is really a lot to ask—that the whole matter is not all that important. This ability to take two contradictory alternatives and find an acceptable way out involves a synthesis. With the possibilities that exist for random whims within the personality to ride off madly in all directions, obviously the person would be torn to shreds were he not able to find some way to *integrate* the parts.

Something there is, therefore, which helps to coordinate the disparate strivings and reactions of the personality. This we call the *synthetic function of the ego.* Its operations are most evident in the negotiation of a bargain between contending impulses, but the function goes beyond this. The synthetic function is invoked in conceptualizing the many processes in which the person strives to find a unifying principle in, or "make sense" out of, his experiences. Gestalt psychologists talk about the tendency to closure, by which we see at quick glance a C as if it were a complete ovoid. Such a mechanism in perception might also be ascribed to the synthetic function.

From the standpoint of developmental psychology, such a function is a necessity for the developing organism. Development, after all, finds the child moving from a "vast buzzing confusion" as William James had it, toward more and more refined categories of experience. The child's first caretakers, for example, gradually differentiate into Mother and non-Mother. As the process of differentiation proceeds, there is the question of how the organism is going to achieve coordination among its increasingly complicated sub-parts. That it does so is evidence of the existence, in most of us, of an ability to integrate that matures hand-in-hand with the process of differentiation. The capacity to integrate, or the synthetic function, if you will, seems to be intrinsic to the warp and woof of the whole ego. As contrasted with particular dynamic interferences, this might be thought of as part of the over-all ego structure. *The intactness and effectiveness of the ability to integrate are part of what we mean by ego strength.*

Just as bright people have a more highly differentiated view of the world than do unintelligent ones, so is their capacity to integrate superior, certainly in terms of the ability to think and to perceive the world. In the intellectual-cognitive sphere, the synthetic function makes its mark in the degree of abstraction one can use in relating disparate experiences. A feeble-minded or brain-damaged person might have difficulty in finding one word to cover a lamp, a desk, a chair. "Well, they are all made of wood except the lamp . . . ," he would say. A normally functioning youngster would immediately respond "furniture." Integration of ideas is unquestionably facilitated by the availability of abstractions in one's vocabulary. To what extent vocabulary also helps us synthesize in the realm of action and feelings remains unclear. There is little doubt, however, that there is something like an over-all synthetic function of the ego, which varies from person to person.

Beyond the silent workings of the synthetic function, a conscious dynamic is at work. Most people not only tend to synthesize but also have a *need to appear integrated*. Consistency is often considered the solitary virtue of small minds. Certainly it is true that one cannot always distinguish the man of principle from the mealy-mouthed hypocrite, especially in religious circles. The need to *appear* all of a piece can be exaggerated into a symptom in the obsessive-compulsive personality who, for example, may feel that once he has said something he is "stuck" with it—whether or not he fully meant it in the first place. But the need to appear integrated can also operate to assist treatment. When a client makes a few conflicting statements, and we point this out, the effort to explain himself *to himself* may be part of what leads him to change internally. Self-deception about the degree to which they are unified and substantial people characterizes some neurotic characters and character disorders we shall discuss in later chapters. But the need to appear integrated seems universal, however variable its strength or closeness to reality.

Looseness of Ego Boundaries

The client bustled into the office and brushed back a wisp of hair from her eyes. This was rather futile, because the hair soon fell back, and indeed, her whole appearance was slightly bedraggled. She was not dirty; she was not clean, either. She hunched forward in her chair, breathed a deep sigh after having hurried up the stairs three minutes late, and said:

"Well, it's the same old sixes and sevens at our house. The children are driving me wild, now that school is out, and I don't know if I really do want to go on living with him. Last night was the living end. Well, everything sooner or later comes to an end. And that reminds me. I've got to get the toes repaired on those blue shoes of mine . . . we were planning to go to Sylvia's wedding . . . weddings are so nice. If I had only known . . . What do you think? What would you advise?"

"About what?"

"Would you let him take me to the wedding, when I'm sure he'll just get sloppy drunk, and spill cigar ashes all over the car. And then he'll want to sleep with me. Boy, I never seem to get enough sleep. It is my aristocrasis acting up."

"Your what?"

"My aristocrasis. At least that's what I think it's called. They call and we fall. Tall against the wall. I should never have let him maul . . . you never tell me what to do."

By now the caseworker is a bit groggy. This lady has him on the ropes. He has been carefully schooled that one should "start with the client where she is." But where *is* this lady? The worker feels helpless, inadequate—if only he were more sensitive and skilled. Undoubtedly the client is communicating something besides general restlessness and some complaints against life. It is the worker's job, of course, to pick out signals that are being passed even in a language not generally understood by laymen. But there is something else of which he should be aware. This client seems unable to formulate her thoughts into any systematic sequence of ideas. She talks, it is true, in what sounds like complete sentences. But the sentences do not follow, one from the other. There is evidence at times that her thoughts are easily distracted. Once or twice we note that the client seems to have been carried away by the sheer rhyming quality of what she said. She used a word that is not a word at all. Either she has misheard it from her doctor, or it is a word she just invented, a *neologism*.

When it is this difficult to understand a client, two major hypotheses are to be considered. Perhaps the client does not wish to be understood. Or, perhaps the client is *unable* to sustain a logical train of thought, which is then reflected in her speech. When this is true, we say that she sounds *loose*. This is an imprecise but descriptive term characterizing the kind of weakness in thought process we see here. It refers to a quality of illogicality and disconnectedness in thinking. It also refers to thought that seems to follow rather arbitrary associations.

Other features are often characterized as *looseness* in thinking. With this client, for example, we are able pretty well to follow how one idea hooks into the next, even if the basis of association is rather primitive. That is, ideas are associated not so much in terms of a problem to be solved or a meaning to be communicated as in terms of "echoing" of verbal sounds. Other associations may be quite mysterious to us. If we had the time we might discover that the client's basis for connecting images is that they remind her of things she once saw together—her mother stooping to scrub her front stoop, or some such event.

This kind of association by propinquity of ideas or similarity of sounds is likely to emerge in free association. It is characteristic of the mental workings of fairly young

children. Another characteristic of their thought processes
is an unrealistic appraisal of cause and effect relationships.
For instance, the logical fallacy known as *post hoc, ergo
propter hoc* is characteristic of children's thinking. This
unsystematic, somewhat magical view of the world we call
the primary process; and we refer to *primary process thinking.* We differentiate it from the style of the mature mind,
with its ability to sustain longer chains of logic and its
closer relationship to reality. Whole sentences, indeed whole
paragraphs, of speech may be integrated around a single
abstract idea that is being communicated. Ideas are distinguished from each other with precision. This type of
thought—characteristic of the mature, conscious mind
especially—we describe as *secondary process thinking.*
Primary process thinking comes to the fore in sleep, when
one is fatigued, ill, or intoxicated. Any one of us is capable
of primary process thinking; it remains in the substratum
of the mind.

We have the feeling that primary process thinking pre-
dominates in this client's mental processes, most of the
time. Perhaps that is partly why she seems so disorganized.
She is. In a more general way, we might then say she dis-
plays *looseness of ego boundaries.* This refers not only to
the disorderly thinking and speech but also to the inability
to hold steadily to a task she has assigned herself. One can
easily imagine her stopping, with one stocking on, to start
the coffee, before returning to her toilet, which will be interrupted by three other activities, and never finished at all.

Looseness of ego boundaries, in more extreme forms,
also permits the eruption into the conscious part of the
mind of ideas and images usually kept repressed. It is hard
to say whether this is pathological, although one should
consider the possibility. After all, unusual ideas and images
are part of the charm of poetry and painting. Important
scientific problems have been solved by sudden insights
brought into being by the availability, to the creative worker, of just such offbeat imagery. A famous example in the

history of science is the well-known benzene ring on which so much of organic chemistry is based. Its discoverer was challenged with the problem of how six carbon atoms might be arranged, spatially, so that they had certain properties. One day he rose from a reverie with an image that, instead of the atoms sitting in a line, as he had thought of them, they had formed into a circle, like a snake who has started to swallow his own tail. (I once got the idea of applying scale-analysis technique to a set of data while I was painting a wire gate made, as they usually are, like graph paper.) As Oppenheimer, one of the greatest physicists of our generation, remarked in a television interview, "If we do not dream by night, we shall have nothing to correct by day." But of course Oppenheimer was capable of rechecking his half-sleepy bright ideas against logic fortified by morning coffee. Persons suffering from true looseness of ego boundaries are not able to displace one style of thought with the other by an act of concentration.

Looseness of ego boundaries refers also to the failure to sustain structure in other realms as well. We think of looseness in connection with extremely impulsive persons. They are said to be unable to *bind impulses,* but must give way to them immediately or else suffer extreme discomfort. An example I like to use involves a dollar bill. In an average class, I could drop the bill on my desk, leave the room, and come back to find it just where I left it. The only problem it would present to most would be whether to comment on it or to put it away for me. Hardly any student would be really conflicted about whether he wanted to steal it. His controls are *well internalized,* which is to say that they operate automatically and with no conscious effort. A delinquent youngster, on the other hand, might also leave the dollar bill alone, but only after some struggle with himself about whether he might get caught or whether he wanted to "treat Polansky dirty," or the like. In the realm of impulse control, his ego boundaries are not so firm as are most of ours. Or, his price is lower! The story is told that when U. S. Grant was stationed at St. Louis acting as procurement officer for the U.S. Army, he wrote to Washington asking to be relieved. Reason? "They are getting awfully close to my price!"

To the extent that ego boundaries are firm and whole, precise thought and planful, coordinated action become the more possible. There is usually also greater capacity for dealing with abstractions. Persons whose thought processes are the more primitive usually are more *concrete minded.* They cannot think in complex units or even take richness of possibilities into account. I shall never forget the psychiatrist who, in reporting to the hospital staff on a new female patient, gave a colorful and hair-raising account of her escapades and harassments by her husband. As the patient seemed to the rest of us very flamboyant, someone asked, "How do you know all this really happened?" This man stared in shocked amazement and replied, "That's what she told me." It was simply not possible for him to listen to so embroidered a tale and simultaneously sift it to see whether the patient might be consciously lying or, as often happens, confusing fantasy with memory—which would be another common form of looseness.

Looseness of ego boundaries is, itself, not a very precise concept, but it does prove helpful in beginning to size up a client with whom we will be dealing. All of us vary in how loose we are, depending on the situation. Nevertheless, there are some persons who unfortunately remain relatively loose under even optimal conditions. Some are psychotic, of course; all schizophrenics betray this pattern. Whether such looseness is inborn or the result of early life experiences remains unclear. There are analysts who believe that the group we call *autistic* children have a congenital defect in their capacity to order the world they perceive. They have looseness of ego boundaries as an inborn trait, persisting even as they mature.

External Supports Against Looseness

We have mentioned that looseness may be an enduring characteristic of the personality, but it may also be a reaction to the immediate situation. Once, for example, I found myself in what I had always fantasied as an ideal job. I arrived for work and was led to a small but plush office (at least it was plush by the standards on which I had been reared in social agencies, prisons, children's camps, and the like). I was introduced to a pleasant woman who, I was told, was my full-time secretary available for any typing I should need. There was a rather good library on the premises and easy access to others. Naturally, I was curious about what was expected of me. The answer was, "Well, hang around a while and see what comes to mind. We want to know what you think of what we are doing." This is not an unreasonable request, actually, nor was mine so outlandish a job for an intellectual. The trouble was that I had come to it after a rather frantic period of my life in which I taught a full course load at a university, while conducting a major research project "on the side"; in addition, I undertook a variety of extra assignments, some because I felt they should be done, some because they fed my narcissism, and some because I needed the money. The sudden shift to this placid and undemanding existence was more than I could take; its major impact was an enormous feeling of inadequacy. After all, the "bright ideas" to be expected from a person so petted by society must be terrific. The price of having no demands made upon you is also that no one really needs you. Such a situation can give full play to any paranoid imaginings or anxieties to which one is prone. He may yearn for a solid assignment, any routine job, into which he can sink his teeth. Although this experience happened later in my life, it is, I believe, not far different from what occurs for many students during their first days, or even weeks, in field placement. They arrive with stars in their eyes and butterflies in their stomachs and are told,

"Here are some case records from last year. Why not look them over and see what sort of thing we do here?"

A young psychiatrist and his chief social worker decided, when they were assigned to take over a mental hospital, to see what life was like for patients in the hospital. They went to one of the back wards and proceeded to follow the patients' routines. They got up, ate a meager breakfast in the cafeteria among a group of withdrawn, somber fellow patients. Then they returned to the main hall of their ward building, where they joined the other patients in sitting in long rows of rocking chairs. There they sat, rocking. Such spasmodic efforts as the staff made were dedicated to "keeping things peaceful." From time to time, one or another patient would arise, grasp the end of a push-broom and shamble the length of the day room, clearing a few odd bits of dust from the polished floor. This routine was interrupted by two major events: meals and trips to the bathroom.

After three days of this routine, our two professionals found themselves no longer observing. Instead, they noted that their thoughts wandered aimlessly; bits of old songs caught their attention and perseverated in their minds; indeed, one of them began to have visions which, fortunately, he could recognize were quite unreal and creatures of daydreaming with his eyes open. They emerged with this question: Was the ward designed to keep peace among a group of schizophrenic patients, or was the schizophrenia supported by the lack of structure and stimulation in the ward environment? Of the two, the second possibility seemed to them the more likely. And this was not an isolated instance. To this day, you can go to almost any state hospital, in almost any state, and you will find this universal feature. Ward personnel are sitting on their bottoms waiting for the end of their eight-hour shifts, and the patients are immersed in fantasies.

From a variety of sources, we have reason to suppose that the absence of clear external structure in one's life makes it likelier that ego boundaries will loosen. This is one of the potent effects of isolating political prisoners from all contact with the outside world, while simultaneously keeping them in a state of uncertainty about the future. It is especially important that the prisoner have no map to guide his actions, and it is deliberately made capricious whether by his actions he can do anything to save himself. Other illustrations come from the now-familiar experiments on stimulus deprivation. Placed in a soundproof room, suspended in a bath at body temperature in the darkness, some subjects hallucinate. Content usually held unconscious breaks through and begins to dominate consciousness.

David Rapaport (1958) said that the ego is *relatively autonomous*. It maintains its autonomy from the id in part by virtue of its continuing responsiveness to external reality. In psychiatric treatment, at least under inpatient conditions, we have learned this lesson well. When the inner structure of the personality is too infirm, a more stimulating external one acts as a counter. Certainly it is to this process of prodding and protecting that one must attribute those successes in some state hospitals of treatment through medical staff inaction which we used to call "spontaneous remissions." It is now possible to design a life-encompassing treatment setting which leads to a higher percentage of remissions, less haphazardly than formerly (Redl and Wineman, 1952).

Just as the absence of external demand may fail to provide needed support to an ego in trouble, so may too much external pressure. It is as if the requirements of the environment lead to a rise in internal tension such that inner boundaries are literally flooded out. Obviously, in offering support to damaged egos through a structured environment, the art lies in imposing sufficient external demand so that ego boundaries are called into play and exercised, without so much demand that they become overwhelmed.

Finally, I should like to comment on the seeming complementarity between the ego and its social setting. In the political sphere, for example, it is customary to blame the regressive, childlike quality found in so many people living under totalitarian regimes on the effects of their dictatorships. It is not customary to ask: Under what sort of regime would it be possible to sustain order among a people with this average level of maturity? It is difficult for me to believe that the average Russian peasant was at all ready for democracy, as we know it in the Western world, and that any effort to offer it to him would not have ended in chaos. One often hears that people get the governments they deserve. Perhaps it is more precise to note that people, and their governments, seem to set up complementary relationships such that if one will not provide necessary controls for himself, he intuitively accepts a government that will do it for him. "Where there is no character, there has to be a system."

There are of course more limited examples of this kind of complementarity. Most mothers who love their children intuitively adapt themselves to a child's needs. It is not uncommon, therefore, to find that the mother of a child with a developmental defect in establishing inner boundaries has fallen into a pattern of providing the child's planning, synthesizing, and self-controlling from the outside. We then say, "She does his thinking for him," but this is an oversimplification. The problem, if there is a soluble problem, may be that the mother is continuing to act as this ego support when the child no longer needs so much. Even mildly retarded children develop, albeit at a slower pace. Caseworkers who meet with their parents often are in the position to help them turn the child loose, freer to find his own way through some aspects of living. In at least some cases, the child makes dramatic advances toward self-reliance out of this mode of treatment. The treatment, let us say, is simple in action, but it is derived from a sophisticated theory.

One final example, before we move on. What is the role of *work* in the psychic economy? We know that through it we earn our financial living; we also know that through it we earn part of our psychological living, too. Is this not because, regardless of the internal conflicts or pangs we may be feeling, our jobs usually require that we brace ourselves, attend to external happenings, solve problems, invest ourselves in getting something done in a world that is real and impresses us with its reality? What a protection against inner devils! It is common to think that a man becomes unable to work because he is neurotic. This may be true. The neurosis may invade the work life as it has so many other functions of the personality. But, because of its outer-directed quality, the demands it makes, and, for people who have become good workmen, there is a sense of accomplishment while on the job, the work life is harder than many other areas to break down. In fact, continuing to work may provide a powerful support against collapsing under a burden of depression and conflict. It is for this reason that one finds so meaningful the psychoanalytic slogan, "Work: the last bastion of defense." This is as true for us as it is for our clients (Polansky, 1959).

Although I have been a social worker as well as a psychologist, I must confess to having catered to my self-indulgence by spending a number of years in contact with some patients who represented great wealth. I cannot join F. Scott Fitzgerald's eternal adolescent when he commented that the very rich are not as others of us. This is not true (even though some of his other remarks may have had more pith, e.g., that Hemingway was ever ready to extend someone a helping hand on the ladder of success—from below). Neither does it seem likely to me that the presence of great wealth is a disadvantage. I have seen many young people whose psychiatric condition was such that they would have landed on the scrap heap were they not provided first-class treatment through their parents' monies. I have seen a woman whose children would have been seriously neglected during a lengthy depression were it not for the presence of competent hired help in the home. But it is true that the son of a man who does nothing in particular in this world has a harder time composing an identity by which to live. Even worse, as he struggles to find something bigger than himself, or at least outside himself, which would stir him from his inner preoccupations, he faces a problem which is vastly simplified for those of us who are poorer. If you are rich enough, it is hard to convince yourself that there is anything that *needs* doing. Worse, even if it needs doing, you can hire it done, so it does not need doing *by you*. Unfortunately, the external demands which poorer men experience as insistent acquire for the very rich a gamelike, playful quality. Only the most dedicated can find "work"!

Protections Against Becoming Overwhelmed

We have discussed a desirable complementarity between internal looseness and external supports, such that the latter can make up for the former. But it is clear that support for a weak ego by outside manipulation is likely to be at best a holding action. We are left with two significant issues: (1) What must character contain in order best to withstand life's vicissitudes? (2) How can such structure be instilled, either in a growing child, or in a patient in need of help?

My intention is not to try now to encapsulate all the literature of child guidance and child development. Much of what is needed for a resilient, reality-oriented, and flexible ego organization is implicit in what has been said above. Let me just mention a few points that have seemed outstanding to me and are not always discussed.

The presence of a strong set of internal standards is not just admirable, it serves as a protection against falling apart. By such internal standards I am of course referring to what in sociology we call *values* and might also call the conscience. Life and happenstance in it are not intrinsically meaningful. We impose meaning on it. For a person to "make sense" out of life disasters, and to manage to ride them out, it is helpful if there are at least some principles to which he can cling, some bulwarks he can use to strengthen ego boundaries, if you will, when he threatens to collapse into a sodden heap.

I have observed that, among people doing casework or therapy, those who were working in terms of a theory were usually more successful than those who were eclectic, provided the theory was not too far removed from reality. The theory seemed to lend their efforts a purposefulness, a directedness which itself strengthened the client's ego. And only if you have a theory can you calculate the direction of errors you seem to be making and correct them.

The same might be said for a person caught in the grip of neurosis. If there is something he stands for, and something he is willing to stand by, then he has a chance of surviving the vicissitudes he will experience. But how is such a system of values instilled? Obviously, it can do its work well only if it is truly part of the person, not something he lives by in order to accommodate to external pressures. The country has always been full of young men who learned to conform either in our boys' industrial and training schools or in our prisons long enough to be discharged. External conformity, going through the motions, does not lend the strength of character which affords resilience.

We went through a long period when many psychologists believed it would be best if children were given maximum opportunities to find their own ways. Rather than imposing values and controls on them, we should let them gradually see the point, themselves. This would be more effective in the long run. It is also easier on the parents, by the way, some of whom are avid for this approach because they do not have enough character to fight the child for his own good. The generation of young Americans who are out of control is not a result of their rearing according to the tenets of Dr. Spock; they are the victims of weak-kneed parents who have distorted the content of Spock because they were too busy "making it."

Therefore, we must add a few points relevant to both child development and treatment. First, controls become internalized only after they have been externally imposed. The child cleans himself first to escape mama's spanking or disapproval; next, he washes up because he can anticipate that mama will disapprove, but she does not have to remind him each time; finally, he washes up because he wants to be clean. It is not necessary to brutalize a child or force him beyond his age-relevant capacities to promote this sequence. But it is necessary that mama be clear in her mind what she wants accomplished and be both realistic and consistent with the child. A high percentage of children who show difficulties with control systems have parents who were inconsistent, or who literally never gave a bit of thought to how one "trains" a child, and usually both.

Second, and this is related to the first point, people seem better able to withstand external pressure if they have strong values that are internally held. Although the wording of this statement is practically circular, it has some interesting derivations. For instance, many progressive educators assumed that the way to foster a self-determined young man or young woman was to provide a permissive environment in which he might find his own set of values, his own vision of truth. This is good to think about, but it is not true to my observations of people. The people best able to stand up against pressures from their neighbors, from their community, to fight for justice and truth usually came from surprisingly rigid backgrounds. Persons from deeply religious backgrounds often made up the hard and fearless core of those willing to stand against McCarthyism or the peculiar group-think which periodically sweeps the South. As Bruno Bettelheim (1943) pointed out in a classic report, it was the Zionists, not the assimilated among the Jews, who were able to survive in the Nazi concentration camp with least deterioration to their personalities.

Finally, and we have made this point before, the presence of firm ego boundaries within the person makes life easier rather than harder. Temptations are more easily withstood if one is certain what he will and won't do. It is the difference between simply turning a faucet as opposed to plugging a pipe with one's thumb. From the standpoint of psychoanalysis, the conscience plays a definite function in one's life. It is not there as a decoration, on which one can solicit and receive congratulations; neither is it a hairshirt one can conceal beneath his coat to feel secretly superior to those who "make it" less encumbered. The purpose of a *healthy* conscience is to keep you out of trouble, and that is what it does, and with relatively little effort on your part.

In reviewing sources of ego strength we find a somewhat surprising note. It appears that another aspect of ego strength is to have a realistic and effective *superego*.

I was once visiting the home of a famous psychoanalyst who had adolescent children. While I was there, a radio in the lower part of the house began blaring some excrescence of rock and roll music grating even to the nerves of a lifelong devotee of jazz. To the analyst, it was unbearable. He left the room and "roared" that they should turn that radio down to a dull whisper. As he was well known for his writing on adolescent behavior, I teased him a bit, asking whether he did not want to be thought an old fogy. His reply was memorable: "I would rather my children thought me an old fogy than that they had a father with no opinions!"

Coping Mechanisms

A strong ego has been described as one which makes it possible for a person to absorb life's punishments and emergencies, to reconstitute himself and go on. Very broadly, we may think of this as an ability the person has as part of his enduring personality, his character structure. In practice, none of us deals with LIFE, but rather with a long series of happenings. In this more specific way, we ask not only how generally resilient the person is, but how he *copes* with stresses and crises.

Interest in *mechanisms for coping* has grown in recent years as clinicians have moved out of their traditional role of dealing only with curative processes in long-term treatment. During World War II, for example, we learned that if a man were evacuated from the immediate vicinity of combat in order to treat his so-called "battle fatigue," it was nearly impossible to restore him to duty. Therefore, the pattern grew up of offering psychiatric first-aid practically on the battlefield, as it were, before the neurotic reaction had become so set—and so overlain with not wanting to get well—that restoration to duty was impossible.

Such on-the-spot treatment was much emphasized in Lindemann's germinal work on handling acute grief (1944). From detailed observations of persons who had just lost someone they loved, it became possible to analyze not only the various ways people spontaneously cope with such a tragedy but also which methods of coping seemed more successful. Of course, no form of responding can bring back the one we have lost and restore life to how it had been. But there are ways of responding that seem to make us less susceptible to enduring damage to our personalities. It was found, for example, that persons who express their grief at once and with open display of emotions are less likely to present severe personality difficulties to themselves and their families than do those who delay and show no immediate response.

From such observations it is possible not only to identify what appear to be the potentially "healthier" forms of grief reaction (which tend of course to occur in people who were healthier to begin with) but also to use the insights gained from such observations to encourage clients experiencing a loss to handle it in such a way that it will be least destructive to them. These efforts to help our clients and patients handle such stressful experiences are called *crisis intervention* (Parad, 1965). Much of what we know about how to help people in crisis has been gleaned from studying the automatic processes of self-healing that have worked well for others. Here, as always, therapy follows the pattern of trying to cooperate with nature.

The function of the coping mechanisms is to restore equilibrium, to get the person back on his feet, and to permit further growth if that is in order. It is nearly impossible to list all the coping mechanisms. For one thing, they are only now being identified and collated. In general, like the defenses, they involve thinking, feeling, and acting—singly or in combination. A simple form of coping with a problem, for example, is to delay action while detouring into thought. Rather than act impulsively, we think about possible solutions, we conduct trial-and-error experimentation in our minds at low cost in energy and for the moment without commitment. When we have finally imagined a course that seems likely to achieve what we want, we are able to act. Obviously, this kind of thinking-as-detour-behavior is not at the disposal of impulse-ridden people. By the same token, casework viewed as a problem-solving process is pitched beyond their grasp (Perlman, 1957).

Coping mechanisms are likely to come to mind especially when we have a patient faced with a sudden external trauma like accidental loss of a limb or desertion by a mate. But there are also universally experienced stress points in the life cycle deriving from maturational processes. Every adolescent has to "cope" with his developing sexuality in his early teens, and so do his parents. How well he does so is determined by the kind of support he is given at that stage of his life, and perhaps more, by the ego strength he had already built up in resolving previous developmental crises (Erikson, 1950). Similarly, each of us must come to terms with aging, and the prospect not only of physical decline but of ceasing to be (Cath, 1965).

Sometimes what needs to be handled is within the person. Each of us who is at all active sooner or later does something about which he feels guilty, and the guilt is completely realistic and appropriate. Whether we are able to learn from the experience and change our way of treating others depends on the coping mechanisms we employ. Some patients, for instance, are overcome with remorse, but only in a general way that does not lead them to examine what they did or seek to prevent its recurrence. Some go into depressive reactions which are well deserved but evidently overdone and perhaps histrionic. Some simply refuse to experience the guilt consciously at all, claiming that what they did was right. For them, the method of coping is to undermine the superego. The absorption of deserved guilt is one of the hallmarks of maturity, and it can be encouraged by proper counseling at the time it occurs.

Finally, we must recognize that it is not easy to distinguish coping from defense mechanisms which may, or may not, prove pathological. A person with a long-term illness that will eventually prove fatal can cope with it best by partially denying it, living as if he had a longer future than he really does. On the other hand, there are well-known instances in which flagrant, primitive denial has led to unnecessary risk-taking and suffering—like the man who climbed a mountain immediately after release from the hospital after a heart attack, and died at the summit. None of us could survive in our part of the twentieth century without some capacity for denial of the military postures under which we do our work, so it is hard to see this defense mechanism as purely pathological. Persons with an exquisite sense of reality and a need for truth-telling often lead markedly uncomfortable lives. It is because there are defenses, then, which aid in coping that we teach the student early to "respect defenses." Just as earlier we reminded the reader of the difficulty in labeling categorically any group of defenses as "symptoms," so now we emphasize that there are softenings of reality-perception which we refer to as coping. Evidently, a judgment of what is evasion and what is adaptive perception must be made with tenderness of spirit on the part of the practitioner.

References

Bettelheim, Bruno. "Individual and Mass Behavior in Extreme Situations," *Journal of Abnormal and Social Psychology, 38,* 1943, 417–452.

Cath, Stanley H. "Some Dynamics of the Middle and Later Years," in H.J.Parad, ed., *Crisis Intervention: Selected Readings.* New York: Family Service Association of America, 1965.

Eliot, T. S. *Collected Poems 1909–1962.* London: Faber & Faber; New York: Harcourt, Brace & World.

Erikson, Erik H. *Childhood and Society.* New York: W. W. Norton, 1950.

Fraiberg, Selma H. *The Magic Years.* New York: Charles Scribner's Sons, 1959.

Hartmann, Heinz. *Ego Psychology and the Problem of Adaptation.* New York: International Universities Press, 1958 (originally 1939).

Lindemann, Erich. "Symptomatology and Management of Acute Grief," *American Journal of Psychiatry, 101,* 1944, 141–148.

Parad, Howard J. ed. *Crisis Intervention: Selected Readings.* New York: Family Service Association of America, 1965.

Perlman, Helen H. *Social Casework: A Problem Solving Process.* Chicago: University of Chicago Press, 1957.

Polansky, Norman A. "The Professional Identity in Social Work," in Alfred J. Kahn, ed., *Issues in American Social Work Today.* New York: Columbia University Press, 1959.

Rapaport, David. "The Theory of Ego Autonomy: A Generalization," *Bulletin of the Menninger Clinic, 22,* 1958, 13–35.

Redl, Fritz, and David Wineman. *Controls from Within.* New York: The Free Press, 1952.

Chapter 4

Character as Personality Structure

AMONG THE MOST IMPORTANT ASPECTS OF EGO PSYCHOLOGY is the study of what is termed *character*. Indeed, the more experienced many of us have become in treatment, teaching, or administration, the more are we impressed with the efficiency of concentrating on the character of those involved in any situation where it is important to us to make predictions. This is as true of complex social situations, at times, as it is in estimating individual reaction.

Imagine you are employed at a hospital headed by a narrow, rigid, stingy person. You must decide whether to remain. Should the director leave, there is no immediate cause for enthusiasm about the opportunity open to the board to improve things. After all, the board appointed him in the first place. Those members who found such a person not the sort they wanted in charge of their hospital probably voluntarily weeded themselves out of the board during his tenure. From the director's personality, in other words, one can already divine a number of things about his board. Therefore, it is only luck when, as does occasionally happen, the replacement proves a more flexible, generous human being, interested in curing people. To part of the board, this will only prove they have made a mistake.

From a knowledge of character one can derive a number of crucial guidelines for helping our clients and patients and, if necessary, ourselves. I shall begin the discussion here, but because of its importance, I will devote another chapter to it also. After listing some of the general ideas involved, I will illustrate by depicting a personality syndrome to which I have previously referred—the obsessive-compulsive personality.

Structure

Many trivia have been written about how one should behave in order to make a good impression on a perspective employer. While this nonsense may be of some use to unusually obtuse young businessmen, the issue is beside the point for most students I have met. What the average young professional needs far more is cogent advice as to how to size up the person doing the hiring. After all, if you are to spend one, two, or ten years working for a man, he has it in his power to make quite an impact on your life.

Suppose, for example, that you have been in correspondence with the Dean of a School. He has expressed interest, you have expressed interest, and now you have come some hundreds of miles to visit him and discuss things further. You arrive promptly for your appointment, but then are kept waiting—not five or ten minutes, but twenty or more. When you finally are ushered into his office, it becomes evident he has been dictating letters. In fact, you soon realize that from the first exchange you are being let know "who is in charge around here." A lot of your interview concerns itself with the great plans and changes this Dean has brought about in his School. He brushes aside details, such as your fringe benefits, you notice, but does take the time for a bit of self-important bragging. In short, you decide he is a little man, even a nasty little man, and no one in whom you want to entrust your job life. Now, you should be warned about turning down an offer from this sort of person. Since he sees only his own needs in the situation, he is likely to be angry if you refuse his magnanimous offer—at a figure lower than you believe you can get—after he has deigned to make it. He will take your refusal as a personal rejection; he will have an urge to retaliate, in some way. If he is sufficiently infantile, he will carry out the impulse.

I once had an interview with such an unlikeable little person, under conditions in which I had agreed to spend two and a half days looking over the terrain, and being looked over. Within an hour or so, it was quite clear to me that I did not want to work for him, but I was there at the invitation of one of his subordinates and so felt obligated not to embarrass my colleague but to go through the routine as planned. Moreover, it occurred to me that this was the sort of person who would try to punish me for refusing to submit to him by withholding travel expenses, despite prior agreement to pay. So I left without making my decision, and waited until my travel had been reimbursed. Then, one week later, I wrote to say I did not think the position was for me. Withholding one's travel reimbursement is a picayune ploy, and for a time I felt a little shameful toward the Dean for having estimated him so low. However, I fell into conversation about him with a professional acquaintance, some years later, who told me that the Dean would do just as I feared. He had done it to a woman who had the misfortune to have treated him quite ethically—telling him immediately when she knew she was not interested, so he could approach someone else. He never did pay her travel expenses, although she wrote to him about it several times.

As used in common speech, the word "character" carries a strong value connotation. To say that a man has character is to imply that he has morals and can be counted on to act in terms of them. Indeed, there is an implication of fixity which can approach rigidity. It is in character for a man of character to stand by his principles even when they are wrong, as long as they are characteristic.

Psychoanalytic theory also employs the word, but without evaluation. The emphasis is on predictability. By *character,* then, we refer simply to patterns that recur in the person under observation. Character is made up of traits that can be counted on to reveal themselves even in markedly varying situations. Put another way, a person's character is his life style, the warp and woof of his personality.

Students who have had some training in sociology and anthropology will recognize the appositeness of character to *structure* as it is used, say, in "the structural-functional approach." What do we mean by this?

Basically we are cognizant of the ancient truism, "This too shall pass." In life, all is change; nothing remains truly constant. But even while everything is changing, some changes are infinitely faster than are others. It has become customary to refer to parameters which are relatively fixed as *structural,* or *structures.* Thus, in speaking of a group, we might mention its *power structure,* reflecting the fact that some individuals in the group consistently possess more influence than do the others. The group's *morale,* on the other hand, is something we expect to see fluctuate from day to day. *Roles* are structured, obviously, because they refer to constancies in how persons are expected to behave toward each other.

Since character refers to enduring patterns within the personality, it is also a *structural concept.* Groups, we have noted, have power structures and role structures. People, too, tend to become *structured:* as time passes, they become more "set in their ways." Why this is so is not well understood, but we can make some tentative explanations. At least we can go beyond remarking that they continue to do what they do because "it has become a habit." This is not explanation; it is name calling.

It is obvious that following an established pattern relieves a person of the effort it would take to produce new responses to the same stimuli. Particularly if there is a problem to be dealt with, it is far less demanding to follow a well-worn solution than to find a new one. Finding new solutions requires us to focus the situation in the full light of conscious attention. And, of all forms of *psychic energy* concentrated, conscious attention appears by far the most exhausting. It is the hardest to sustain over long periods.

Even though I am making an effort to make it easily readable, this book is not the sort one can read steadily with unwavering attention. I know this, and that is why I put in little breaks and buffer zones, from time to time, in the form of examples, side remarks, and the like. These add some color, I hope, to the presentation; they also provide instances where the reader knows that if he does not pay close attention at the moment, he still will not have missed a major point. In short, I try to allow for the waxing and waning of conscious attention. Because it "takes so much out of us," it is not surprising, therefore, to discover that an inability to sustain attention is a frequent symptom among persons whose psychological energy is already depleted. Most neurotics suffer some shortening of attention span.

Structuring responses conserves energy; it may also avoid pain, which is another powerful force leading to structuring. Defenses, for example, are likely to become fixed, or structured. After all, any habitual way of doing things may well be part of a defensive maneuver. Should one seek to change his ways, he takes the risk that old conflicts and the anxiety associated with them will rear their heads once more. It is partly for this reason that symptoms tend to become part of a person's character, and ego-syntonic as well. Similar processes, by the way, are observable in groups. Social institutions often serve to preserve compromises among conflicting subgroups which were originally arrived at after a bloody battle. An attempt to change the institution is the moral equivalent of penetrating a defense. Group resistance will take directions analogous to individual forms.

Finally, any pattern that has become a part of character usually serves also as a means of yielding satisfactions. What starts as a defense is reworked by the shrewd ego in order that, even as he is warding off anxiety, the person is concurrently getting some other benefits. A homosexual may be caricaturing and mocking his mother; simultaneously, he uses "camping" to keep himself in a state of low-level erotic excitement—and, of course, he may even be paid or supported for his sexual services. All this goes on while he is renouncing what he finds threatening in normal sexuality.

When an action or pattern which was originally developed in the service of defense becomes useful as a channel for drive-discharge and gives pleasure, it is likely to be *structured*. We may say that it has become a part of character, a *character-defense* (Reich, 1933). This all comes about through the skill of the ego in converting a liability into an asset. Because of this skill, symptoms that have existed for years are likely to have been diverted to non-defensive uses. An untreated symptom, therefore, is often much harder to remove after a number of years; it is also common for such a symptom to "spread," involving more and more of the personality. The symptom is the more *embedded* because it has acquired numerous extra functions, reminiscent of a bureaucrat building his little empire as an indispensable man. Because the symptom has made itself so "useful" it is hard to dislodge, not simply because it has been around a long time. As the psychologist John McGeoch used to say of his memory-drum experiments, "Time *qua* time does nothing." Those Freudians who understand the issue will agree.

When one speaks of character in an adult human, one is discussing a melange. Included are channels for sublimating drive energies, defenses, habitual adaptations, and so on. An almost infinite variety of individual styles can be evolved, and this makes our field so fascinating. No two patients or clients are ever identical, even if they fight all the time because they are so much alike. But, even among the diversity, psychologists have had some success in establishing general types or categories of humans.

These typologies are not satisfactory. No definition one

devises ever completely fits the human being in one's office, unless that definition is so general it would fit nearly anyone. Moreover, a patient we have in mind usually has features that fit into more than one category. Why, then, do we bother to teach them at all?

The important thing about these typologies is that they do not represent neat pigeonholes, but *syndromes.* Some personality features go together with other personality features. They do this consistently. The reason there is so much consistency is that the styles in which character comes together are not accidental. The personality as a whole constitutes a kind of *gestalt,* whose parts are interdependent one with another. We have already had reason to comment on this, in discussing the fact that even treatment which concentrates on symptomatic improvement is likely to result in at least some shifts in the underlying causes of the illness.

There are basically two major reasons why syndromes exist with relative consistency. The first is historical. An event or a distortion in one's life at an early age is likely to have effects which, by now, are more or less predictable. These effects will show up in the several spheres of human functioning. Even though the spheres are different, if one knows the historical origin of the difficulty, one can predict its effects from sphere to sphere. The second reason for the consistency is functional. One may have a source of anxiety and cover it by a defense. If the defense in turn is unacceptable to one's consciousness, he may add a layer over this in the form of a reaction formation. Thus, a person preoccupied with sadistic impulses may display exaggerated concern for suffering. In our examples, I shall emphasize the functional basis of the fitting-togetherness of character more than its historical causation. This is because in my experience the latter style of explanation, which Kurt Lewin (1936) termed *ahistorical causation,* is more significant both in predicting behavior and in treatment.

To reiterate, it is no contribution to establish that a "type" exists if all we have in mind is to take a patient and find a label for him. The real contribution comes if we are trying to understand someone and we know a few things about him, but not a lot. Our knowledge of "types" will then be valuable when, from limited information, we can guess a good many other things about the person. Thus far, our knowledge of character, or of character types, is seldom sufficiently great to permit certainty in such extensions from the known to the unknown. But—as with the Dean I never worked for—we often do know enough to make predictions based on good odds. At least that is my impression; the reader will have to try things out himself. People vary in their ability to predict intuitively, even without formal training. But a good theory added to natural intuition makes a formidable combination for understanding our fellow humans.

A Traditional Characterology

In psychoanalysis, the character typologies first established were based on the early work of Karl Abraham (1927). As id psychology was most of what they had in those days, it was natural that the character typology in vogue should represent the drives and their vicissitudes. Most readers are well acquainted with the theory, and indeed the observation, that there appears to be a sequence in the development of humans such that certain body areas are charged with pleasure in a fixed order. These pleasurable areas are called the erogenous zones, of course. The sequence goes from mouth, to anus, to genitalia as maturation proceeds through the earliest months and years of life.

Students of an earlier generation were told that there was an *oral-receptive* phase, followed by the *oral-biting* phase. The latter would be more or less displaced by the *anal-expulsive* and then the *anal-retentive* phases. Eventually, the attention is shifted to the pleasure derivable from manipulation of the genitals, which in boys was called the *phallic* phase. It is important to recall, however, that the phallic phase was not seen as equivalent to mature genital pleasure. For one thing, it was masturbatory, lacking a desire for the mutuality found in what is called *mature sexuality*—simultaneously giving and receiving pleasure. Also, childish genitality consists only of low-level eroticism in the form of stroking or rubbing, without building up to peaks of orgasm or ejaculation. At this stage, there is no peak, but just the kind of slightly exciting rubbing that unhappy children and anxious adults often continue to indulge in as a means of comforting themselves in the face of an unfriendly world.

That there are in fact such things as erogenous zones hardly warrants demonstration today. Although students used to look upon such a listing as that given above with adumbrations of the forbidden, risqué, or disgusting, these ideas now seem much more mundane. Even if there is a sequence in the zone to which the child is supposedly chiefly attentive as he matures, in most of us the pleasurable potential of each does not disappear with middle childhood. Who, that enjoys a pipe, will deny the lip pleasure of holding it in his mouth? Certainly, some of the delight of sea food is its chewy quality—gum-pleasure from biting. The tension relief associated with bowel evacuation is undeniable, and this may in fact be heightened into a kind of exquisiteness after retention.

If a person develops normally, and fortunately, after adolescence his greatest source of pleasure is concentrated on the genital area (which seems plausible). In addition, he seeks to satisfy himself in a relationship of mutuality with a person of the opposite sex. It was recognized that the course of development does not run smoothly for all of us. Some are unable, or fearful, of maturing toward mature sexuality. Instead, they continue to exploit erogenous zones which luckier people have largely given up for genital activity. The question of homosexuality raises all sorts of legal, moral, and ethical issues on which psychoanalysis can claim no particular expertise. But it seems demonstrable that physiologically male and female humans are so constructed as to maximize the chance of giving each other pleasure simultaneously in normal intercourse. The psychological problem of homosexuality, therefore, can be reduced to this: How come the patient has settled for less than the best?

Continued concentration on a body area for pleasure after that childhood phase of life has passed is called *fixation*. For example, we might say, jokingly, that a man who seems more interested in his food, liquor, and cigars than he is in sex was "fixated at the oral stage." This description encompasses a fair proportion of the courthouse politicians in this country, however, so it is wise to be careful where you make the comment. It is not too clear what is meant by fixation in Freudian theory, although it is conventional to mouth words about failing to develop, and the like. Nevertheless, it does appear that if the infant was either totally indulged at a given life stage *or* badly deprived, he is more likely to show evidence of being stuck at that stage in his mature personality. It is as if, on the one hand, he had no need to progress toward other satisfactions; and, on the other, he had no reason to look forward hopefully, based on his experience thus far. But this is "as if." We have no basis for judging whether our infants really do carry on a Benthamite calculus of hedonism in their minds. We do have some evidence, however, that puppies which have been either deprived or overindulged tend to "fixate" at the oral stage.

We shall next sketch two character types as they were originally taught. One reason we do this is that such terms as "oral type" and "anal type" are still present in the vocabularies of some expert social workers and therapists, and the reader will want to have a sense of what they are trying to convey. The terms have survived because, despite subsequent advances in theory, they do in fact provide good shorthand descriptions of a fair number of fellow humans one encounters. Finally, one will notice that reflections of these original analyses of personality are still to be found in the personality descriptions presently more in vogue (Reiner and Kaufman, 1959; Kaufman, 1963).

The Oral Character

The outstanding characteristic of the oral character is his greed. This may be shown in his patterns of eating, drinking, and smoking. It may even be found in his work habits, in which he throws himself completely into the job, as if trying to engorge himself on work as he otherwise does with food. I once had a patient who was an alcoholic, and an extremely successful one, too. One reason for this was that he alternated several months of working twelve- to sixteen-hour days with a binge of a week or more, followed by a few days in a middle-class drying-out spa, euphemistically termed a sanitarium. One might say that he worked as he drank, *addictively*. Indeed, students of alcohol and drugs have found it useful to identify an *addictive* personality.

If the oral character is primarily oral-receptive, he is likely to be quite *passive,* wanting the nourishment to be trickled into his mouth as he lies supine. The emphasis on passive receptivity is at variance with the standard requirements for males in our culture, and many men, who have such passive longings, do much to hide them from themselves and others. Just as all persons who are acting a part, they tend to overdo it, with a great show of ambitious striving in an effort to prove they do not really yearn for purely passive gratification. This discrepancy between the reaction formation and the underlying wish often produces a great deal of tension in such a person, especially when the desire for *oral supplies* is so great that he simultaneously has an inordinate need to please, to be liked. It is no wonder, then, that many persons thus constituted end up with ulcers or cardiovascular disease.

Fixation at the oral-biting phase is more likely to be represented in the *demandingness* which also is a frequent attribute of oral characters. This demandingness applies, of course, to food and other ingestible stuffs, but it is likely to go beyond. Such persons frequently "get their feelings hurt," which is to say they are not able to get the *unconditional love* they feel is their right, their need—or their preference. "Love me just because I'm me." Demandingness may also lead to an impatience with others, an "I want what I want when I want it" attitude. Perhaps it is for this reason that, Shakespeare to the contrary, life demonstrates few truly jolly fat men.

An oral-biting person may also be demanding in another sense. He is greedy for perfection. The best is never good enough. When this kind of perfectionism is turned toward one's view of himself, he may be as angry with himself for not performing up to what he requires as he might be toward an external object. From this derives depressiveness, in its classical formulation: depression as aggression turned inward against the self.

This is but one of the dynamic constellations out of which depression may arise, but it is common to find that a chronically depressive person is also a covertly demanding one. Ofttimes, the first casework step in relieving depression is to encourage the demandingness to come out into the open, into free verbal expression. Oral-biting persons, by the way, often have biting tongues, although they are not the only ones with this characteristic. Perhaps it is no more than fair that if one has a biting tongue, he should so often put his own foot in his mouth.

In interpersonal relations, a man or woman with strong oral needs is likely to be recognizable from the way in which he tends to engulf others. The more passive person establishes a clinging, appealing sort of symbiotic tie; nevertheless, it is as firmly fixed as is that of the more obstreporously requiring man who *insists* on being taken care of. This feeling of being entangled, of being *incorporated,* derives from the steady flow of speech which, as it were, fixes your attention in its grasp, and will not release you even after—having still said nothing—you feel sucked dry. We shall say more about this in Chapter 10.

A noteworthy feature in many oral characters we encounter as adults is their *expansiveness.* They are given to large schemes and big dealings; they have no patience for details and, in fact, may be so insistently optimistic as to exhibit questionable judgment. When such a promoter succeeds, he is hailed as a genius; when he fails, he is very susceptible to depression. Many creative people alternate the two. Expansiveness is often exhibited in smaller ways. Many fat people cannot reduce because they find it impossible to think in terms of losing a pound a week. They immediately set their goal at thirty pounds, only to become discouraged when, after a month, they have "only" lost six or seven. The expansiveness, then, is to be seen as a facet of the all-or-none style of thinking and feeling that we associate with the oral phase of development. And this same oral-phase, all-or-none quality in thought will recur, in our discussion, when we mention the *splitting* within the ego that occurs when the child cannot integrate his love and his hate of the same person (see Chapter 6).

Even though oral elements are present in an adult, they typically come through only in much *modulated* form as compared with the infant's urge to take the world into his mouth. This process of modulation, of altering the original drive so as to fit better into the life led by an adult who is in contact with the real world, dampens the raw drive energy originally involved. The drive energy may then be said to have been *neutralized*. We can detect the original drive, and deduce its origin, but we do not find it so directly expressed. Instead, it is as if the spurting water from an artesian well has been fed through a series of pipes and reducing valves until, when it reaches our house, it can be controlled by a small and inexpensive sink faucet. Most persons who develop normally experience drives in neutralized forms only, once they are adults. Thus, rather than consciously feeling an urge to kill the person who does not give when they want, they merely are annoyed or irritated. To an adult, this does not warrant annihilating the one who deprives you; it is enough if you can tell him off.

Similarly, oral needs are the more likely to be expressed in diverted, sublimated fashion—as with the literary critic who spends his life sniffing and tasting others' writings, and then exclaiming or complaining about them. Such a critic might be said to have partially *regressed* should he abandon literature for gastronomy, and if he went on from there to gluttony we would be quite sure he had done so. At that stage the oral needs are not being expressed so symbolically, under control, and no longer dedicated to earning his living. Of course in daily life we find oral needs more typically expressed, by the same person, openly at times, and in symbolic, neutralized fashion at other times. The same is true of sex. Our judgment regarding how far a person has matured, psychologically, is based on whether he is able to be realistic and appropriate in choosing his times and places for primitive discharge.

The Anal Character

The traditional mnemonic device for keeping in mind what is meant by anal character was the four p's. An anal character was said to be parsimonious, prurient, petulant, and pedantic—see whether this does not apply to someone you know. These adjectives are not flattering and, indeed, there is little connotation of the cheerfulness we associate with the oral fellow, so indulgent to himself and others.

The parsimoniousness or stinginess in the anal character has usually been the facet most remarked upon in professional circles. If a woman was married to a stingy banker, accountant, lawyer, or psychologist, one might find her complaining about his being *withholding* in a number of other areas. Tight lipped, such a person often withholds words; certainly, he finds it difficult—he would call it unnecessary—to be generous with demonstrations of affection. "She should know I love her. Don't I let her buy anything she wants?" In direct treatment, too, one has a sense of the *stubbornness,* which is also a marked facet of this personality type. Whereas some clients are stubborn about changing because they are so fearful of becoming nothing at all, the stubbornness to which I am here alluding seems to derive from another attitude of "I won't give you the satisfaction." This person has resumed the battle of the potty over which he fought with his mother, insisting on evacuating when and where he wants, and refusing to produce when *she* wants him to.

Prurience is visible in the tendency of anal characters to see things as dirty. Sex can be expected to be interlocked with bowel movements. Certainly, their view of sex is typically as a matter for sniggering, leering, a "behind the barn" sort of approach. Sex is dirty, just as bowel functions are dirty. Although there may be great pleasure in little-boy sex jokes, the funny-bone is really touched by bathroom humor. Because this may be embarrassing, many anal characters avoid the danger of being exposed by their laughter by showing practically no sense of humor. Hypocrisy is rife among such people, for they are preoccupied with questions of shame and blame.

Young caseworkers confronted by such intrinsically sullen folks are prone to credit them with somewhat more maturity than they have achieved. They will tell their supervisor, "I don't think he can be active and outgoing because he feels so guilty." The client may not have matured far enough for guilt, which is, after all, a feeling that you have wronged *another person,* and warrant being punished for it. The shame we have under scrutiny here is much more self-centered. It takes the form, "I have messed up my pants, and now I smell bad, and people will point and laugh and say 'Shame, shame on you.'" The relation of this feeling to what happens in toilet training is quite direct.

If anal characters are preoccupied with shame and blame, they are also often caught up in varieties of sadistic fantasies. They are likely to get a quiet pleasure out of criticizing, "For your own good," while joyfully defecating on the others' works. Meanness, in its implication that one is both small *and* nasty (like a Klan member in the deep South or a Hell's Angel in California), is common. Because of the tendency to withhold, the meanness seldom erupts in major outbursts of rage. It is as likely to be expressed in niggling ways, as *petulance,* carping, and nagging. Not a few elderly folks who may have had such traits well mastered in their healthier days regress to them under the impact of aging and the constant threat of death. They are then converted from people into "management problems," in nursing homes. The relation of the petulance and the prurience to taking malicious gossip into one's joyful embrace does not need spelling out.

We have been sketching the manner in which the anal character used to be discussed. We have covered three of the four p's—parsimonious, prurient, and petulant. That you, as well as I, cannot resist wondering what happened to the fourth tells us something about what is meant by *pedantic!* Along with being stingy, the anal character was also commonly said to be extremely orderly. If a person not only were willing but also seemed positively anxious to sort and file his miscellaneous papers, we would immediately accuse him of being anal, although not so anal as if he saved his money and kept his dictation up to date. The pedantry extends also to style of speech, and especially to written communication. If the anal character has a great desire to control, and overcontrol, and generally exercise sphincters, this is closely related to his desire, and his fear, that he will give way to his other urge, which is to smear feces. The practice of putting ideas or papers or objects into neat little boxes becomes part of enjoying the process of holding back. Not all anal characters are pedantic. Some are happy simply to wallow in disorder and filth, not as a matter of laziness or even of defiance (which it very often is). Rather, it is derived from the original urge to gain pleasure from one's bowel action.

There was a time when psychologists took a great deal of pleasure in trying to reduce a variety of complex human activity to its ultimate motivational roots. A painting by Leonardo might be said to derive, in the long run, from a childhood urge to smear feces on the sides of his crib. Painting then might be said to be a kind of *drive-derivative*. We are not in good position to analyze whether this was the case with Leonardo, although there is ample evidence that he was a man with problems. But it is silly to talk about the painting of such an adult as if it were smearing. For one thing, we know that da Vinci was fascinated with the optics of painting, and that he made efforts to formulate laws of perspective, ideal size-relationships among parts of the human body. He also experimented with various ways of mixing paints, with results so disastrous in a famous instance that one great picture he produced began to fade after a relatively short time. If Leonardo were displaying an urge simply to smear, he could have accomplished this more easily by concentrating on another position he once held, a designer of weapons.

We want to note that the observable behavior in a reasonably mature adult may derive, ultimately, from anal pleasures, but they have by now gone through a long series of *vicissitudes*. The impulse to paint would be, at most, a neutralized *drive-derivative* of the impulse to smear, but this would not be the only motivation at work. The identification with an admired teacher and the wish to please him might be active; so might be a desire to prove one's father wrong in forbidding this career. In short, any activity as life-encompassing and significant as a career choice assiduously followed must satisfy not a single drive or represent one set of drive-derivatives. It is more likely to constitute a blending, a compromising, a common outlet for energies that come from several sources. This blending is evident in the formation of a workable *identity*.

Why, one might ask, did analysts become so interested in tracing an adult activity to its infantile motivational roots? There were two reasons. One was the desire to advance theory, to understand how man functions. The other was nearly equally pressing—to cure patients. Suppose a person in treatment earned his living as a playwright, but had become unable to write plays, even though there was evidence he still had the technical capacity to write. A possible explanation might be that the original drive that led him to write had somehow become entangled with other urges in a way that made it forbidden activity. We might try to trace the impulse to its earlier roots to see whether we could help him find a new reason for writing that was not likely to become so intertwined with his neurotic conflicts.

We began this chapter by noting that the personality does, in fact, seem to fall into a finite number of broad constellations because its various facets must "make sense" one with another. We noted, further, that the interdependence of the parts can be understood in terms of commonalities of outcomes from an identical historical root and functional interdependence that arises from the interplay of present facets. We have just discussed two character types commonly taught to students in social work and psychology, the so-called oral and anal characters. We had a number of reasons for this discussion, not least of which is that these typologies still have a certain usefulness when summarizing sets of dynamics we encounter. However, it must be clear that by and large the features thus far put together are together primarily because of the patient's life history. Nearly all facets of the oral character are to be seen as thinly veiled expressions of oral-receptiveness or oral-biting urges. In describing the anal character we see some evidence of reaction formations, but generally the picture is again derivable from a study of the anal drives and their derivatives. These analyses might be included under ego psychology, but in truth they represent primarily summarizations from the study of instincts and their vicissitudes. The next section will be exemplary of a later approach to characterology, as we consider the obsessive-compulsive personality.

The Obsessive-Compulsive Personality

No adult can survive with reasonable comfort in our society if he does not plan, keep most appointments, put his papers and tools where he can find them, and exercise prudence in important decisions. To be unable to maintain reasonable order and cautiousness may doom one to a lifetime spent under someone else's supervision. Should the interest in order become more important than the purpose for which it is kept, then it stops being useful and becomes a handicap. We have commented that there are functions of the ego which, in normal limits, are adaptive and beneficial. They may, nevertheless, be exaggerated to the point at which we think of them as symptoms. Rarely is this better illustrated than in the bundle of machinations we have come to call the obsessive-compulsive personality.

Many "splendid specimens" of obsessive-compulsives are to be found on college campuses throughout our country. They were even better concentrated in European universities. The story is told of the German philologist who had spent his life studying the uses of the dative and ablative cases in Tacitus. Although he was well regarded by those who care about such things, our scholar was prone to self-doubts. On his deathbed he moaned that he had accomplished nothing. His friends gathered, anxious to reassure him. They reminded him of his numerous books, his many published papers, the footnotes and citations he had enriched. The old man roused himself and said, "Ah, yes. But how much more could I have accomplished had I confined myself to the study of the dative alone!"

The key dynamic in understanding the obsessive-compulsive is his strong need to sustain *control*. It is basic analytic theory that drive energies will seek expression either through action or in ideation. The same may be said for defenses against anxiety. When the need to maintain control shows up in the form of rumination, excessive preoccupation with one idea, we say we are dealing with an *obsession*, the aim of which is to "control one's thoughts." *Compulsions*, on the other hand, have to do with externally visible behaviors, with rituals and actions. The counterpart of the statistics professor who required us to calculate all correlation coefficients to five decimal places (regardless of how meaningless they may have been) is the Army officer intent on close-order drill.

The presence of an obsession or a compulsion does not by itself mean we should classify the person as an obsessive-compulsive personality. Either, or both, may occur as an isolated symptom in a person who otherwise seems essentially normal. It is also common to find these symptoms in persons who are extremely ill psychiatrically. When, then, do we make the character diagnosis? It is when the emphasis on control and on "playing it safe" has become a total way of life. Although no real person will fit *all* these characteristics, we can make a number of related statements about most obsessive-compulsives.

We have alluded to the delight in orderliness and fascination with precision. Although this has its uses, it is frequently accompanied by an inability of the obsessive-compulsive to look up from his worm's-eye view of the world—"He cannot see the forest for the trees." The officer may claim that close-order drill produces discipline in an Army, despite the appallingly good fighters we have witnessed who do not salute. We become aware that he loves drill for its own sake. Moreover, he is aghast at any lack of skill in drilling. He is *rigid* and finds change extremely hard to take. This is because many of the disciplines by which he lives are set up to prevent his feeling anxiety. Change endangers a whole defensive system. While the rigidity is usually quite unconscious, and can be assessed only by the therapist, his *stubbornness* is not. Of this he is likely to be quite conscious, and even takes a quiet pride in it.

At first glance, the stubbornness seems paradoxical, for it occurs in a person who is otherwise plagued by *self-doubts* and *indecision*. Only gradually do we come to understand that these seeming paradoxes in the personality disorders represent a problem and then an attempt to counter it. If it were easier for the obsessive to make up his mind, he would be less fearful of changing it. For change requires him to make a whole new decision.

Sensing that he has this trouble and thus appears weak and vacillating, the obsessive-compulsive sometimes swings between the extremes of indecisiveness and hastiness. Where another man might find it quite appropriate to stay a decision pending more information, an obsessive will sometimes busy himself with *appearing* decisive. The chief functions of commitments he makes at such times are to relieve him of the discomfort he feels at having things undecided, and the boost to his self-esteem which he experiences from having vaingloriously taken a stand. Reality may then run a poor third in influencing the judgment.

The more typical stance, however, is to remain undecided and proceed with extreme caution. Psychologically there are several reasons for this. To begin, we have in mind the rather obvious derivation of this personality structure from fixations at the anal phase of development. There is some satisfaction in *withholding* decisions, especially if they affect other people, just as there is pleasure in withholding love, money, feelings in general. Commitment is like a hard bowel movement. But this describes only the part of the pattern derived from drive-satisfactions in one zone. It is rare to find a person who remains immature in only one sphere of his psychosexual development. In my own observation, obsessive-compulsive personalities are typically extremely *oral* as well. They have difficulty in making up their minds partly because they are *greedy,* just as they are greedy for *perfection.* Most decisions require that in order to get one thing, you have to give up the other. The sort of person we are discussing has a secret notion that he can beat life at this game. He believes he will find a way to get both choices, and give up neither. So he stalls for time.

Finally, we note that the indecisiveness is also a defense. This is where ego psychology takes us beyond the original formulations on this character type. What is he being so cautious about? Despite his emphasis on orderliness, restraint, and containment, the obsessive shows signs from time to time not only that he fears he will make a mess but also that he wants to make one! This masking of a wish by experiencing it as a fear is termed a *phobic defense.* The strong emphasis on order derives not just from anal-retentiveness but from a desire to be anal-expulsive.

I once knew a young woman who was an excellent pianist and majored in piano in college. However, it was impossible for her to pass her required recital as a music major because she froze when facing an audience. There were several reasons for this, but one that gradually came out was her fear that she would "make a mess of things." It was true: she might well have. For she resented her mother's treating her successes as a personal triumph, as if her daughter had done nothing herself. The only way the patient could retaliate was to "make a mess of myself."

Making a mess of one's self has been graphically described in Rabelais as "beshitting one's self." True enough, the pleasures of anal-expulsiveness precede and accompany toilet-training, in the life-history. It is no wonder, therefore, if the person who is so meticulous, so ultra-refined in certain ways, should not be a bit messy in others. These are not paradoxes, really. They are questions of the extent to which drive overcomes reaction formation, and what compromise has been worked out. In the spending of money it is not unusual that such a person will suddenly indulge in a major splurge after months of the most self-denying parsimony. Diarrhea follows constipation. The same may be true with his handling of rage, alternating passivity with outbursts.

It is not *de rigeur* to be indecisive in this culture, especially for men. There are, therefore, a number of screens that such persons put up to avoid facing the problem. They take pride in being judicious: "I like to see both sides of any issue." Or, as I prefer to put it, "I'm a man of firm convictions, one on each side of the question." Often, they simply avoid any situations requiring decision-making, and are spared having to face this disability in their personalities. The regulations of bureaucracy are welcomed by personnel who merely have to "look them up" to have made a decision. In social work, by the way, this is known as "making positive use of agency structure." Sometimes it is. Life is similarly simpler for certain followers of Learning Theory in psychology.

Beyond the questions of pleasure in withholding and greed, it is obvious that persons with this makeup are *fearful* of deciding. As one would expect of a person with an urge to besmirch himself, he is preoccupied with questions of shame and blame. After all, these are the levers primarily counted on by mothers to get young children to use the bathroom as they want them to. The fear is not just that a wrong choice will lead to a financial loss, let us say. What is worse, he could be criticized for having had poor judgment. But, to reiterate, his anxiety is over being *shamed*. Because of this sensitivity, the obsessive-compulsive hates to be held responsible for his actions. In conversation, for example, he may be a counterpuncher. He does not offer an opinion outright; he prefers not to deny yours too obviously. He does not argue, he only "qualifies." He is a great "Yes, but" . . . er.

Another way to avoid responsibility, of course, is to pretend that one never exercises an act of will, but only reacts. "Where are you rushing?" "I *have* to go down to buy a suit." "Why do you have to? Don't you own one?" "Yes, but there is this terrific sale, and I can't resist sales!" "Oh, you *want* to buy a suit." "I suppose you could say that. Well, see you around. Got to go now." This poor victim of circumstances is about to be *forced* to spend money for a new suit, with a color that everyone is favoring, in a tweed that his wife likes, because *he* can't resist its appeal. How many burdens must one person carry? His arrive in Job lots, by limousine.

In order to side-step responsibility for a decision, the obsessive *feels forced*. Indeed, he prefers to feel forced, but this creates new difficulties which themselves demand solution. By avoiding responsibility and the danger of blame, the price he pays is to experience life as a long session of being pushed around. While overdoing exactly what he wants to do, he manages to feel coerced. He eventually becomes resentful, not to mention the backlog of frustration built up by withholding pleasure from himself. This, in turn, leads to more need to control himself, lest his angry feelings burst forth. It is no wonder, therefore, that so many obsessive-compulsives are sardonic, slightly vitriolic characters who do not express hostility; they leak it. But, even these, if humorous, are easier to live with than persons who take refuge in an odor of sanctimony, like the frozen-faced, self-righteous politician protecting his Klan behind the flag.

The obsessive is concerned with "moral responsibility" and, in a limited way, with shame. That is to say, he may otherwise be a moral man, but this is not part of his "problem." From the standpoint of those who have business with him, the obsessive-compulsive is usually a responsible person; you can count on him and his word is good. This is not always true, however, and there is a subtype we label the *irresponsible obsessive.* He is an immature person, really, indifferent to his wife and family, who will devote days to tracing a minor issue in his family's genealogy, tuning his sports car, and so forth. For many such a man, when the season is ripe for fishing, you might as well forget that he has taken the roof off your house. He *must* go fishing, and your house is your problem.

These are the absorptions of small boys playing games, not to be interrupted by the needs of others. A few such persons, incidentally, through special talents or luck become extremely successful at their compulsive hobbies, and support their families very well. They are used as hopeful examples by the women who marry them, to buoy up their spirits, but this is self-deluding. Most irresponsible obsessives are simply childish, and remain that way, without acquiring wealth except by inheritance. They usually live longer than conscientious compulsives.

There is a group of famous men whose habits represent an overdetermined form of irresponsible obsessiveness. These were the men, great artists of the printed page, who nevertheless were continually in debt, usually because they spent so recklessly that even their assiduous writing could not counter their extravagance. It has been common for their biographers to express dismay at the even greater things they might have written had they not been driven by their own profligacy into supposedly excessive productivity.

A fascinating instance of this is Balzac as portrayed by Andre Maurois in *Prometheus* (1965). Here was a man sufficiently versed in business matters that he wrote of them shrewdly and in detail. Yet he managed his own finances in such a way that he was constantly in debt, hiding from the sheriff, impoverishing his aged mother in her efforts to rescue him, and mortgaging his writing months ahead. All this because of his selfish, impulsive buying, his ostentation, and apparent lack of judgment. If one were to ask Balzac, he would undoubtedly complain that he wanted nothing but to rest and he wrote only to stave off bankruptcy. But this man who played so much the childish slob in his personal affairs spent as much as one hundred hours a month correcting proof; he is said to have rewritten supposed potboilers as many as ten times. It does not seem to have occurred to Maurois that Balzac wrote because he wanted to write, but that he also feared it. The financial need into which he trapped himself acted to spur his productivity *and* to permit his creativity. Only in a situation so maneuvered that he created under compunction could he defeat his fear of asserting his own ideas, lest they be criticized. He arranged his life to "force" himself to write. Of course there is more to the infantile side of Balzac's character. I merely want to assert an artistic advantage which the egos of such men as Dickens, Wagner, Scott, and Mark Twain may have wrung from the disaster of their poor handling of money.

It is now possible to be a bit more precise about the chief mechanisms involved in this syndrome. The average obsessive is, to be sure, a great ruminator. An idea gets fixed in his mind and he cannot let it go; it turns over and over and he complains that it keeps him awake. It is important to remember, therefore, that if the thing about which he is *consciously* worrying were what is really troubling him, the odds are he would find some solution for it, one way or another. The typical function of an obsessive idea is to *keep us from thinking* about something we dread having come into consciousness. He *is* being kept awake, but not because of the conscious worry. This is largely a diversionary tactic by the ego to maintain repression. Still, the young case-worker would not be wise to ignore the conscious worry. It usually is associated in some way with the idea it is being used to conceal, and it is as good a place as any from which to try to trace the real source of concern. But it is even more unwise to take the conscious obsession, the defense, as if it accurately represented the whole conflict.

In my experience much of the rumination plays the function of *undoing*. This mechanism, classically associated with the obsessive-compulsive, means, symbolically, that the person tries to pretend he can call back an action, "undo" the past. Undoing resembles the witty rejoinder we wish we had thought of, which occurs to us only while driving home after the party. Much of the rumination of the obsessive consists in going over and over an event in which he took part, trying to remake it in his own image, or, more properly, in the image he wishes he could sustain. In short, he needs to look good, and he redigests the evening until he has established this in his mind.

Undoing is very much implicated in compulsions. The client with a hand-washing compulsion reminds us of Lady Macbeth. Preoccupation with undoing leads to another well-known obsessive-compulsive act: the need to spoil an action at the end. He may refuse to take the final examination in a course or impatiently destroy his own masterpiece.

Another facet of the obsessive-compulsive is his vacillation between *gullibility* and *suspiciousness*. The obsessive psychiatrist is apt to accept as true everything a tearful, angry wife tells him, if she is his patient. The social worker, in such a case, will have a hard time introducing the husband's version of reality into the therapist's mental processes. As a result, the therapist may join the wife in her neurotic machinations and stupidly permit a salvageable marriage, and a salvageable life, to go down the drain. Or, should you have such an obsessive in a position of authority over you, you must be wary. Because he believes the first person who gets his ear, and thereafter finds it extremely hard to hear new evidence, any liar on the staff can make your life miserable.

The suspiciousness, then, is a defense against the gullibility. The obsessive in his rigid, awkward way senses from time to time that "he has been had." Therefore, he tries to protect himself by doubting everything told him, as indiscriminately as before he accepted all. Rather than alternating these attitudes in time, however, the obsessive is more likely to divide them among others. A female patient, having trouble with her husband, may decide that her therapist can say no wrong; her poor husband, whom she formerly treated as an oracle, now is never right. This arrangement often leads to a happy and prosperous treatment relationship in which, unfortunately, neither the patient nor her marriage recovers.

Entire books can now be written about this character type, once regarded as untreatable. Despite the difficulties his patterns create for himself and others, the person with this character, or with *many obsessive-compulsive features,* as we say, does much of the work of the world. It is possible to rank character structures from very primitive to quite mature. In any such ranking, the obsessive-compulsive scores rather high.

When we find an obsessive who is more analyzing than being analyzed, we say he is *well compensated.* By this, we mean simply that his defense system is collaborating well enough with reality to keep him happy and productive. Should the defenses begin to collapse, we say he is *decompensating.* Decompensation is sometimes first visible as compulsions which become more and more frenzied, more and more life encompassing—a small boy literally trying to stop a hole in the dike with his thumb, and then with handful after handful of mud. If an individual is put under enough pressure, and if his customary limitations in life style are interfered with, such decompensation can proceed to the point of psychosis. When someone with this character becomes psychotic, he is likely to experience paranoid states. There is reason to believe Stalin was a case in point.

Fortunately, most people with many obsessive-compulsive features remain reasonably well compensated and seldom become psychiatrically very ill. However, the pattern is likely to be progressive. A somewhat perfectionistic and reserved young man may become a constricted, pedantic middle-aged one, who "never wants to go anyplace." The trim and well-dressed young woman who proves so good a housekeeper when first married may turn into the lady who makes her family remove their shoes before entering the parlor. We have already discussed some reasons why any defensive pattern tends to spread and become fixed. Why this particular character structure should be outstanding for its progressive nature into middle age, we do not fully understand. Neither is it clear why, in many instances, there is such a mellowing in old age. Perhaps the anger against which the syndrome is primarily erected becomes banked. And many older people do report their pleasure in no longer caring so much about being shamed in the opinion of others.

Limitations in the Concept of Character

This chapter has introduced the major ideas most relevant to the general notion of *character* in ego psychology. We have demonstrated some of these ideas in our discussion of the obsessive-compulsive. In the next chapter, we shall continue exposition of character types, choosing those types the reader seems likely to meet frequently in his work and whose appellations recur in conversations among analytically oriented clinicians. Before going on, however, it seems wise to review the limitations to what we are doing.

It is possible to reify the character type, just as one might the ego. Indeed, one might rather easily move from his experiences as a caseworker and therapist to writing in a Chekhovian short story a composite of all the obsessives one has known. But in real life only a few persons one sees constitute textbook examples. Most clients fit only in some ways, and their discrepancies matter. For this reason it is better to say someone has "many obsessive-compulsive features" than to label him an obsessive-compulsive.

Besides, nothing much is accomplished simply by labeling. Unless the classification implies a cause of the condition and suggestions for its treatment, it is at best useless and at worst derogatory. Therefore, it is well to think of the character types more as syndromes of dynamics. As we have seen, such psychological features are found together for either of two reasons. Historically, the fixations of childhood express themselves in correlated ways in adulthood. Functionally, a given impulse is likely to lead to a given reaction-formation, or other defensive maneuver—as we saw in the alternation between messiness and meticulosity in the compulsive. The teaching of characterology, then, is as good a place as any in which to describe to the student a concrete series of frequently encountered defensive maneuvers. If nothing else, the functional analysis of character is instructive of dynamics that can occur in all of us.

We cannot stop without a note about theory and theory construction. The reader will undoubtedly have recognized the link between the so-called anal character and the obsessive-compulsive. It is instructive to see how much further the latter conception, utilizing ego psychology, is able to lead us than the former. By taking into account not only the drives but especially questions of defense and synthesis, we can give a much richer picture of the personality involved. This, in turn, affords many more handles with which one might try to take hold in offering treatment. Although the picture is more elaborate and more complete, it is also more parsimonious. We can synthesize infinitely more about this person from the observation that he has a great need to "keep things under control and play it safe" than from simplistic attempts to trace all his mannerisms to pleasure in withholding feces.

References

Abraham, Karl. *Selected Papers.* London: Hogarth Press, 1927.

Kaufman, Irving. "Psychodynamics of Protective Casework," in H.J.Parad and R.R.Miller, eds., *Ego-Oriented Casework: Problems and Perspectives.* New York: Family Service Association of America, 1963.

Lewin, Kurt. *Principles of Topological Psychology.* New York: McGraw-Hill, 1936.

Maurois, Andre. *Prometheus: The Life of Balzac.* New York: Harper & Row, 1965.

Polansky, Norman A. "The Professional Identity in Social Work," in Alfred J. Kahn, ed., *Issues in American Social Work.* New York: Columbia University Press, 1959.

Reich, Wilhelm. *Character Analysis.* New York: Noonday Press, 1949 (originally 1933).

Reiner, Beatrice S., and Irving Kaufman. *Character Disorders in Parents of Delinquents.* New York: Family Service Association of America, 1959.

Salzman, Leon. "Therapy of Obsessional States," *American Journal of Psychiatry, 122,* 1965, 1139–1146.

Chapter 5

Familiar
Character
Formations

WE ENDED THE LAST CHAPTER BY BEGINNING TO SEE SOME
of the ways in which the traits associated with the obsessive-
compulsive make sense dynamically and historically. Now
we shall proceed to other personality structurings. These
have been chosen for presentation because they include personality syndromes widely recognized among mental health
professionals of psychoanalytic background. Knowing what
is meant by the terms involved is necessary for ready communication in our field.

The Hysteric

Think of a female who exudes more allure proffering
her cigarette for a light than Cleopatra achieved floating
in her barge. But how to describe her without sounding
sarcastic? If her actions are touched with charm and sen-
suousness, they must also be seen at times as more than a

little ludicrous. Let me say, to begin with, that I find hysterics very likeable patients. Moreover, I regard the effort by some therapists to strip such folk of their flair, in the course of reducing their anxiety, as leading to an unsatisfactory treatment result. The flattened remnant of personality represents a waste of a natural resource.

Let me again illustrate the personality type by a composite. I shall refer mainly to female patients in this section, but I want to note that many men are hysterics. Most of what I shall have to say seems to apply to them too, except that in our culture there are a number of pressures that lead to important differences in the way the pattern expresses itself.

The patient was a thin-waisted, large-bosomed woman with lovely features and a skin that had not aged. She had finely formed legs, and helped me to be aware of this fact by wearing snug skirts. Some days she wore a blouse carelessly undone at the throat; other times, a sweater; occasionally a semi-bare midriff. Against the studied dishabille of her expensive clothing, her face was always meticulously made up, her nails were nicely polished in an unusual shade, and above them flashed her boulder of a diamond with matching wedding band. Both arms were decorated with bracelets. Here, indeed, was a woman making the most of the physical equipment with which she had been endowed.

The patient's excitement communicated itself whenever she made her entrance for a conference. Her eyes shown; she spoke rapidly and energetically. Her feelings carried her away, so that she laughed, wept, scorned, raged, and depicted deep thought within the compass of fifty minutes. Her conversation seemed scattered at times, childish and illogical, as if one were dealing with a schizophrenic. But her judgment of reality was not bad, usually shrewd. Nor was the excitement confined to the patient's manner with me. If her life had been marked by tragedy, at least it had not been dull, and certainly she had not stinted living at high emotional stakes. To be her therapist was an invitation to a ride on her emotional roller coaster.

The *craving for excitement* is one of the most characteristic features of the hysteric, even if outwardly her life seems routine and decorous. One can make a desperate struggle out of sewing a dress; a polar expedition of going to the mailbox in the snow; a disaster of a child's sore throat. What is the excitement all about?

At one level, the excitement represents *displaced sexuality*. Indeed, it has been well understood for a long time that the hysteric is likely to be preoccupied with sex. Many readers will have heard already that the word hysteric is derived from the same Greek root as uterus. It has been said that if you scratch a compulsive defense, you will find rage underneath; scratch an hysterical symptom, and you will find conflict about sex. The excitement is seen as an attempt to discharge sexual stimulation in neutralized, sublimated fashion.

A number of characteristic features can be understood in these terms. If the hysteric is addicted to sex, she is also conflicted about it. She invites, and then she flees: she is a *tease*. The delight in teasing may be ego-syntonic and conscious, when it has been displaced—like wanting to be coaxed to play the piano for guests. With respect to sex, however, the hysteric is surprisingly often only dimly aware of just how much of a tease she is.

The client who waves her exposed thighs at you may be evading her own seductiveness. If you point this out to her, you stand in some danger of being accused of making a pass at her! This would be in line with her tendency to *sexualize relationships,* that is, to experience sensual associations in otherwise matter-of-fact heterosexual encounters. Doctors, dentists, caseworkers, ministers have all learned this from experience, even though Freud, in his Victorian fashion, first resisted acknowledging it. As a result, he interpreted transference fantasies toward himself as real memories of childhood sexual experiences with elder males in patients' families, thus committing one of the major blunders of his career.

Professional men who tend to sexualize intimate contacts have been known to have affairs with hysterical female clients or patients. Despite the intense feelings of manliness some of them derive from such actions, it is they who typically have been seduced. When a woman in therapy has intercourse with her psychiatrist, (a) she is typically an hysteric; (b) she, not he, is manipulating the situation; (c) her action is in the service of resistance to treatment ("How can you confront me with unpleasant things, when you're a man and I'm a woman?"). Whatever else one might think of such occurrences, and perhaps they are not so rare as one might hope, they represent poor treatment technique. The therapist has been rendered therapeutically impotent.

The major defensive maneuver of hysterics is said to be *massive repression,* referring, in this instance, to the inability to recall much of her early life when she starts treatment. This interference with memory plays a role in the seeming scatter of her speech. Once the therapist is convinced the client is neither brain-damaged nor psychotic, he becomes aware of her tendency to skitter from topics that would lead to insights she does not want to have. She may seem illogical, but this, too, is in the service of maintaining repression. After all, if she were to follow certain lines of thought to their ends, they would lead to conclusions she cannot stand to face. So she pretends to a little-girlish flightiness.

Two satisfactory methods for avoiding unwanted insight into one's own fantasies are *projection* ("You are trying to seduce me!") and *somatization* ("What's wrong with me is physical."). Hysterics commonly suffer "pains for which no organic basis can be found" or exaggerate the significance of symptoms which do have ascertainable physical causes. By concentrating on her bodily discomforts, the hysterical patient may successfully distract herself from the guilt-laden images which otherwise threaten to break into consciousness. It is partly for the same reason that hysterics so often seem to *court hardship and turmoil* in their lives. The "need to suffer" used to be ascribed to *masochism,* with the implication that the client gained sexual pleasure from pain. However, in my experience, the defensive function of the real-life emergencies they seem to invite for themselves often outweighs the titillation.

Many physicians find it odd that patients known for overconcern about trivial illnesses often prove remarkably brave and reasonable when confronted by a serious physical crisis. This becomes less paradoxical if we remember that the major source of the anxiety is derived from unconscious images, sexual fantasies, and attendant guilt. Having a tangible, conscious danger on which to focus comes as a relief, because they can make active efforts to cope with it externally. There is a corresponding increase in ego strength. We observed, for example, that during World War II the number of mental hospital admissions in Detroit, Michigan, dropped substantially, not just among the young men taken into the Army, but for all age groups.

The most characteristic form anger takes is *righteous indignation.* Hysterics are not satisfied to retaliate for hurts suffered, they seem to seek out incidents about which to feel abused. Then they pursue the person they hold responsible with accusations relentlessly stated in a penetrating voice calculated to arouse as much guilt as possible. The burden of the piece is the moral reprehensibility of the other party. Recrimination of this sort is frequently found adding to the other discordant sounds of marital squabbling.

Such outbursts of moral indignation often end by costing the client more than they are worth, psychologically. Although he may feel unusually well put together when in the midst of a tirade, afterwards he feels depleted and guilty for having gone too far. Yet he finds it impossible to give up such tantrums, even though they leave him shaken, disrupt relationships with people he loves, endanger the mental health of his children. If a female hysteric has no provocation in her immediate life, she is likely to find herself brooding on more general injustices to humanity or resurrecting hurts from the distant past. However, a factor distinguishing the hysteric from, say, the paranoid character is the extent to which there is some foundation for the accusations.

Why is it so hard to give up this pattern which, among other things, leaves the accuser frequently more shaken than the accused? What are the functions of *righteous indignation?* First, of course, it is a *projective defense.* How satisfying it is to escape self-recriminations by saying, in effect, "Compared with you, I'm not evil at all." The high moral tone adopted is the tip-off that guilt and shame are in the mind of the accuser. Second, it is a defense in which *one affect is substituted for another.* Just as sex is not just sex for the hysteric, so anger is not just anger. The complaint being filed usually has the content, "You don't really love me. . . ." The instinctive reaction to this abandonment is not necessarily anger: a more natural one would be depressiveness and anxiety. However, while she is busy with her anger, the hysteric feels strong and sure of herself, rather than crushed and unlovable. Finally, there are a series of other rather obvious functions of the anger: keeping the other person involved in a *hostile-dependent* contact; provocative verbal wrestling with connotations of *sexual foreplay;* the desire to distract oneself from threatening insights by sustained tumult in the environment; and the close tie between righteous indignation and *fantasies of being raped.*

We have referred to sexual preoccupation, and I have just noted that "sex is not just sex" to the hysteric. It is usually easy to establish that the sexual functions have been invaded by conflict. The man with a "Don Juan complex" seems obviously trying to reassure himself there is nothing wrong with his abilities. The woman accused of nymphomania, or who acts so provocatively, seems bent on hiding from herself her own difficulties in achieving orgasm in a stable, love relationship. Similarly, we would expect defense to be piled upon defense. Thus, the woman who seeks sexual reassurances may try to find them in casual affairs. As a reaction formation against such impulses, she may then become studiously *asexual*—in manner, in dress, and even in body build. One way to secure herself against temptation is to make herself undesirable. Then we end with a large-bellied woman, hastening to her doctor with recurrent gynecological complaints or even what used to be called polysurgical addiction—inviting multiple operations. Meanwhile, she may have become so manipulative in her use of sex with her husband, giving or withholding for extraneous reasons, that she is by now unable to achieve orgasm. Or she may have to insist she never feels anything —she has produced three children from a succession of rapes.

There are numerous variations we could list, because the hysteric is, after all, usually—developmentally speaking —a rather mature sort of person, and defenses are correspondingly rich and flexible. The *pseudofeminine* woman, the *pseudomasculine* man, the *neuter,* the *histrionic* homosexual all represent compromises and reaction formations around the fact that normal sexuality has been invaded by conflict. In the treatment of an hysteric, attention must be given to his problems with sex. This layering of defense cannot be skipped in treatment. It would be a serious mistake to assume, as we used to, that this layer represents the ultimate source of the difficulty. For among the uses and misuses of sex one finds this: sexual feelings, themselves, may be diverted to the service of defense!

What, then, is being defended against? Given the *exhibitionism* of a woman with many hysterical features, and a penchant for wearing her heart on both sleeves, we are reminded of a wisecrack often used by third-year psychiatric residents: "I think there is *less* here than meets the eye." They were referring, of course, to the frequent hollowness of the protestations of love, concern, or even guilt of such people. Actors and actresses in daily life, they seem unable to distinguish the role they are playing from reality; and they, like chameleons, will shift roles to meet the immediate situation in which they are. We may suddenly see the hysteric as an *empty person,* lacking enduring values and even attachments.

It is natural that our perceptiveness be accompanied by shock and even contempt. But why? Because suddenly we are face-to-face with an emptiness that can afflict any of us! We want to dissociate ourselves from it because it is frightening, and that is why we are contemptuous of the hysteric. While our judgmental attitude is understandable, it may prove unfortunate for the hysteric, for we miss a significant insight into what she is most desperately defending herself against. It *is* the sense of emptiness and the accompanying loneliness.

If at times she is greedy for sex, we see it as an effort to assuage her anxiety about being bereft by escaping into pleasure. Even the sort of pleasure is indicative. Mature sexuality consists of an encounter in which there is a progression from interest, to sensuality, to higher and higher peaks of pleasure culminating in orgasm and followed by relaxation and satiety, for the time being. The sexuality of immature hysterics, especially, lacks this *orgasmic* quality. It is more like the gentle stroking of her labia by a little girl comforting herself because she misses her mama and can think of nothing else that makes her feel better. The need for stimulation is chronic; there is no latent phase. Similarly, an hysterical man may react against the loss of a loved one, or the threat of rejection by his wife, by becoming all the more importunate for intercourse. It is as if he could re-establish the tie to his loved one by entering her. He tries, figuratively, to suck through his penis.

It is because of her fear of loneliness that an hysterical young woman may become involved in an affair. What she really wants is to be held and cuddled by a warm and tender mother-daddy, but the man becomes excited, and the result is intercourse. Dependency needs have become sexualized, and this creates reverberations as we have listed them, but the core of the difficulty usually lies more profoundly in the unresolved sense of emptiness. The emptiness also accounts for the *histrionic* and *exhibitionistic* facets of the syndrome. While the overt behavior says, defiantly, "Look me over," the covert message is "Don't overlook me." Rather than contemptible, the client now seems appealing, even poignant. But our pity will be misapplied if it distracts us from the necessary psychological surgery. The fact that our hysteric is so often a great "ham," clever in mimickry, skilled in manipulation, and funny need not prevent the treatment so long as one principle holds: if the client cannot distinguish between the drama she has created and her real life, the caseworker or therapist had better not have joined her—at least not in the same script.

I cannot end this section without including for the reader's pleasure another gem from Eliot, which needs no exegesis.

> Grishkin is nice: her Russian eye
> Is underlined for emphasis;
> Uncorseted, her friendly bust
> Gives promise of pneumatic bliss.
>
> The couched Brazilian jaguar
> Compels the scampering marmoset
> With subtle effluence of cat;
> Grishkin has a maisonette;
>
> The sleek Brazilian jaguar
> Does not in its arboreal gloom
> Distil so rank a feline smell
> As Grishkin in a drawing-room.

And there, my friends, is the casework problem.

Mixed Marriage

What happens when an hysterical woman marries an obsessive man? This combination is found rather frequently in marital counseling. The wife is invariably experiencing the greater discomfort and showing the most symptomatic reaction. As she works out of her depressive, martyred stance of "I feel trapped," she may conclude that her husband is going to have to change or she will divorce him. This is not to be taken as an idle threat; often that is exactly what she does. The husband, meanwhile, finds it difficult to take the whole matter seriously. He is embarrassed to be talking about feelings, in the first place, and preoccupied with making a living, in the second. He wishes she would just calm down and do a better job of balancing their budget.

Such cases are painful to encounter. They often involve a woman in her early thirties, whose chances of a satisfying remarriage are not so great as she likes to think, and a husband in his later thirties, about to be pushed toward bankruptcy. Typically it is a marriage of about ten years' standing, with the fate of several children hanging in the balance. As one husband, less stodgy than many, burst out: "Ten years and three children later—*now* she decides she doesn't love me." What has gone wrong?

Although the wife claims she never really loved her husband, something attracted her to this man originally. As a young woman she was obliquely aware of her emotional lability, her preoccupation with flirting, and the chance that she would get herself into trouble. The husband, let us say, was a man then in his later twenties, single because he was too conservative and shy to have rushed into marriage with a contemporary. To the girl, he seemed successful, mature, solid—just the person to help support her controls against impulsivity. So one basis of her attachment to him was his defensive function and her need for a mother-figure in her husband.

The husband's maturity was actually being overestimated. She mistook his stolidity for solidity. It was not that his emotions were so judicious, rather that he feared to express any. At the same time, he was aware of a vicarious sense of freedom and pleasure from watching this girl's vivacity. She added variety and entertainment to his life, even as he felt he had to slow her down at times. And so they were in love, and were married. Such a marriage can work for a time, and it usually does. If neither partner exhibits too much of the pattern I am describing, they may meet each other's needs for a lifetime. Indeed, they may help each other mature. But there are dangers.

A common danger is that the girl who was fearful of

her impulses becomes a woman who, after coping with life for a number of years, is no longer so afraid of them. She wants more excitement and is impatient with a husband who will not give her even a good fight. As she no longer needs a man who will support her defenses, she now views him as a wet blanket, a drag, a party pooper. Some of her feelings are realistic, of course, but some are not. It is inevitable that this immature woman will sooner or later grow ambivalent toward anyone she loves. She carries over her sense of emptiness and disappointment in her feelings toward her mother, and punishes her husband for them. She now can project the cause of all her neurotic despair onto her husband. Gullible or unethical marriage counselors and psychiatrists may accept at face value her statement of what is wrong. In that case, there may be a divorce and only afterward will she discover she still has many of the same feelings the divorce was supposed to alleviate.

Such a marriage cannot always be salvaged. Sometimes, when both partners no longer need the defensive functions they served for each other, they find they have no other basis for love. Or, if the parties involved are extremely immature or stubborn, the level of friction in the household may rise to a point too high to risk while one tries to treat the personalities and their marriage. Shooting of one's mate has been known to occur even among apparently successful and sensible people. At a less menacing level, we find that they are making each other worse—that is, as she regresses and acts more hysterical, he withdraws and becomes more anxious and rigidly compulsive. Each would like to think the other is "making me sicker." The truth is they are exacerbating each other's neuroses, but each would still have a neurosis if the other went away.

Fortunately, many such marriages can be treated, and are. Even if the couples exhibit the character-structures just described, they often achieve a downward spiraling of tension through ventilation and insight. Then it is possible for each to look at his own contribution to the trouble and think about changing. How much help will be needed depends of course on how extreme the patterns were in the first place.

Although this is not a book about treatment, let us mention that the caseworker's task is to step in and become the "good mama," satisfying dependency needs. By comforting, rewarding, and occasionally admonishing, it is possible gradually to get them to stop acting like two children fighting in the back seat of the family car during a tedious auto trip. When their love of their children and the desire to recover what they once had takes precedence over their spitefulness and bitterness, they will have stopped the process of regression. At that point, our job is to help them satisfy their dependency needs, needing us the less as they do so, until we make ourselves therapeutically unnecessary. For the sake of their pride, we can call this "re-establishing communication," but we must remember that primitive, violent forces are also at work.

The Paranoid Character

Most educated people associate *paranoia* with the serious mental illness *paranoid schizophrenia*. All schizophrenics suffer from thought disorders. They show vagueness in thought and gaps in reasoning, are concrete-minded; they are thought to be psychotic because they have lost the ability to recognize reality in the way others see it *(consensual validation)*. A paranoid schizophrenic suffers from these general symptoms. In addition, he is recognized by his extreme *suspiciousness,* by which he infers maliciousness in the actions of others to an extreme degree. He may have hallucinations and *delusions of persecution.* Typically, too, the paranoid schizophrenic is *grandiose;* he has a great sense of his own importance, his role in history, or the like. It was not uncommon for such patients to think of themselves as Christ, or Napoleon, or Caesar. Today one hears less about such colorful delusional states, perhaps because our psychoses, like the rest of our culture, are growing more sophisticated and less delightfully eccentric. When reality offers the hydrogen bomb, who needs *delusions of omnipotence?*

A *paranoid character,* however, is not psychotic, or not currently psychotic. The term encompasses a person with some of the features just mentioned, but they are greatly modulated and well-masked. A paranoid character is not thought to be in the midst of an acute, labile, schizophrenic illness. Rather, as the word *character* reminds us, he is in a relatively stable state. His reality testing is adequate; indeed, it may be hypertrophied in an area of special concern, because of either his *suspiciousness* or his tremendous need for *power*. Hence, it is not uncommon to find paranoid characters who are highly successful speculators, on the one hand, or shrewd diagnosticians on the other. There are a great many more persons who are paranoid characters, or have marked paranoid trends, than the average new practitioner conceives possible.

The paranoid character, like the hysteric, often feels sadly abused. What distinguishes him from the ordinary hysteric, however, is the *rigidity* with which he pursues the person he believes injured him. Many obsessives, as we have noted, are argumentative yes-butters. The paranoid character does not find it necessary to be a yes-butter; he does not accept your point even for heuristic purposes. If you place a fence on what he thinks is four inches his side of the property line, he not only will take you to court about it but also will pursue the case as long as it takes to win. He is *litigious,* and with all his suspiciousness is as much the shyster's friend as the inadequate hysteric is the support of unprincipled physicians. The paranoid character feels friendless without an enemy; as long as he has at least one person with whom he is actively feuding, he is in balance. The paranoid character need not be brave, so it is not uncommon for him to select as his enemy a person over whom he has power and whom he can then prosecute *mercilessly.* If your employer has many of these characteristics, and you find yourself his target for this year, leave. Now.

It is seldom possible to mollify such a person, except temporarily; he respects only counterforce. An hysteric can be helped to correct her distortions about another person through reasoning and evidence. But the paranoid character "needs" his projections and suspicions far more, and this accounts in part for his rigidity. There is something more than stubborn about the way he clings to his ideas and persists in his intentions. It is as if we were dealing with defenses that are brassy, or somehow brittle, and you get the feeling that if he were to give ground even a little bit he might collapse totally. This is reflected in his *intolerance for criticism,* which may be so strong that it seriously interferes with his ability to learn from his mistakes, certainly not from the advice of others.

Where the obsessive is perfectionistic, the paranoid character is *hypercritical,* especially about people. There is hardly anyone about whom he does not have serious reservations. This trait may make him an excellent psychodiagnostician, for he is preoccupied with smelling out the crannies of others' motivations, anyhow. Many first-rate psychometricians have marked paranoid features. The hypercritical attitude about others often extends to himself, but this he keeps unconscious. Still, he is *pitiless,* and rather than sympathetic is actually *contemptuous of weakness* in himself or others. He is likely to experience attempts at self-examination (casework or psychotherapy, for example), as a series of psychological assaults. He assumes you have the same contempt at remarking his difficulties as he would feel were your roles reversed.

Paranoid characters are not usually very humorous, and least so about their own foibles. They subscribe to the doctrine of personal infallibility. One patient hated to call the railway station to ask when the train left. Not only was she shy, but it turned out that she felt, somehow, she should already know the train schedule; to have to ask for information was an admission that she did not already know it. Actually, this is rather ludicrous, and many patients would be amused to discover their inability to ask directions had such a basis in their personalities. This young lady, however, was not amused. For her the stakes were too high: to be uninformed was a violation of her defensive *illusion of omniscience*. In plain English, this means being a know-it-all.

Lack of humor in the paranoid characters I have known has seemed to be multiply determined. First, they are unable to enjoy jokes at their own expense, for the stakes are always too high to be taken lightly. They prefer bathroom humor and cruelty jokes—like little boys. Second, much humor involves an element of surprise. We see a sudden juxtaposition of images we had never thought possible, it makes a weird kind of sense, and we laugh. But the professional know-it-all cannot afford to be surprised. Third, he cannot *surrender* to humor; he can tell a joke, but he cannot enjoy one, let us say. He "tops" your story, or he has heard it already. The need to control is even more desperate, even more brassy, than we saw it in the obsessive. Indeed, some paranoid characters are warding off open psychotic breaks. Others have had temporary psychoses, and the personalities we deal with represent instances of poor healing after such illnesses.

In my experience, the sort of personality we have been describing often rises rapidly in bureaucratic structures—the Army, the university, the mental hospital, and even the large social agency. Few of us have the drive toward power which frees the paranoid character to fanatic efficiency in pursuit of status. We may, in fact, be handicapped by concern for our subordinates or pity toward someone with whom we are in competition. But this sort of person has few such qualms, consciously, and allays such as he has with claims that he does what he does "for the good of the organization."

Moreover, some of the energy others put into love relationships is, for paranoid characters, drained off into their fascination with *intrigue*. They are expert backbiters and office politicians. As soon as they meet someone new, the question is, "Who will be on top?" Their interpersonal relationships tend to be largely *manipulative*, however

superficially warm they may appear. The best-known example is Stalin, but we cannot forget the British double
agent Kim Philby, who betrayed his country to the Rus-
sians, and John Foster Dulles, who placed our country on
nearly the same pedestal of concern as he did his narcissism.
It is of passing interest that studies of the Russian national
character seem to show that the group who becomes the
managerial class has much in common with the personality
of the U.S. managerial class—many paranoid elements.

It used to be thought that the crucial dynamic in all
paranoid states was *unconscious homosexuality*. So abhor-
rent was self-recognition of this propensity that the client
or patient would project all sorts of evil, accusatory
thoughts into the minds of others, thus giving rise to his
suspiciousness. Nevertheless, I learned from a patient who
was homosexual and recurrently paranoid (and who de-
feated my attempts to treat him) that the reverse may also
be true. That is, it is because the young man is deeply hostile
and suspicious that he cannot tolerate any long-term relationship. Certainly he could not endure the commitment
and intimacy which, in our culture, go with marriage. Hence
the homosexual relationship—fleeting, jealousy-ridden,
interrupted by side-affairs with casual pickups—was his
only refuge against being left completely alone.

The paranoid character utilizes a number of defenses
found in both the obsessive-compulsive and the hysteric. A
major distinguishing feature is the desperateness, the hard,
turtle-like exterior, if you will, with which these defenses
are organized. This is what we mean when we speak of his
rigidity. Obviously this character structure represents a
developmentally lower stage of maturation, with many anal-
stage remnants, whatever his success in manipulating the
world. The social caseworker is usually more in the position
of recognizing the trends, and dealing with the client realistically (which is *not* to say frankly) in terms of how he is,
rather than anticipating much change. The etiological roots
of this distressing character-formation will become clearer
when we discuss the *schizoid* and *paranoid* positions.

The Depressive Character

It has been said that a cynic is a person who, when given a choice between two evils, chooses both. A similar comment applies to the depressive person. It is not always clear whether we label him depressive because of the state in which he exists or the talent he has for inducing a sad feeling in us. There is a kind of client of morose demeanor who is actually so *affect-inhibited* he feels scarcely anything. The depressive person does permit himself a modicum of feelings, but they are consistently in one direction. They range from dreadful to "not too bad." It is as well not to ask him how he feels.

Other prominent characteristics include a *self-derogatory* attitude so that he seldom admits to having done well. If he did so, it was "an accident." There is an *apologetic* manner that accompanies the self-deprecation and says "excuse me for living." Constantly bracing himself to cope with *impending doom,* the depressed person lives by his forebodings. Needless to say, he seldom has, or permits himself, any fun out of life. *Er vergonnt sich nicht.*

These attitudes are found in persons experiencing acute depression, usually in response to something that has happened in life—death or illness of a loved one, a major career defeat, loss of caring by a person to whom one has become attached. When we refer to a depressive character, we do not mean an acute state, reactive to some identifiable event, but a chronic one. It is characteristic of the depressive personality that his mood cannot usually be ascribed to any concrete event; rather, it is as if he always finds something to feel depressed about. In short, we are discussing depression as a *modus vivendi.*

Much of what we believe to be true of the dynamics of acute depression also applies to the more chronically depressed person, but with the usual qualifications regarding a symptom that has long endured and become part of character. The technical interpretation of depression is *aggres-*

sion turned against the self. The client is angry but unable to express it directly toward the true object of his rage, so, *faute de mieux,* he attacks himself. Why does he not express it openly, "get it off his chest," rather than letting it "eat at him" without even consciously knowing he is mad? The most usual reason is that the adult has too *rigid* a conscience to permit the outburst; we say he has a *primitive superego.* Many people, for example, have been mistaught religiously that to feel hatred is sinful. Obviously such emotions as rage and hate were well known among those who set down our Bible, and they were taken for granted as part of the nature of man. Rage is an automatic response, something like a reflex, if you will. One cannot decide whether he will be angry; one can decide only whether he will show it or express it destructively. Many clients believe that by some act of will they can feel what they do not feel, or not feel what they do feel. It would not be surprising, then, if their rage were to come out in some other form—like depressiveness.

In my experience, while religious doctrines may contribute to, or exacerbate, the overly strong constraints against expressing anger, they are seldom the primary reason. More typical is the childish association that because one was originally most angry at mama, all later rage is as if one were attacking mama. If one destroys mama (children *do* remark, "I'm going to cut off your head and throw you in the garbage pail"), then one will be left utterly alone. Therefore anger is desperately dangerous. It may also be dangerous if the client or patient is immature in parts other than his conscience. For example, he experiences anger still as the raw, violently colorful explosion of childhood. To a grown man, who has some power to let his thoughts find reality in action, this is frightening. If we ask *why* the ideas of rage are still so primitive, we find in many cases there has been a circular process. Never, since childhood, has he felt free to express such feelings. Therefore, he has had no practice in how to get mad, but to do so in modulated forms, as most of us gradually had to learn through practice and from being punished for uncontrolled expressions. In short, he was held back from the life experiences out of which he could have matured in his handling of anger. Therefore, as an adult he can only alternate between holding it all in, and sudden, violent outbursts which become proper cause for much subsequent guilt.

A frequent concomitant to this set of dynamics is the personality constellation we call *passive-aggressive*. Literally, this usually means a person who expresses his aggression in passive ways—the husband in the comic strip who frustrates his wife by reading the paper while she nags at him. *Spite* is the form of aggression the weak can dare. Thus, spitefulness is common among passive-aggressive, depressive people. It takes many forms, but the one of greatest interest to caseworkers and counselors is *hostile-compliance*. This consists of carrying out a suggestion (experienced as a command) in such a way that it fails. Artful hostile-compliance takes the form of overdoing as directed, thereby reducing the prescriber to complete helplessness. The patient does not just peel the potato for her mother: she ends up with a small pebble which she carefully sets in the pot. The Southern Negro used to be an expert at this. Northerners discovered that the Southern Negro was being paid thirty or forty cents an hour (while Northern help was getting a dollar) and he was often managing to give just about that proportionate amount of effort. The danger with spite is that it can lead to guilt feelings, especially when it is unconscious. And it, too, can be turned against the self, begetting depression. "Cutting off one's nose to spite one's face." The sullen housewife refuses to make herself attractive to her husband, but then she also ends up with no sexual relationship.

Finally, there may be an inability to express aggression directly because the true object is unavailable. Following a death, one will hear the lament, "How could you go away and leave me?" But the mourner would be outraged were we to suggest that he was mad at the departed for abandoning him. This would really add to his burden of conflict! So he rends his clothes and covers himself with ashes, while he weeps at his lot.

These formulations of depressiveness and its roots are applicable to many people, in acute as well as chronic states. But they may have become "classical" as interpretations, accepted too glibly. If we routinely *assume* that any depressed person we see is secretly angry, it becomes impossible to verify whether this is true in any given case. An angry outburst will demonstrate your assumption; failure to get it is interpreted as "covering up." Therefore, I must emphasize strongly that while depression may emerge as a *result* of a defense (i.e., the need to redirect anger), depressiveness may serve as a defense itself.

One defensive function of depressiveness is as a form of *security maneuver*. These are a series of psychological operations carried on with the general intention: play it safe. Among the peasants in Southern and Eastern Europe, there used to be a good deal of fear of the evil eye and the evil spirits. The Jews, for example, felt it was bad luck to acknowledge pride or satisfaction verbally, as this would call down the vengeance of the evil spirits. This idea spreads, often, until it seems safer in general not even to think of good fortune lest it be taken away from you. Another familiar version of a related phenomenon is the effort to *control* the experience of disappointment. If you do not hope for much, indeed if you expect the worst, then you cannot be taken by surprise, and you are braced to receive bad news. Of course the price one pays for all this internal preparation is that in preparing for the worst, one preoccupies himself with morbid thoughts.

Another version of controlling by anticipation is the manner of self-abnegation and self-recrimination, to which we referred earlier. By blaming oneself aloud, one can get in the punch before it is thrown at him. At the same time he can try to soften the blow by being the person who throws it. Hence, the punitive superego is encouraged to stay immature, for it continues to have a function also in the present. It is intended to soften criticism. In fact, a skillful practitioner of the art of self-blaming can even select the charges he wants leveled at himself.

These psychological processes tie in with other congeries related to "playing the morality game." These are maneuvers by which one attempts symbolically to wrest success from defeat by claiming a moral victory. When I was at college and our football team never won a game, we would pretend to a massive indifference to the childish sport or else we would say, "Well, our coach is building character again." The defect with such moral victories is that there is no substitute for achievement in the real world. The advantage of setting up life as a series of moral issues—a policy that vastly increases the penetration of the superego into all aspects of living—is that one cannot lose. After all, one can always say, "I could have won, but I would not stoop to such tactics as studying before an exam," or the like. Although the person seems to be taking major chances with his life, he is, actually, "playing it safe." We readily see, therefore, why the depressive person often has a punitive superego. He has reinforced it even in adult life, as a security maneuver. While he wrests defeat from the jaws of victory in the service of his moral superiority, he must suffer from the blows he inflicts on himself in order to keep things under his control.

Depressiveness is a symptom and a pattern from which other patterns can be derived. One is the occasional erection of a *manic* defense. Literally, it is as if the ego becomes tired of living down in the sewer and, from time to time, decides to throw off the whole attitude by a sharp reversal. Unlike the droopy showing that accompanies depression, then, we may suddenly find ourselves with a hyperactive client, who can be—and is—on the go all night. A general sense of euphoria replaces dark, dismal feelings. Absolute certainty and a brassy unwillingness to be crossed or corrected replaces the self-doubting and misgivings. The hint that all is not really so well as the patient likes to pretend to himself comes from the fact that he is now as rigidly optimistic as he was formerly pessimistic. The rigidity in the personality, in other words, continues and is now increased, if anything, by massive denial not only of his own self-questionings, which may have been unreal, but of reality and its limitations as well.

What is the etiology of this pattern? By what series of life events does one become a depressive personality? Basically, the depressive is chronically dissatisfied. He is dissatisfied, ultimately, because he did not get, or feels he did not get, all he should have from his mother. Therefore, he is demanding of the world about him, constantly trying to make up for what he feels he has missed. The result is that he is *greedy,* and his constant complaint is that life has not given him enough. If a cynic is a secretly disillusioned romantic, a depressive is disappointed because he asks more from life than it gives. Or more than it gives to adults.

If the depressive could express some of this openly, he might at least come to grips with it, and perhaps even resolve some of it. But it feels insulting to be conscious of these thoughts and emotions. Consequently, he may cover his whining and demandingness completely behind a reaction formation of bravery and self-sacrifice. This cheerfully bitter front has the effect of creating considerable guilt among those close to you. The spouses and youngsters of depressives who become regressed and hospitalized are among the most interested, respectful, and attentive relatives one will find. We must feel admiration for the resolution with which the depressive fights against the feelings that threaten to overwhelm him.

A depressive's extreme *pride* may not let him know how much he yearns to be taken care of and mothered. Pride is certainly a concomitant of this character formation, extending into overconcern about others' opinions, the self-demand for achievement, and so on. This pride, however, also contains a suggestion as to the ultimate root of the problem. What is the pride of a little boy whose mother leaves him to go to work, or the little girl required, at too young an age, to care for her younger siblings? The pride is a way of saying, "If nobody else loves me, *I* will."

We now see the link between this character type and the obsessive-compulsive. Indeed, for those with chronically depressive feelings, constant achievement and activity toward achievement are the only defenses they may know. The ultimate etiology for the depressive person lies in the early mother-child relationship. It is well to remember that no therapy can make up for what has been, and for what may never be. But we can at least seek to dislodge some of the later elaborations on the neurosis which make things worse: the self-demandingness, the dependency on others' opinions for reassurance, the pride and jealousy, the self-hatred, the redirection of reasonable desires for succoring; the denial of needfulness, the tendency to play the morality game and its consequences, the general defensive maintenance of funereal outlooks, the fear of experiencing fun. We may not be able to eliminate all these subsequent developments, but at least they are modifiable in many instances.

It is not necessary to hurt the pride of the depressive person when meeting the needfulness behind his self-sacrificing front. It is not required that one *tell* him that one is being nice, or why one is being giving. If you burlesque his own despairing feelings toward himself by saying, mock-solemnly, "Yes, you are just awful," or, "We might as well bury you now," he gets the concern—and the message.

Infantile Personalities

One of the secrets of the adult world to which many of us are not privy until our own middle age is that most people never really grow up. I first became acutely aware of this in my professional attempts to use the form of characterology on which I had been reared. In trying to formulate a case as an example of the anal character, I would become cognizant of the number of oral traits also present. People did not fit their genotypic pigeonholes. Gradually it dawned on me that despite my efforts to place them in neat categories, some folks seem to move through adult life with *all* their psychogenetic underclothing still flapping on the wash-line. Stages of development which should have been passed through have not been; images and feelings which ought to have been repressed are still blatant in consciousness.

Nearly all neurotics and certainly all psychotics show evidence of failure to mature. The lack of adaptability that accompanies childishness makes for greater vulnerability to emotional breakdown. There are some clients and patients, however, who do not impress us as having clearly definable illnesses, in the traditional sense. We hardly know where to begin in trying to understand their "problems." At one and the same time they have no symptoms, and a myriad; they are odd; they generate troubles for others and for them-selves. In the end, we have to recognize that whatever the surface manifestations, the *immaturity* is itself the illness.

Persons grouped together here have been variously de-scribed in the psychiatric nomenclature. Some were called *constitutional psychopathic state,* until it became apparent that the psychiatrists most favoring such genetic diagnoses were themselves constitutionally incapable of insight. Other terms, of more recent vintage, include *character disorder, inadequate personality, impulse-ridden character.* There is some value to these distinctions, but not a great deal. To some of us, it seems more relevant to emphasize the com-mon element in all these uncomplimentary diagnoses: these are children in the bodies of adults. This is well pointed up by Ruesch's term (1948) the *infantile personality.* The reader should be warned that my preference for this expres-sion is not based on general usage. The term *character disorder* is perhaps more common, as exemplified in the excellent monograph by Reiner and Kaufman, *Character Disorders in Parents of Delinquents* (1959).

What are some prevalent features among infantile per-sonalities? Ruesch first used the term in discussing psycho-somatic illness, so perhaps we might start with the physical consequences of this personality problem. Children have a limited repertoire of response, and this is true of grown-up children as well. Instead of dealing with a frustration or an interpersonal conflict by using words or by effectively manipulating the world, the infantile personality is apt to *somatize* (Hill, 1952). His adrenals are activated, his pulse rate and blood pressure go up. This happens to anyone under stress. But if the stress persists long enough, stubbornly enough, and the person develops no satisfactory alternate means for handling it, there are expectable medical consequences—including ulcers, high blood pressure, coronary thrombosis. If the infantilism includes falling back on childish greed to assuage anxiety, the patient is likely to be grossly overweight, which can only exacerbate the cardiovascular difficulties he is already inviting. Another somatic ailment is colitis, a condition which, if it persists, can become ulcerative. Lest the reader discount the impact of functional physical ailments, I should mention that while hemorrhoids are usually a nuisance, and warts and various skin blemishes readily treatable, the conditions mentioned above are all potentially lethal.

One reason the infantile personality somatizes is that he lives with a massive amount of subjective frustration. He is frustrated because he is still childishly demanding—more open than the depressive person, but nonetheless extremely needful. When he cannot get "what I want when I want it," he becomes explosive. Although it might be better for him physically simply to express it, or psychologically safer to be annoying than depressed, it would be best of all not to be so angry all the time! But it does not take much perceptiveness to realize that injunctions from his physician that he "must not get emotional" are not only useless, they complicate the problem.

The frustration felt by the infantile person is based on his demandingness; it is compounded by his limited competence in dealing with the world. Because he wants his gratification immediately, he is incapable of setting himself long-range goals, of planning toward success, of accepting temporary setbacks philosophically. In the language of Kurt Lewin (1951), he has foreshortened time-perspective. Similarly, he seldom sticks with an activity long enough to acquire a high degree of skill at it. Therefore, not only is he ashamed of being thought inadequate, he *is* inadequate. This incompetence may apply to limited aspects of his life or it may be quite general.

As I write this, I have just finished reading a biography of Picasso written by a former mistress—an account that cannot be taken as unbiased. Still, if any of it is true, Picasso is certainly in his daily life *outside his work* a boringly infantile man. Yet he has produced some work that is certainly great art, and even more work that is calculatedly expensive. The same man who requires to be coaxed out of bed, and who cannot bear to be measured for a pair of pants, also has survived one marriage and several long-term liaisons without dissipating more than a tiny fraction of his fortune.

Similarly, there are some impressively verbal, and verbose, people who are nevertheless infantile. The general trend, however, is a lack of verbal skill. They literally do not know many words. The words they know tend to be concrete, as one finds with children. They have neither the vocabulary nor the capacity for complex grammatical structure to support a complex train of ideas, and this further incapacitates them for long-range planning. The net result is a kind of concrete-mindedness approaching behavior we associate with schizophrenia. This feature makes adaptation difficult, just as it limits what can be accomplished in therapy. All these are personality features which emerge from the *culture of poverty;* they are said to be attributes derivable from *cultural disadvantage.* I must note, *en passant,* that these are also features of the infantile personality, and one effect of *cultural deprivation* is the production of generations of markedly childish people. Because of the limitations of ability and judgment mentioned above, we realize it will not be enough to put money into the hands of these people—necessary though that may be. There will be too many others around ingenious at taking it away from them!

In his interpersonal relationships, the infantile personality can exhibit many things, but it is well to be on the lookout for his *selfishness.* Mature love involves a giving and taking between two people who could exist independently of each other but prefer not to. Even though the childish person make a fetish of his "independence," this is not the way he relates. When he does form an attachment, it is apt to be a type of clinging and clutching which we call *anaclitic dependency.* This kind of sucking on the other person is bound to irritate him, sooner or later, so that the very needfulness of the infantile person eventually leads to his being rejected by those he has left drained. Because of the continued dominance of *separation anxiety* in his personality, by the way, the infantile person finds it uncomfortable to break off relationships, even after they have become unsatisfying to all involved.

Childish persons are, of course, not without urges to give, but the giving is always in danger of being impulsive, overwhelming, well-meant but insensitive. I recall the instance of a wealthy man who was in treatment with a psychiatrist who lunched with him between appointments at the clinic. Out of gratitude for the "help" he had received, he presented his doctor with a motorboat. I am glad to say the doctor refused it, pointing out simply the criticism to which he would be subjected if he took so handsome a gift from a patient. Of course the patient was not thinking so much of the effect of the gift on the recipient as of how good he would feel in making the present.

A frequent accompaniment of "giving" among infantile persons is the tendency to *infantilize* the beneficiary. This is especially true of their children, as in the case of the "Jewish mama," but the same sort of person encourages dependency and childishness in her husband as well. It is as if they cannot bear to see those dependent on them grow up, lest they become so mature they can walk away and leave. We recognize a closely related phenomenon in child guidance work when we see a mother who seemingly does well with her children until they have reached a developmental stage critical to the mother's makeup. She may be comfortable with a helpless infant, but the toddler is capable of more mobility and, we hope, begins to assert a mind of his own. At this point the infantile mother is threatened with both physical and emotional separation and she becomes discombobulated (Polansky *et al.*, 1968). Many such women deal with the anxiety by having another child, and discarding rather abruptly the next elder when the baby arrives. In such families there is naturally a vicious sibling jealousy. Incidentally, women are not the only ones with problems of accepting the burgeoning personalities of their children. The world is full of successful men, mature in many ways, who yet cannot stand to see their sons grow up. They are happiest with fellow-infants, and make far better grandfathers than fathers.

Immature personalities will show characteristic malformations of the superego as well. According to Freudian theory, the function of the mature superego is rather clear and simple. Its *purpose* is to keep one out of trouble. In that sense, it is properly to be seen—as its name implies— as a specialized function of the ego. Most of what we learn about how to avoid pain comes from our direct experience. But it is also possible to derive useful guidelines from the lives of others, if we admire them, and take over their patterns by *identification*. This organization of identifications and partial identifications with individuals and groups we term the superego.

Childish people typically have spotty superegos. Many of their standards are thinly held and poorly integrated, and they sense this. Hence, we often find a reaction formation against the sense of being so easily corruptible. Such persons become extremely *rigid* in their standards. We can see a great deal of this in the Bible Belt in this country where part of the population gets roaring drunk whenever it can afford the bootlegged whiskey, another part of the populace is sanctimoniously abstinent, and a third part, perhaps the majority, alternates between the two positions!

A youngster whose mother was childish and impulsive is unlikely to have been held *consistently* to any set of standards to have sufficiently internalized them. Moreover, if one's parents are immature, and have a limited ability to give love, another link in the chain leading to internalization is missing. The child is unable to respond to his parents' disapproval as if it threatened the loss of love, when he has never been that comfortably loved. For a variety of reasons, therefore, one can anticipate that the consciences of infantile personalities will be childishly oversevere, on the one hand, or corruptible and poorly-formed on the other. Often they are both. The man who is absolutely reliable in business dealings may be a complete liar and cheat in his relationships with women. Such folks may be described as having "Swiss cheese superegos."

Related to the defects of internalized standards is the lack of ability to appraise one's personality and weaknesses. Using the term loosely, we say these patients have no *insight,* by which we mean the *self-observing function of the ego* is sadly underdeveloped. The capacity for self-observation, after all, also requires the internalization and organization of a set of standards that come from outside the self but exist as a network of ideas within the self. For reasons similar to those involved in the faulty superego development, the ability to appraise one's faults realistically is also impaired. Therefore, a distinguishing mark of any infantile personality who gets involved in treatment, for whatever reason, is that he really sees nothing wrong with himself or with how he does things.

The woman who eats herself into a state of grossness "cannot understand" why her husband's eye should wander; the man who works obsessively while rubbing up his own narcissism about success, sees no reason his wife should be unhappy with her lot. Typically, we find infantile people in treatment because they have been forced into it, by the threats of losing the comforts of married life, say, or by their physical symptoms. To expect a childish man to want to change for the sake of his wife's happiness is ridiculous. The only thing that will induce an effort at change in such a person is a simple answer to an age-old query: "What's there in it for me?" As soon as the threat of divorce is dissipated, for example, such a man is ready to stop further marital counseling. Although he may have made some grudging obeisances, he never really saw anything wrong with his way of operating. The same applies to the woman who is being seen for the sake of her child's treatment. It is a major evidence of growth for such a person if she even decides she will have to change what she *does* (never what she *is*) for the sake of her *own* long-run comfort as a mother. Yet despite their obtuseness about others, they often expect great sensitivity where their own feelings are concerned. Infantile people are constantly "feeling insulted" in treatment. We find the lady who would not dream of asking her husband to give up a business trip that falls on her birthday, "If he *really* loved me, he would know how I feel." In short, they demand *unconditional love*.

It is natural to ask, finally, how it happens that some of us get this way. We distinguish, to begin with, between two mechanisms by which a person may become childish: fixation and regression. If a man were once mature but, under a series of life blows, psychological or physical, he has become more primitive, we say he has *regressed*. Most primitive personalities, however, are not people who once had it but lost it; they are people who never had it. We say that emotionally they have failed to develop beyond a certain phase and they are *fixated* in this childhood phase.

Speaking very generally, there are three major reasons for such fixation. First, and most common, is a life situation in which the person has received insufficient love and attention and stimulation in childhood. The personality has not been sufficiently *nourished* to provide for growth. In discussing superego dysfunctioning, we noted a few instances of how this might happen with childish parents. The second reason, common especially in the upper-middle class, is that there has been insufficient *demand* for growth. If the youngster gets all his wants satisfied without trying to reach progressively higher peaks of personal competence, he feels no reason to abandon the pleasures of childhood. This can happen with an infantilizing mother; it also happens with mothers and fathers too self-centered to be willing to fight the child on any issue so that he is permitted to remain un-couth and selfish despite the long-run danger to his life.

Third, there are people who, either because of their parents' personality disorders or because of life misfortunes, have experienced what we call *defensive progression*. The eldest daughter left motherless at age ten may, in her loneliness and anxiety, seek to jump into adulthood and take care of her five brothers and sisters. Her father may praise her, she may be "Daddy's big girl," but the fact is she is trying to skip adolescence and jump into adulthood. It is not possible to do this, in my observation. Sooner or later, life catches up with us, and the victims of a forced-growth childhood are revealed not to have progressed beyond the point at which they put on a mature front, *pseudomaturity*. Others who jump into pseudomaturity include persons who had severe childhood neuroses and somehow hoped that by leaping into adulthood they could leave their miseries behind. Here, too, life catches up with them, even though we cannot but admire the valiant efforts they make to sustain the solution they found as a child. As noted earlier, many obsessive-compulsives reveal this etiology in their histories.

References

Eliot, T. S. *Collected Poems, 1909–1962.* London: Faber & Faber; New York: Harcourt, Brace & World.

Hill, Lewis B. "Infantile Personalities," *American Journal of Psychiatry, 109,* 1952, 429–432.

Lewin, Kurt. *Field Theory in Social Science.* New York: Harper & Row, 1951.

Polansky, Norman A., Christine DeSaix, Mary Lou Wing, and John D. Patton. "Child Neglect in a Rural Community," *Social Casework, 49,* 1968, 467–474.

Reiner, Beatrice S., and Irving Kaufman. *Character Disorders in Parents of Delinquents.* New York: Family Service Association of America, 1959.

Ruesch, Jurgen. "The Infantile Personality: The Core Problem of Psychosomatic Medicine," *Psychosomatic Medicine, 10,* 1948, 134–144.

Chapter 6

The Theory of Object Relations

WE TURN NOW TO AN AREA OF THEORY THAT IS AMONG THE most exciting and promising contributions by the newer ego psychology to our work with people. It is called, in a general way, the theory of object relations.

By *object relations* we refer to the way in which our patient relates himself with the other humans who have more than passing meaning in his life. The use of the term is partly determined by historical accident. Originally in Freudian psychology a personal object usually referred to the *object of a drive*. Suppose you feel sexually excited. A person may then come to mind as the one with whom you seek to satisfy the need—or at least you fantasy doing so. That person is conceived to be the drive's "object," the image of a person associated with the act which is the aim of the drive. Our thoughts about other people serve many functions in our lives besides their roles as drive-objects. We use them also in the service of defense. But the term object relations has continued to be employed in a way that means

141

nothing more precise than did the notion Significant Other in the psychology of George Herbert Mead (1934) or Harry Stack Sullivan (1947).

I will begin the discussion by presenting some ideas taken largely from the work of Fairbairn, a Scottish analyst, whose writings have been extremely important for many workers involved in direct treatment of severely regressed, hospitalized persons. Of course, my presentation is not intended as a summarization of Fairbairn (1952); rather, I will give him the interpretation that has made the most sense to me. For a more exact description of his theory, and indeed of those English and continental analysts who have done so much to advance ego psychology in recent years, I strongly recommend the excellent volume by Harry Guntrip, *Personality Structure and Human Interaction* (1961). Let us return to things observable.

Some Common Phenomena

Anyone who has seen persons suffering from schizophrenia cannot fail to be impressed with their isolation. Sometimes they go to the extreme of physical withdrawal, by either running away or shutting out stimuli. Always there is emotional detachment and interpersonal coldness. Psychiatrists used to refer to the schizophrenic's characteristic handshake: it is a fervent form of human contact, roughly like clasping the tail of a dead fish. Even the schizophrenic with more capacity for relationship prefers a noncommittal stance. If, for example, you give a Likert-type attitude test (1932)—meaning you ask whether the subject Strongly Agrees, Agrees, or Strongly Disagrees with a series of statements—you get a typical pattern of response. They choose the noncommittal responses: weak agreement or disagreement or, preferably, "Doesn't matter" (Polansky *et al.*, 1957). The most severe forms of withdrawal require discounting reality altogether, so that the patient experiences hallucinations and the like.

We used to think that one either was or was not schizophrenic. Now we find it more helpful to think about patients as falling along a continuous dimension we call the *schizoid spectrum*. A person suffering from active, acute schizophrenic illness is far out on the spectrum. But let us discuss a more "normal" person who is not psychotic, the *schizoid personality*.

In daily life we come into contact with many schizoid personalities. They are not nearly so withdrawn as the ill schizophrenic; indeed, it may require some acquaintance to appreciate just how *detached* the schizoid person is. He has often made strenuous efforts to compensate for and mask his pattern. The college professor who acts so engrossed in his books and papers that he scarcely notices his surroundings, much less his wife and children, may well be schizoid. So may be the backslapping politician, salesman, or banker who seems warm and friendly, until you discover how indiscriminately he distributes his warmth and how reserved the expression in his eyes remains. Even the physician who exudes bedside manner may suddenly stand revealed as essentially shy and shrinking from any human contact not ritualized into his professional role.

The schizoid personality, then, is frequently odd, self-centered, basically unfeeling toward you. But he does not feel much about anything. He suffers from what we call severe *affect inhibition*. This does not mean he has no feelings; it does mean that he blocks out his feelings so that he is literally unable to be consciously aware of them.

Let us cite still another example. You are a caseworker in an institution for delinquent youngsters. For the past two months you have been having regular interviews with a boy named Pete, struggling to try to breach his wall of toughness and bravado to the point at which you can involve him in treatment. At the last interview you finally had a glimmering of hope. After all the interest and affection you have proffered him, he muttered, "Well, I guess you'll do." You spoke hopefully about his progress at the staff meeting this morning, only to be coldly informed by the

supervisor of cottage life that Pete escaped from the institution last night. Here is a clear implication that another
gullible young social worker has been outfoxed by a four-
teen-year-old "psychopath." Flashing through your mind
is the sneering voice of an elderly psychiatrist describing
the psychopath as "the asp in your bosom." At the moment,
you hate this kid, and all his kind. Even after you calm
down a bit, there remain the questions: Why did he do this
to me? And, why, just when we seemed to be getting somewhere?

Here, then, are examples of people who pass through our
professional lives. Obviously, I believe they are all related
to one another. But how? To answer this question, let us
leave our cases for the moment and take a little excursion
into developmental psychology. I will talk about life as an
infant feels it.

A Developmental View

Nobody really knows how the newborn experiences life,
perhaps he least of all. And all reconstructions of the emotional life of the very young infant are necessarily specula-
tive. Why, you may ask, bother to try to theorize in such
terms at all?

The answer derives from a fundamental precept about
human growth and development. *Earlier experiences pre-
determine the later.* This follows from the proclivity of
the organism to change following experience, otherwise
known as learning. Once you have enjoyed lemon pie, your
anticipation of it will never be the same. The next piece is
approached with a hopefulness based on the way you last
tasted it, and with a standard that may well be disappointed.
The older you get, the more you have already experienced,
the more your later responses are already influenced by
what has gone before. When you have become totally incapable of new or spontaneous reactions, you are said to
be middle-aged. Because early life experiences have such

far-reaching consequences over the total personality, it is obvious that any good theory of personality functioning must pay great attention to the earliest months, and even weeks, of life.

Even though we do not know the neonate's mind, we can make some rather solid inferences. In the first few hours of life, the principal preoccupation of the organism is with obtaining food. The milk from the mother's breast offers two essential ingredients: water, without which the whole internal bodily environment comes to a halt, and nourishment. We may extrapolate, therefore, that the hungry, thirsty infant experiences terror that he might shrivel up from lack of water or collapse from lack of food-energy. In a vague, unformulated way there must be a sense that he can wither away and, literally, cease to exist as an organism. I believe the *terror of loneliness* that older patients feel derives ultimately from this primordial childhood fear of death by desiccation. From less marked forms of the same emotional root we get the dread feeling of *emptiness* reported by so many of our schizoid patients as well as the somewhat intellectualized version described as the sense of *meaninglessness.*

The child needs desperately to be assured that nourishment will be forthcoming as he requires it. If he does not get this assurance, he is overcome with *futility,* one of the most distinguishing marks of the schizoid personality. This is the feeling that "nothing will do any good," because in the long run there is only disaster. A young patient once exclaimed, "What's the use of eating dinner? You will only be hungry by breakfast." The feeling of futility is not the same as depression: a depressed person may be miserable, but he still feels. The sense of futility is accompanied by a relative absence of feeling, taking the forms, "I feel empty. . . ." "I am a nothing. . . ." "I feel dead inside. . . ." From all accounts, it is a paralyzing inner state, resting on childhood despair.

It is common to implicate the inadequacies of the mother in producing or reinforcing this feeling in the young child. That is, any of us is liable to it, because this is the nature of life, the ultimate existential anxiety if you will. But if we are regularly given supplies, we may dare to hope. However, I no longer presume the root of the trouble can always be definitely identified in the maternal personality. Some infants are born with highly sensitive or incompletely matured digestive systems. We found once, upon closely rescrutinizing the early history of a series of schizoid adolescents, that a series of five out of six had had early feeding difficulties. Several were still unable to stand the taste of milk, and all five had been shifted from milk to a formula in infancy. Whether due to something in the early mother-child relationship, or to the infant's physiology, the net result is his feeling that "the milk of life itself is poisoned." Such a reaction hardly helps to ward off the feeling of futility, to which each of us is potentially heir.

In popularized psychology it is common to speak of "insecurity." From the examples given, the textbook writer has something terribly dramatic in mind. The sorority sister is "insecure" about whether her hem is straight or her boyfriend will like her lipstick. When we talk about *security maneuvers* in ego psychology, we are referring to defenses against ultimate dreads regarding life and death to which every man is necessarily subject.

Paraphrasing Fairbairn, we say that every infant has to come to some conclusion about how hopefully he will approach life, how he will resolve the *schizoid position*. Depending on the kind of mothering he is offered, and how he experiences that mothering, he may emerge with what Erikson (1950) described as "basic mistrust" or "basic trust." In relationships with others, the question is whether he believes human contacts can be relied on to be ultimately rewarding. Or does each new close attachment already promise to end in anger, anxiety, and disappointment? Patients described as having problems in the schizoid spectrum are those who have jelled their fundamental attitudes around a combination of *futility* and a *fear of closeness*.

From the *fear of closeness* we can already derive a number of insights into a class of defensive operations we call *distance maneuvers*. If closeness threatens hurt for you or for the object, if tenderness makes you vulnerable, if warmth and taking love bring tears to your eyes, then you have to erect defenses until your basic responses are somewhat alleviated. However, before we proceed with our discussion of distance maneuvers, let us consider another set of ideas, those of John Bowlby (1961).

Separation Anxiety

Fairbairn's theories are especially instructive in understanding the fear of relationship present in schizoid personalities and, indeed, in all of us. He has also formulated a conception of "splitting" in the ego which helps to understand some of the concreteness and disorganization encountered in the thoughts of deeply disturbed people. Bowlby's observations, however, seem to me to clarify certain issues beyond the point where Fairbairn left them.

Bowlby began his work with a major attempt to understand the effects on the young infant of being separated from his mother (1951). Thanks to Hitler, this was a problem of urgent social as well as theoretical impact. Eventually it became clear in Bowlby's research (and that of others) that maternal separation as such is not a univocal phenomenon with consistent sequellae. Its resultants in the child depend on the age of separation, the presence of substitute objects, and so forth. But Bowlby did clarify a concept that had not previously been so emphasized: *separation anxiety* (1960).

Separation anxiety can be typified by this scene. Picture a very small child, helpless, easily damaged, who is being held to his mother's breast. Should the mother suddenly let go of the child, he would find himself wrenched from security, and falling alone and desolate through space, just as so many of us did in nightmares in childhood. Or imagine the feeling we have momentarily when a high-speed elevator drops beneath us—again the terror at falling through space. To Bowlby this terror is the primordial form of all anxiety, which is to say the various other forms of anxiety—super-ego anxiety or the fear of internal punishment for guilt, ego anxiety, the sense of being overwhelmed by stimuli—all ultimately derive from this basic form.

Certainly it is true that separation anxiety plays a powerful role in object relations. A woman will remain in a loveless and exhausting marriage not, really, because she is "masochistic." She may be unable to tear loose from an attachment, once it is formed. Another reason schizoid adolescents keep their distance is that as soon as they start to like someone, they already begin to dread the pangs of the relationship's ending. To avoid the ending, they decline the beginning. Because of their dread of separation anxiety, they starve themselves of human warmth in the first place. "Playing it safe," they guarantee their loneliness.

Bowlby became interested in the reactions of infants old enough to be attached to their mothers when the mother left them. He reports a regular sequence of events, three stages through which the human infant seems to go. First, after his mother leaves, he looks uncomfortable and threshes around. Then he becomes angry and *protests,* reminding us that the basic function of anger is to push the external world around. If the wailing has no effect, and mother does not return, he eventually stops his outburst, but lapses into a phase of *despair* in which he looks and acts depressed. Eventually this seems to pass, too, and the infant comes to terms with his fate. But he comes to terms without joy, sullenly. His calmness represents no peace but resignation. To Bowlby, he is now *detached.*

The phases following separation from mother may then be listed: *protest, despair, detachment.* I do not pretend to know a lot about young children, but I have found Bowlby's identification of these phases meaningful in working with adolescents and adults. It is not necessary to dig through case histories other than our own to realize that we all employ detachment as a kind of ultimate defense against the pain of loss of someone we love. And not to have felt this pain is to have been so unlucky as never to have loved.

I have often noticed that when working with a delinquent or a schizoid adolescent who may not be delinquent at all, one gets very similar reactions. Each youngster begrudges liking—for you as for everyone else. He is both *detached* and *affect-inhibited.* Oh yes, he can express anger quite well. Hostility serves to support the basic removal. *Tenderness* and *love* are the dangerous emotions. Should the youngster begin to like you, should his resolute detachment begin to crumble, it is not uncommon to find him immediately overcome by sadness. His eyes fill with tears, he gets a catch in his throat. The reaction is unconscious, seemingly automatic. He feels unmanly, and wants to run away. No wonder, then, that the delinquent child in the institution fled the caseworker just at that point when he was admitting he liked him. Intermixed with the depressiveness, by the way, there is often anger. Instead of the cold and arrogant front, you are suddenly dealing with a miserable, angry child. In my experience as a therapist, I have never seen any real change occur in a schizoid adolescent when we did not repeat in treatment this sequence of penetrating the detachment not once but a number of times (see also Thomas, 1967). That the detachment is only a defense and not a final resolution is readily demonstrable in our own lives. There may be a girl you once loved, but of whom you have not really thought in years. Should you suddenly confront her, however, you are swept by unexpected emotion.

Let us return to Fairbairn and Bowlby. Each has independently made some acute observations; each has formulated an engaging and fruitful set of concepts for relating the object relations formed by our clients to preoccupations of the first year of life. But the two theories are not ready to be brought together in rigorous fashion and detail. Bowlby's emphasis on separation anxiety and its derivatives certainly clarifies many points concerning both infants and adults. Fairbairn is far the richer in insights regarding the ego operations of schizoid personalities and schizo-phrenics. We become sharply aware that everyone, without exception, has problems in the schizoid range. The notion of the schizoid position provides insights into the workings of hysterical and compulsive personalities, too, and further simplifies our understanding of these character structures.

The Paranoid Position

While many American analysts have busied themselves with becoming rich and acquiring high office in their pro-fessional and academic organizations, the serious and crea-tive work of advancing ego psychology has taken place in England. We come now to a few ideas of Melanie Klein, whom we must regard as quasi-English, as she came origi-nally from central Europe. Although Mrs. Klein was well-known as a child analyst, her ideas have attracted an impor-tant following in England among those practicing adult analysis. Indeed, there is now something referred to as a "Kleinian analysis" distinguished, *inter alia,* by its unusual length even by the standards of our affluent society.

The Kleinians are a controversial group, perhaps in part because of the difficulty in deciphering the key ideas in Klein's writings, and their leaders have been accused of substituting a kind of mysticism for theory. Nevertheless, there are two concepts associated with Mrs. Klein's work which I have found quite valuable in understanding some patients (1952). One has to do with the *paranoid position;* the other, which is also present in Fairbairn, is *splitting the object.* Let me illustrate what I mean.

There is a kind of woman we encounter who is extremely unpleasant. Not only does she nag, she does so in a harsh, penetrating, accusatory voice which carries through doors and walls; you can even hear it in your dreams. She is filled with self-righteous indignation; indeed, she is addicted to it. There is a hardness, a brittleness, a mercilessness about her, which gives no quarter to the one with whom she is angry; forgives no weakness; understands no toleration. It is only after you know her for a time that you realize she is in pain nearly as often as she gives pain. She is equally intolerant with herself and constantly under tension to demonstrate that she is not fallible and not to blame. If this description recalls the paranoid character, and some of those we otherwise think of as hysterics, the resemblance is intentional.

Gradually, in treating such a person, you become aware that she lives with an inner voice quite as nasty as the one she exposes to view. It is as if there were a small person in the back of her mind constantly *persecuting* her, in the same merciless way. The image is not conscious, at least at first. Is it the voice of a real person? There is certainly a real image which the patient carries around with her and which is *part of the patient*. The image is real, also, in that it has effects on the patient's feelings and how she acts toward others. But who is the source of this persecutory anxiety; whom does this internalized icon resemble? Who seems to be saying, "You are worthless; you always were a nothing; you never will be anyone?" Eventually it turns out that the bitter image is the patient's mother!

This seems odd, for often when the worker goes over his notes he finds that the patient either spoke of her mother only in adulatory terms, at first, or else did not mention her at all. It was her father at whom she was the more consciously enraged. But now it proves to be her mother who is so unyieldingly demanding.

When I first encountered this, I believed the patient's mother was in fact the virago finally described, but the patient had not dared say so out loud. From Klein and others, however, we learn the situation is more complicated. The patient walks around with two mother images. One, who is all-giving, all-wise, tender, and beyond criticism is the "good mother," and she is the one to whom we are typically first introduced. The other is evil, filled with malice, implacable; the "bad mother." Usually neither is the real mother, of course. If the patient had really been born to the bad mother she carries around in her mind, she would not have survived the first year of life. She has taken the real person who was her mother and *split* her into two walled-off, mutually exclusive images. We refer to this as the *good mother –bad mother split*.

A tendency to split the object may reveal itself in a variety of ways. One pervasive effect is to have the kind of personality that deals only in extremes—everything is either black or white, with few grays. The patient lacks "tolerance for ambiguity." Kernberg (1966) has pointed out that the tendency to split the world into walled-off categories represents a failure to develop the ability to synthesize, which we expect in more mature minds. Such childish people live in a world peopled by saints or devils.

Our patient, just described, has split her mother into two images, and then has done another typical thing. She *personified* each image by a single person. Thus her mother was all good; her father became all evil. Take these same dynamics and apply them to young men whose hatred of their fathers was formerly ascribed to the Oedipus complex. We now recognize that, quite as often, the threatening, hated father actually derives from one-half the ambivalence experienced toward the mother. Patients also do something very like this in more current relationships. While the individual therapist is a sweet, dear man, the ward administrator is an ugly, mean tyrant. We have to watch for the danger of such splits in marital counseling. The lady who comes to work out a better marriage may fall into the habit of regarding her caseworker as the good mother. Her husband, with whom she was to have repaired relations, is now dismissed as the bad. An understanding of the dynamics involved teaches us forcefully that there is no such thing as a consistently "positive transference" (cf. Garrett, 1958). There is only suppression or displacement of the negative elements of an essentially ambivalent relationship.

What is the source of these powerful, conflicting emotions? They derive from the ambivalence toward our mothers which all of us must experience. Because we are infants when we have these feelings, they are intense, raw, primitive, powerful. The reason we have mixed emotions toward our mother derives from the fact that we have love for her. The mother who cuddles, who warms, who feeds us and relieves our pain is the same woman who inevitably lets us down. She angers and frustrates us because she is, after all, human. She cannot always offer gratification and security immediately. There are delays—because she does not hear us immediately, because others also make demands on her, even because she is momentarily tired. The person who is so invested with love is necessarily exposed to becoming the object of rage. The infantile mind, like the *primary process* in the adult, knows no reality limitations. How common it is for childish patients to assume that if their parents do not give them what they need, it is because they do not *want* to! They accuse them of evil intent. There is no room in their schema for inability. They need their parents to be all-powerful so they can be all-giving, and they hate to be reminded, "You are sucking on a dry tit!"

The part of the maternal image against which the hate is directed, then, is split off in the infant's mind to form the bad-mother image. The attitudes of this bad-mother image are venomous, violent, mordant. Where did these feelings originate? They came, originally, from the patient. They are his own feelings of rage now associated with, or *projected,* if you will, into his mother. Let me say, once again, that the bad-mother image whispering scornfully in the back of the mind of our driven, overmeticulous and bitter lady is *part of the patient*. It is evident that the feelings involved are, in fact, the patient's own, from the time of earliest childhood. It is easy to understand why a person dominated by such an organization should have such a need to project the persecutory anxiety. How good it feels to be able to say, "I am not evil; you are."

What I have just presented is not, of course, pure Melanie Klein, but my integration of her concepts into other observations and other theories as I have learned from them. Still, it is evident that her ideas offer powerful leads to parsimonious and effective formulations about our cases. The relationship of her ideas to Fairbairn's is fairly clear. Both emphasize traumata potential in the infant's early relationship with his mother. Bowlby, in turn, is aware of Klein's conceptions and disagrees with some of them. Once again, we are left with a nugget of the theory of object relations not quite ready to be integrated with the remainder— or, at least, not until there has been further work on both theory and clinical observation.

As the student of personality theory might infer, these various ideas are evolving side by side because the time seems ripe for them (Winnicott, 1955). They are all representative of a particular *Zeitgeist* which, it seems to me, has come to fruition much more in England than in the United States. They have roots, by the way, in certain conceptions of ego psychology that were not so popular earlier in the Freudian movement, those of Horney (1937), Rank (1947), some in Adler (1917), to mention schismatics. Some of the ideas were developing among the Berlin group of psychoanalysts before Hitler. I shall later refer to the equally penetrating, if fragmentary, ideas of Hellmuth Kaiser (originally a member of the Berlin Institute) which were, to the best of my knowledge, evolved independently of the English school. Nevertheless, the reader will recognize in Kaiser's emphasis on the human's dread of loneliness, and his need to create a defensive *delusion of fusion,* assumptions about man that are quite compatible with the work of Bowlby and others.

References

Adler, Alfred. *A Study of Organ Inferiority and its Psychical Compensation.* New York: Nervous and Mental Disease Monograph Series, No. 24, 1917.

Bowlby, John. *Maternal Care and Mental Health.* Monograph Series No. 2. Geneva: World Health Organization, 1951.

Bowlby, John. "Separation Anxiety," *International Journal of Psycho-Analysis, 41,* 1960, 89–113.

Bowlby, John. "Separation Anxiety: A Critical Review of the Literature," *Journal of Child Psychology and Psychiatry, 1,* 1961, 251–269.

Erikson, Erik H. *Childhood and Society.* New York: W. W. Norton, 1950.

Fairbairn, W. Ronald D. *An Object Relations Theory of the Personality.* New York: Basic Books, 1952.

Garrett, Annette. "The Worker-Client Relationship," in H. J. Parad, ed., *Ego Psychology and Dynamic Casework.* New York: Family Service Association of America, 1958.

Guntrip, Harry. *Personality Structure and Human Interaction.* New York: International Universities Press, 1961.

Horney, Karen. *The Neurotic Personality of Our Time.* New York: W. W. Norton, 1937.

Kernberg, Otto. "Structural Derivatives of Object Relationship," *International Journal of Psycho-Analysis, 47,* 1966, 236–253.

Klein, Melanie, Phyllis Heimann, Susan Isaacs, and Joan Riviere. *Developments in Psychoanalysis.* London: Hogarth, 1952.

Likert, Rensis. "A Technique for the Measurement of Attitudes," *Archives of Psychology,* No. 140, 1932.

Mead, George Herbert. *Mind, Self and Society.* Chicago: University of Chicago Press, 1934.

Polansky, Norman A., Robert B. White, and Stuart C. Miller. "Determinants of the Role-Image of the Patient in a Psychiatric Hospital," in M. Greenblatt, D. Levinson, and R. Williams, eds., *The Patient and the Mental Hospital.* New York: The Free Press, 1957.

Rank, Otto. *Will Therapy and Truth and Reality.* New York: Alfred A. Knopf, 1947 (originally 1929, 1931).

Sullivan, Harry Stack. *Conceptions of Modern Psychiatry.* Washington, D.C.: The William Alanson White Psychiatric Foundation, 1947.

Thomas, Carolyn B. "The Resolution of Object Loss Following Foster Home Placement," *Smith College Studies in Social Work, 37,* 1967, 163–234.

Winnicott, Donald W. "The Depressive Position in Normal Emotional Development," *British Journal of Medical Psychology, 28,* 1955, 89–100.

Chapter 7

The Pursuit
and Dread
of Love

OURS IS THE GENERATION OF TOGETHERNESS. IN CONTRAST
with an earlier era in which social functions were generally
instigated for such respectable motives as excluding others,
sexual stimulation, and cheerful gluttony, we now make
elaborate plans to be with, share with, talk with others.
Privacy is a rare and expensive commodity in urban living.
Nevertheless, we seek each other out.

Such restless searching for human contact can only
reflect famine in the Promised Land. Never have so many
owed so little to so many. While constantly tossed together, people feel overwhelmingly alone. Much of our professional activity consists in providing prostheses against this
void. Group workers encourage group cohesiveness, caseworkers support, and "your analyst is the best friend money
can buy." What is missing in the relationships people have?
Why can these empty people not replenish each other?
What is most frequently missing is the ability to get close.

Dilemma for Our Time

Since before 1900, sociologists have written about the process of impersonalization as an accompaniment of industrialization and urbanization. Even popular magazines tell about "alienated" youth, using the jargon in about the same way as does the *American Sociological Review* (cf. Seeman, 1959). Philosophers and theologians have looked up from their self-preoccupations to notice the estrangements among men. New aspects of human inhumanity are under discussion by the humanists. In a warm, tedious dissertation, Martin Buber has discussed the "I-thou" relation (1958). Students sometimes call this to my attention as if Buber had made a unique discovery which, perhaps, he had. It is not necessary to innovate for the culture in order to invent for oneself, and each man's uncovering of the extent of his aloneness is, in fact, unique.

Of those who write about the problem of dehumanization in our time, most hold out hope of solving it *alloplastically*—that is, there is the wish that by changing his environment, a person will have somewhat resolved his difficulties. Certainly, it is each man's privilege to seek salvation in his own way. Who can say that a restructuring of one's external world will not make it easier when he confronts his inner wasteland? Psychoanalysis, however, emphasizes *autoplastic* change. This field has been sensitized to the same phenomena of modern society since at least the 1930s.

Masud Khan begins a most important paper, published in 1960, by referring to "a new type of patient that has come into prominence in the last two decades" (p. 430). And, paraphrasing Fairbairn, he remarks that "a fixation in the early oral phase . . . promotes *the schizoid tendency to treat other persons as less than persons* with an inherent value of their own." (*Ibid.* Italics mine.) In other words, the deindividuation and devaluation of men is attributed by some to the growth of totalitarianism, by others to sheer population pressure. Now we see that the same sort of phenomena are thought about in ego psychology as part of a constellation of "problems in the schizoid spectrum."

Guntrip, also much influenced by Fairbairn, has aptly sketched what he calls the *schizoid dilemma* (1962). This is a conflict that is heartrending and ludicrous at the same time. Should the patient begin to feel emotionally involved with another person, then powerful feelings are stirred in him which leave him terrified and ashamed. Should he seek to evade this anxiety by maintaining an aloof isolation, he is overcome by devastating loneliness. Torn between the two forces, our patient is truly a victim of the *pursuit and dread of love*. The best he can hope for is to strike a bargain between the two. Searching out his optimal distance between closeness and emotional starvation eventuates in what Guntrip has termed the *schizoid compromise*.

Although much of this thinking is peculiarly relevant to the *schizoid personality,* not everyone who has experienced the schizoid dilemma need be urgently in need of treatment. From our discussion it should be evident that these are likely to be rather ubiquitous human reactions. Therefore, a review of theorizing associated with the schizoid personality will serve more than one purpose. Beyond understanding that personality type, it should offer a set of insights applicable to all characters with *schizoid elements.*

Encounter

When I came out to get him, the young man was lolling in the waiting room, and holding a magazine. His response to my greeting was silence—not aggressive, not obviously frightened, just bland and noncommunicative silence. Of course, I already knew something about him. He had a severe upset in college and had to withdraw in his freshman year. Since then, he had been surviving a marginal sort of existence at home, and was neither productive nor happy with his idleness. Pressure from his parents had brought him to our hospital, and to me. About *me,* he knew practically nothing; it would be months before he would admit curiosity if, indeed, he had any.

As he preceded me to the office, I became aware of his gait. While neither deformed nor unsteady, he walked as if he were afraid of staggering, in a kind of mincing lurch. Gradually I became aware that he was unusually stiff from knee to navel. For a youngster from a well-to-do family, his clothing was also noteworthy. He wore faded blue jeans, a red flannel shirt, and a pair of expensive flight boots. His hair was long, but looked neglected rather than deliberately styled that way. His only concession to the raw weather was a nylon windbreaker.

In the office, he stood dumbly waiting to be asked to be seated, took the proffered chair, and finally yielded a passing smile. He began the interview by staring at a spot three feet, two and a third inches beyond my right metatarsal arch. Later, he shifted his gaze to a point four miles and seventy-six yards out the window. He evaded eye contact and, in fact, appeared never to look at me. Yet I soon discovered that he was preternaturally alert to my inflections, expression, general demeanor. Evidently, he was an acute observer of feelings, in his darting fashion.

I asked him why he had come to our hospital. He took me by surprise. From his pout, I had expected him to say he was here because his folks made him come. Instead, in a slightly shaky voice, he said, "I have problems." There seemed a desire to do something for himself, perhaps a good bit of surviving reasonableness, so I encouraged him, "Care to tell me a little?" He lapsed immediately into silence, and to contemplation of the Bigelow rug on the floor. Was he fearful of beginning? Did all beginnings make him anxious? As the silence lengthened, we were no further along, really, than if he had blamed his presence in the hospital on his parents.

He emitted signals that he was unhappy sitting with me. There were beads of perspiration on his forehead, and he looked glum (did he always?). Finally, however, it dawned that he was waiting to see whether I, in my turn, might not become uncomfortable with *him*. He seemed completely capable of letting our time pass without anything much having happened on any spoken level. I decided for the moment to overlook his *withdrawal* and *negativism* and try to get a line on another of his possible gambits.

I had no clear evidence as yet, but I knew from bitter experience that, with nearly all schizoid people, any new relationship presents a chief issue: *who will be on top?* As his "doctor," I present a problem. He takes it for granted that I will want to control the situation. After all, it is *my* office. He has to figure out how to let it appear that I do so, while guaranteeing that I do not, in any area he really cares about.

He can say the right words, but he has no conviction that two people can become involved in a cooperative venture as independent but still close and equal partners. He believes one must absorb the other, and one must dominate. He thinks he fears being absorbed, but his thoughts on this do not involve me. He really wishes to play the helpless infant and is afraid I will let him get away with it, at great cost to his dignity. How rigidly, out of how much desperation he plays this game, I still do not know. At the moment, anyhow, he probably is not even conscious of any need to control the situation, but only of a dogged determination that his outline of an identity, scratchy as it is, will not be erased. It is more than likely that what is on his conscious mind is a series of fantasies and experiments he has gotten into about sex. Even though he has the general impression that this is what therapy is all about, he does not see how he can bring himself to talk about these "problems" right off. But he feels he should. Because therapy, like everything else, is *all-or-none* for him. There are no halfway measures.

He does not know that I agree with him. I do not see how he can expose a lot of intimate details on first acquaintance, and I would find it ominous were he to begin that way. So I decide to offer him a way out. I remark that all we can hope to do today is get acquainted, and perhaps he can begin to fill me in on some basic information about himself. I have read his record, but I need to hear more from him. Where was he living before he came to the hospital?

Although this sounds matter of fact, I am really taking a chance. In truth, all I hope for is to get acquainted and to make some preliminary estimates of his condition. Regardless of how mundane or lurid the tale he unfolds, all it means at the moment is a way to assess the ego strength of the person sitting with me. This is the first order of business. But the patient may have his own preconceptions about therapy. He may decide that, in offering to ease his way, I have already surrendered to his tactic. He may become contemptuous. I watch his reactions for such signs, as it is a feeling he would not bother to conceal. I will then throw it right back at him. Meanwhile, I ask myself whether he will accept my way as sensible and realistic. If he can, it is a hopeful sign. I have no reason thus far to think him psychotic, although he was described as eccentric. How eccentric and suspicious I will soon know.

My patient accepts the question as reasonable and tells me he has been living at home, with his parents. I begin to ask about the conditions under which he was living, moving gradually toward inquiring about feelings and, before long, about possible symptoms he might have been experiencing. By now we are over our first hurdle, not because of my masterly interviewing skill, but because this fellow is not that odd in his response to a simple indication of interest on my part, and he knows I ought to have a straightforward approach to collecting information. Evidently, along with his peculiarities, he has wide islands of intactness in his personality.

Thus the first five minutes of getting to know each other have passed. The processes of forming a relationship and of diagnosis and evaluation have begun. Eventually I know him nearly as well as he does me, and we get along. I can virtually predict some of the steps in this sequence. For example, after about six sessions we go through a phase in which he obliquely questions my motives, and I remark that he does not seem to trust me. After some hesitation, he agrees. The hesitation is meant to convey polite concern for my feelings, but its true purpose is something else. Addicted to *indirection,* this young man simply hates to say anything directly. At this point, I tell him, again quite honestly, that I am pleased he does not trust me. If he did, on such short acquaintance, it might indicate that he is more childish and less realistic than I had hoped. He does not know quite what to make of my reaction. He would like me to try to prove to him I am trustworthy, as this is a gambit that has worked well in frustrating others in the past. But I decline the ploy in advance, commenting merely that trust is something you feel, or you don't feel, and it comes from experience with a person, not from his protestations. For instance, I don't trust him very much, either.

And with good reason. I once treated a man for nearly a year with similar problems. From time to time I expressed concern that he was using up his inherited capital on the long hospitalization and wondered if the benefit to him were worth it. Only after about ten months did he let slip the fact that, while still a youngster, he had invented an electronic device that had been adopted by a large corporation. His monthly royalties alone far exceeded his hospital expenses, leaving aside income from accumulated investments. What he feared we would do if we knew of his wealth, or what labyrinthine satisfaction he gained from letting me make a fool of myself in my overconcern, I never did find out. I can guess, but I lay fewer claims to infallibility after each such incident in treatment!

The Schizoid Personality

The most noteworthy affect of the schizoid personality has been described as a *feeling of futility,* to which we have already referred. The attitude is that nothing is worth while, no effort will do any good. It is typified in the remark

"Why eat supper? You'll just be hungry before breakfast, anyhow." Another patient, author of the classic comment, "Once a slob, always a slob," put it differently: "If at first you don't succeed, the hell with it." Whether the sense of futility be grasped with desperation, or waved about with bravado, the message is always the same: if the milk of life itself is poisoned, why bother?

The feeling of futility would seem to emerge from the defense of *detachment* in the three phases of an infant's handling separation (see discussion of Bowlby in Chapter 6). It is different from *depression,* with which it may be confused, clinically. The feeling of futility is a defense against depression, a refusing to care at all. Yet, as so often happens, the cure may be worse than the disease. With the detachment comes a kind of massive blocking of feelings which we have called *affect-inhibition.* The patient does his best literally to feel nothing. The price for succeeding may well be terror. For one way we know we are alive, exist, are persons, is that we are filled with feelings. Not to feel and not to care gives rise to enormous *emptiness* and a *numbness* with awesome *connotations of death.* It is a bleak and hopeless state of mind from which, fortunately, not even suicide promises much. The danger, on the other hand, is that it does not threaten much, either.

One would expect futility to be accompanied by a withdrawal from personal relations, and from the life about one, and indeed it typically is. Yet there are persons whose behavior reflects this affective syndrome, but we do not immediately make the association. Take the delinquent, for example. The stereotype of a delinquent youngster is of a young man, eyes flashing, face hardened, in motion and aggressively beating someone, or driving away recklessly from the scene of his latest escapade. These are rare occasions, even for the truly delinquent personality. More typically, we find him slouched against a wall, eyes half closed, cigarette dangling, flaccid, bored, and boring. His normal stance is an overt demonstration of indifference to the life about him. He has trouble getting pleasure from the milder forms of stimulation most of us enjoy. Among other things, professional criminals are said to be poor lovers, which is also a price paid for psychologically induced anesthesias.

Danger is usually involved in criminal acts, and a punk's face may light up as he tells you how much he enjoyed being chased by the police. Why the love of risks? I was once taught to think about danger as an urge toward self-destruction, but I no longer believe this the most parsimonious explanation. There is *indifference* to self-destruction, to be sure, founded on an illusory omnipotence. But the driving force is a *craving for excitement*. Only at moments of crisis, pain, intense pleasure does the delinquent feel fully alive.

The craving for excitement, with its ugly and frightening consequences, must be seen as itself a defense against massive affect-inhibition and its emptiness echoing of death. Were he able to enjoy smaller pleasures, the typical delinquent would not need such heroic forms of entertainment. Similar logic applies, of course, to the sexual sprints and gymnastics of such persons, *including hysterics with marked schizoid features.*

The schizoid youngster, like the detached infant, wards off feelings in order not to be overcome by his anger and despair. The cost of this defense, alas, is the desolation and emptiness which, in turn, demand another layering of defenses in order to overcome them. I have also alluded to the *stubbornness* and *negativism* so frequently prominent in this character. Stubbornness has many roots, but one of them may well be the sense of emptiness. The client feels that if he permits himself to be influenced, something will have been taken away from him, and he already has too little to work with in any case.

The *negativism* has a closely connected source. For a person who feels himself a vacuum, a nothing, to stand *against* something provides a sense of being. His firm grasp on *futility,* with its claim that no goal is worth the effort and no good can come of striving, affords him the luxury of avoiding failure and defeat. He can even surround the feeling with elaborations of superiority, telling himself that he is onto a secret other mortals have not penetrated. But, again, the feeling of futility cannot be so successfully maintained if the youngster admits something matters to him, and takes a positive stance. The only way he can integrate himself into a person is in negativism. Paraphrasing Descartes, he says, "I oppose, therefore I am."

Let us face it. Whatever his admirable qualities, the schizoid individual is typically an odd, gawky personality, rigid when yielding might be graceful, un-with-it. He knows this; he has known it since early childhood when he already had thoughts that he was not like other children. Indeed, he was not, for he already suffered from a childhood neurosis. Such self-recognition is of course frightening to a child. Many of these patients reacted in the only way that must have seemed possible to their young minds. They hoped that by *acting* like other people, they would *become* like them.

It is important to bear in mind that this struggle to break through his self-imposed barrier of detachment is no trivial matter in the life of such a child. Not to be like other people is to be less than human, an object in terror for his very existence because he is *unlovable*. No wonder, then, that the business of *appearing to be human* should be gone at with such dead seriousness, such solemn self-preoccupation and self-consciousness, such strained and rigid role-enactment. It is for this reason that the schizoid adult seems teetering and odd in his mannerisms when he tries to be warm and spontaneous.

Given any new role, each of us is likely to overplay it at first. This patient may well overplay being a person. Perhaps it is because of this I have so often found, in dealing with such a patient, that it may clear the air if both of us recognize sooner rather than later that much of how he acts with me is *phony*. It seems to help him to know that I know. And it helps me to like him in spite of his spuriousness—although he prefers to think he is engaged in an act he can turn off at will, I know better. I recall a patient who liked to think he was escaping unpleasantness at home by feigning being crazier than he was. In poignant truth, he was sicker than he pretended.

We can list a number of other characteristics of this fascinating syndrome. Without training or therapy, such a youngster often exhibits and articulates an unexpected *insight* into others' dynamics. Repressive mechanisms normally to be anticipated simply do not exist in him, and their absence contributes to an *excruciating sensitivity* in limited spheres. The same absence may make him the more masterful *manipulator,* and it is not uncommon to find that the patient has been tyrannizing his whole family despite his own difficulties. In fact, when in the first interview you find a patient with no previous treatment already explicating his own dynamics with reasonable accuracy, it is likely he is fairly far out on the schizoid spectrum. Often this represents an overvaluation, on his part, of the contents of his own thoughts as compared with remaining open to the world about him. Like the Jews confined to European ghettos, he knows much about motives and feelings because that is all he has had to preoccupy his mind. He is Proust sans pen.

All these features of the schizoid personality are a woefully incomplete description if we leave out his characteristic inability to form warm human relationships.

Distance Maneuvers

We have already described at length the early experiences leading to alienation among persons with markedly schizoid features. To help us understand the schizoid's *fear of closeness,* let us add a characteristic of mental functioning discussed earlier, *looseness of ego boundaries.* When he begins to form a tie to another person, the schizoid youngster tends to "go all the way." It is not enough to approach each other as two loving but independent beings. Out of greed founded in his deep sense of emptiness, and the indefiniteness of the outline of himself in his own mind, he has a tendency not so much to relate as to want to *absorb* the other person into himself, or to *lose himself* in the other.

For many such persons, talking is simply not enough; there must also be physical contact, cuddling, caressing, often sex relations. Because of such needs, the schizoid youngster may mistake his therapist's interest in him as a homosexual pass. Adding to the projection of his own desires into the relationship is his feeling of unworthiness: "What could possibly make me of interest to you unless it is my body?" Similar feelings exist in the pseudo-hysteric nymphets one encounters in high schools. One cannot help also but remark the emphasis in hippie cults on total fusion between two people—intellectually, but also preverbally, physically, and erotically regardless of the sex. In such a subculture, the desire to fuse physically with the other is permitted full expression. For most schizoid youngsters, however, the childlike needfulness and desire to be cuddled which they experience on coming close are embarrassing and disconcerting. They are also dimly aware of the ravenous orality that makes them wish to devour the people to whom they are attached. Hence, such a youngster signals, more in kindness than in anger, "Stay away, or I will hurt you." There follow from these dynamics a group of mechanisms calculated to keep other people at arm's length. We call these, graphically, *distance maneuvers.*

Distance maneuvers make up one of the most interesting collections of psychological operations identified and associated with ego psychology, and we have had frequent reference to them already throughout this book. Now we shall bring them together into a more compressed outline.

1. *Flight.* An obvious way to prevent others from coming too close is literally to flee them physically. There are various ways of doing this, some more obvious than others, and some offering evidence of severe disturbance. The boy who runs wildly into the woods and disappears out of fear of his growing dependence on his therapist. The chronic "loners," hermits of the lakes and seas, and forest cruisers.

The professors who are comfortable only in their studies; teachers who hate to teach. The youngsters who cross the street rather than greet a person. The girls who shrink from the touch. All are physical forms of withdrawal.

Psychological withdrawal is more subtle, of course, but it usually can be easily sensed. I have commented on the "schizophrenic handshake" in which the schizoid person goes through the motions of sociability while shuddering from relating. The most frequent withdrawal, however, is found in the person who, in the midst of his family or other company, simply is not there. He is said to be absent-minded, and there is no doubt he is absent, in thought and spirit.

2. *Fight.* Bion, who brought some of these formulations into the area of group therapy, described phases through which a group might pass as "fight, flight, and work" (1951). "Fight and flight" are highly visible in the schizoid pattern of operating; and the fighting serves some of the same purposes as fleeing. Not all aggression, of course, is in the service of running away: far from it! But squabbling and battling can facilitate taking distance.

I have seen a number of patients who, after involving themselves in a reciprocal love relation, nearly always provoke the person they love. The *usual* reason for this goes back to the basic ambivalence we often feel toward those on whom we are most dependent. We form a love-hate relationship, and as we love, we also begin to get somewhat hostile. This is but part of the explanation in cases where the pattern is fixed; to label it a *hostile-dependent relationship* may obscure its full meaning. There is the person who, having become attached, becomes frightened. If he is unable to leave the one he loves, either out of guilt or simply out of separation anxiety, he provokes the other to take the initiative in breaking off. "You will have to fire me, because I can't quit." The fight is a distance maneuver.

Others fight as their peculiar way of resolving the schizoid dilemma. They want to be in contact, but they cannot tolerate the open expression of affection and caring. So they camouflage their loving behind a good deal of bickering, thus keeping their feelings at just that state of ambivalence which makes affection possible for them. Nagging, querulousness, teasing, or even good-humored kidding suffice to dilute the degree of warmth they are feeling. Others require so strong a camouflage against open recognition of their tenderness that the resulting battles may become physically dangerous. Wilde said, "You always hurt the one you love." Yes, if you are Oscar Wilde.

3. *Emotional Coldness.* A socially acceptable form of withdrawal is contact without feeling. I have mentioned the intellectualized college professor; I also mentioned the doctor, or other professional, who can tolerate impinging on fellow humans so long as he is relating from within a professional role. Quite a few schizoid individuals, by the way, resolve the dilemma between the Scylla of being engulfed and the Charybdis of loneliness by finding positions in which they too can "meet the public" without getting too involved. This group includes waitresses, sales personnel, clergy, hospital attendants, secretaries. You do not have to have a doctorate to barricade yourself behind occupational status while maintaining fleeting and stereotyped contacts with your clientele. Who else but a doctor can absent himself from wife and family during all but minimal time for sleeping and eating, while seeing people and serving humanity at the same time?

In such desiccated relationships, money need not always change hands. The friendly, impersonal prostitute can use her occupation to earn an emotional living in the same way as does the reservations clerk. In my observation, many schizoid young men are needlessly concerned about whether they will be sexually capable. Often, so long as the relationship is primarily erotic, sex without affection, they are quite adequate to achieve satisfaction.

It is much easier for the schizoid adolescent to rail against his parent than to confess the rest, which is that he loves him very much. Once, for instance, we needed to measure openness of communication of children in an institution for the treatment of the emotionally disturbed. Ratings of the children's *hostility* proved relatively meaningless. Angry expressions toward adults in the institution were common and even more or less encouraged by the therapeutic atmosphere. Hence, the readiness to express hostility did not discriminate among our subjects. A measurement based on willingness to verbalize liking or affection, on the other hand, proved much more valid as an index of *verbal accessibility* (see below), since it came harder and reflected individual differences. The open expression of *tenderness* is most devastating; such admission may be accompanied by tears and genuine sadness.

4. *Noncommitment*. The schizoid individual finds it very hard to become *committed* to another person. When the tie becomes closer than he can bear, he finds ways of breaking loose, for example, by precipitating a fight and being ejected. As he feels himself being committed, his discomfort increases. It is her schizoid element which ofttimes leads the thirty-year-old mother of two, so apparently hysterical in other ways, to come for marital counseling with the announcement, "I am trapped." There are other variations on this theme. One of the more interesting, and amusing, is the *verbal denial of commitment*. At the same time as the patient is arriving early for his appointment, and otherwise showing his attachment to you, he will have to take time out to let you know that all this means very little in his life and he has been thinking about quitting treatment. He needs words discrepant from his actions. These are the same sort of men who must soon announce to their girl friends, "I am not ready to get involved, so I hope you will not take all this seriously." Such a young man may be terribly chagrined should the girl take him at his word and begin to date others.

The fear of commitment afflicts men who in other respects seem rather intact personalities. Many stories are told about reluctant swains. One is of the maid, Mathilda, who had been dating Jasper for fifteen years. Finally, one night she said, "Jasper, don't you think it's about time you and me was marrying up." Jasper reflected for five or ten minutes before replying, "Tillie, I believe you're right. But at our age, who'd have us?"

Commitment to another person is dangerous because it makes the schizoid patient aware of his extreme vulnerability. *Who loves has given hostages to fate.* The schizoid person, therefore, feels lonesome at times, but he also has a smug feeling that he will keep secret even in therapy. Making a virtue of necessity, he believes, "Nothing ventured, nothing lost." While the young caseworker tires himself encouraging him to find outside interest and companions, he barely conceals his conviction that he is much smarter, he knows a better way.

Because of their fear of closeness which, in turn, involves tremendous infantile separation anxiety, schizoid persons, as we have reiterated, keep their distance. For persons with schizoid elements in otherwise intact personalities, we see a related mechanism. To play it safe, and avoid becoming vulnerable, they must remain in control of the relationship. To love and feel love is to risk becoming unloved, because of something over which you may have no control. This they cannot stand. Consequently they are preoccupied, at the beginning of a relationship, about the circumstances of its termination. Just as it is easier to take leave on the train than stand on the platform and wave good-bye, so they much prefer any rupture to occur at *their* initiative. Therefore they repeatedly play out the scene, "You can't fire *me;* I quit!"

By controlling the timing of the ending, the schizoid feels at least somewhat more the master of his fate. By meeting the rupture actively, the weakened ego is somewhat better able to tolerate the anxiety. All this has a logic and a purposiveness. What is not purposeful, unfortunately, is the tendency repeatedly to break off ties at the least threat. In this way friendships are broken needlessly by a person who yearns for friends. The same mechanism, of course, can easily invade the treatment, spoiling the patient's chance of getting help because of just the thing for which the help is needed! And I have alluded to the jockeying for position from the beginning of therapy.

The difficulty of commitment is most visible in relation to personal objects, but it typically pervades the personality. There may be a fear of becoming tied to a place or to a job; hence, a drifting existence. During World War II, I worked in an Army Disciplinary Barracks. We saw many soldiers charged with AWOL or desertion. A fair proportion of them had no civilian record. They were now in legal difficulties because, for the first time in their adult lives, they were required to remain in one place, among one group of people, and this they found intolerable. When we received our first shipment of General Prisoners at the disciplinary barracks, we were still (unknown to them) desperately closing gaps in its barbed-wire wall, on a distant side of the compound. While we sweated in the midday sun, we heard our blithe, former comrades caroling, "Don't Fence Me In" as armed GI's herded them into our care.

There is usually an associated noncommitment in attitudes and beliefs, with the exception of a few that are rigidly held for defensive purposes. The schizoid man or woman professes no opinion on many, many aspects of living. This includes religion, which otherwise might have been a considerable solace against self-imposed isolation. Naturally, one will find many evidences of what Erikson (1959) has so marvelously described as *identity diffusion.* Along with her other problems, the schizoid young woman may have avoided deciding which sex she really wants to claim as her own. Homosexuality and bisexuality often occur. Even more frequent, however, is the sexual neuter, the person permanently poised in pre-adolescence—the man who feels he somehow is not yet mature enough to take command among other men, or the lady golfing champion.

5. *Selfishness.* Alienation, isolation, detachment, preoccupation are some of the words we have used to describe this syndrome. To these I must add another: A striking feature of the constellation is *selfishness,* in just about the meaning we attach to it in everyday speech. The ability to

love others has been shunted backward: the love is turned toward the self in a combination of *primary* and *secondary narcissism*. Primary narcissism refers to the infant who is not even aware there is anyone worth attending to but himself; secondary, to the infant who has started to be attached to his mother but who, out of disappointment, has made the defensive switch, "If no one else loves me, then I will."

The selfishness became markedly visible to me in hospital work. Whatever the parents' defects, and they were manifold, they had tried to provide their daughter with treatment and to help with the treatment as they could. The patient, on the other hand, patently could not care less about the expense, or their feelings, or their fate. Indeed, it is a mark of success in treatment when one notices a letup in selfishness and a developing considerateness for others. Some withdrawal, for instance, is within the patient's control; that is, he can make an effort to pay attention to his wife and children, if he will bother, rather than be so obsessed with "work," whose main aim is to increase his status in his own eyes. Even though he may need to withdraw, he can fight against it rather than yield to the symptom without a struggle. His wife's complaint, that he simply does not care, may have more justification than she dares to know.

It is similar if you are the caseworker or therapist for such a person. You may be concerned for him, even go out of your way to see him. Do not be surprised if he repays you, for a very long time, by scarcely noticing your existence beyond the times he needs you. He is truly incurious about your life except as it impinges on his life. He can transfer from one therapist to another with equanimity. Whereas an adult depressive whom you saw briefly and helped with little effort will write you at Christmas time for years afterward, the schizoid adolescent whom you labored and fought for two years to drag back from the brink of psychosis often sends no word until there is something he wants. In seducing the schizoid personality into treatment, the path to follow is the same as for any other extremely narcissistic person. There is no point in appealing to his love for his family or his duty to some higher ethic. His interest in change derives from the questions: "What's there in it for me? Now?"

Should the schizoid personality succeed completely with his distance maneuvers, he will have failed. For the price of freedom from the threat of separation and from the more current anxieties of intimacy is utter loneliness. Thinking to play it safe, he wants to "quit before I'm fired." By seeking to gain absolute security through refusing to take a chance on losing, he only guarantees his loss. After all, the person who has never loved, nor ever dared to seek to be loved, is as much alone as if he had been loved and then abandoned. Indeed, most of us would think him worse off. His life, too, passes just as inexorably as if he had lived it with pleasure.

Many comments scattered throughout this book are based on the ideas of Hellmuth Kaiser. Although his theorizing was intended to deal with problems in treatment broader than the schizoid personality, his formulations seem to be related mainly to this particular character type. Therefore, we shall end the chapter with a summary of Kaiser's fusion-fantasy theory.

The Delusion of Fusion

I have described the looseness of ego boundaries that so often accompanies the schizoid personality. Partly because of his empty greediness, and partly because of this vagueness in self-definition, the schizoid personality may try, symbolically or even physically, to become absorbed into the person to whom he is attached. Yet, such statements as "being absorbed," "devouring" and the like are only similes, of course. Despite our colorful speech, as therapists, there are physical impossibilities of which the schizoid person is fully aware. A major contribution of Hellmuth Kaiser has been to put these impulses, certainly very real, into a logical perspective that goes beyond figures of speech.

Kaiser began as an orthodox Freudian analyst (Fierman, 1965). After some time in practice, he began to question the efficacy of the method of treatment he had been trained to use. The classical technique did not help a large proportion of his patients, and there was the unsettling knowledge that even when results achieved were successful, they could not have been predicted precisely. Trained originally in mathematics, Kaiser was also sophisticated regarding the desirable characteristics of any science. It was evident to him that the technique employed in analytic work was not strictly derived from any rational base. "Insight," for instance, so often regarded as a proximate goal in treatment, is scientifically of indeterminate status. Does having an insight "cause" one to get better? Or, as seems more likely, is it that when the patient has already improved for other reasons he can then afford to let something previously repressed come to consciousness?

Seeking to answer the classical question of what, after all, is *the* specific in treatment, Kaiser eventually arrived at a formulation of extraordinary parsimony. He expressed his final thoughts in three related conceptions: the *universal conflict,* the *universal symptom,* and the *universal therapy.*

The *universal conflict* derives from the tremendous dread of loneliness and the consequent need to cling which is observable in all men from infancy onwards. Each of us is alone; this is the ultimate existential anxiety. But this truth is extremely hard to live with. To avoid awareness-of-separation anxiety, men erect a fantasy by which to live. This is the *delusion of fusion* in which boundaries between self and some other are weakened—in one's mind. To maintain this fantasy, or this delusion, we engage in a variety of maneuvers, each of which is dedicated to supporting the defense. In this way, if our need for the delusion of fusion is great, we may take great comfort from being part of a tradition; we may gain security from close-order drill, rowing in a crew, playing in a quartet. Another expression is to be found in the *avoidance of decision,* for decision is experienced as an open declaration of individual responsibility, hence, of one's aloneness. Thus, the *desire to feel forced* by circumstances, rather than exercising choice, may be in the service of the fusion-fantasy defense.

The fusion-fantasy is, of course, not a final solution. The loneliness feared can be combatted more realistically by communication with other men, through direct and honest talk. But for one to be so direct requires that he recognize his separateness from the person to whom he is speaking; the effort to communicate fully, in short, concedes the separateness of the participants. And this threatens the delusion of fusion. Therefore, the *universal conflict* is between the desire to achieve real contact and the fixation on a delusion which prevents it. This is reminiscent of Guntrip's *schizoid dilemma.*

Kaiser went on to theorize that most persons who become neurotic have had little reason to hope for comfort from communication in their lives. Therefore, they betray a *universal symptom* in their speech, which tends to be indirect and marked by what he termed *duplicity.* Putting it strongly, he found one and only one characteristic common to all neurotics: they are unable, or unwilling to "stand behind their words." From this it follows, said Kaiser, that the *universal therapy* should be an experience of a direct, open, and spontaneous relationship, and it is the responsibility of the therapist to make this possible. If one asks what the criterion is for deciding whether a given tactic will be therapeutic, the answer is (deceptively) simple: whatever will help the patient to "stand behind his words."

Kaiser's theory has adumbrations to other psychoanalytic writers, from Rank and Fromm to Fairbairn and Bowlby. We share his misfortune that the Germans gutted the middle of his scientific life, so that he never had the leisure to place his ideas in context. But, he was unique in moving from a completely psychological theory of neurosis to a testable hypothesis applicable to talking-treatment, with neither metaphysical nor metaphorical presumptions. While it is difficult to take seriously his hope of finding "universals" and "the specific" in treatment, a search more reminiscent of nineteenth-century philosophy than our own, there is no doubt his theory is of great elegance and potential power. On the one hand, it casts new light on the *predilection to indirection* which we have identified as a schizoid element; on the other, it has far-reaching implications for social psychology and group theory.

Although he writes, somewhat loosely, about "the neurotic," it seems to me Kaiser's theory has its greatest applicability in respect to the treatment of problems in the schizoid spectrum. I have used techniques based on Kaiser's theory with very satisfying results. Although to "help the patient stand behind his words" is not nearly so simple a matter as it may appear to the unperplexed, being roughly equivalent to removal of all distortions and pathological defense, it is a remarkably efficient focus for treatment effort. My interest in *verbal accessibility* was stimulated largely by Kaiser through processes conscious and—I must assume—also unconscious as well. After all, had I achieved true verbal accessibility in my own analysis, would I have had to study it for the next decade as a scientist? The laws of the mind that fit our patients also apply to us.

In the next chapters, which deal with work on *verbal accessibility,* I shall share with the reader what seem to be the objective fruits of my continuing process of *working through* and, quite probably, resistance as well!

References

Bion, Winfred R. "Experiences in Groups: VII," *Human Relations, 4,* 1951, 221–227.

Buber, Martin. *I and Thou.* 2d Edition. New York: Charles Scribner's Sons, 1958.

Erikson, Erik H. "The Problem of Ego Identity," in *Identity and the Life Cycle.* Monograph 1, *Psychological Issues.* New York: International Universities Press, 1959.

Fierman, Louis B., ed. *Effective Psychotherapy: The Contribution of Hellmuth Kaiser.* New York: The Free Press, 1965.

Guntrip, Harry. "The Schizoid Compromise and Psychotherapeutic Stalemate," *British Journal of Medical Psychology, 35,* 1962, 273–287.

Khan, M. Masud. "Clinical Aspects of the Schizoid Personality: Affects and Technique," *International Journal of Psycho-Analysis, 41,* 1960, 430–437.

Seeman, Melvin. "On the Meaning of Alienation," *American Sociological Review, 24,* 1959, 783–791.

Chapter 8

Verbal Accessibility

"ONE MAN'S MEDE IS ANOTHER MAN'S PERSIAN," IS A PUN
attributed to the late Charles MacArthur, husband of Helen
Hayes. As we shift from our explication of ego psychology
to its applications to related sciences and problems, a similar thought comes to mind. *One field's gossip is another
field's datum.* Seldom is this better illustrated than in the
cross-disciplinary study of communication.

We have just come from a discussion of Kaiser. He has
emphasized, perhaps more strongly than any other theore-
tician, the nature of the ultimate existential anxiety: that
each man is, in fact, biologically alone, afloat in a potentially meaningless universe. Kaiser refers to the delusion
of fusion as a neurotic effort to escape this anxiety. There
are in fact more realistic and satisfying ways by which we
can try to get close. It is perhaps uniquely human that one is
able to do this best through the spoken word; it is even more
human that this same power of speech is vulnerable to distortion and abuse so that, instead of combating loneliness,

it contributes further to alienation and despair. Out of my concern with why people cannot reach each other, and why we therapists and caseworkers often have trouble reaching our clients, I became fascinated with a concept I now call *verbal accessibility—the readiness of the client to communicate in speech, and to permit others to communicate with him, about his most important attitudes.*

Although this definition seems simple and straightforward, I came to it after a rather long process. Note that I do not take sheer volume of speech as indicative of accessibility; indeed, as we shall see, verbosity is often used to evade the expression of feelings. By now, there has been a considerable body of work on verbal accessibility, as well as a substantial literature reporting work on closely related conceptions.

In this chapter, I am going to try to synthesize the theory surrounding the phenomenon labeled verbal accessibility (VA). I regard this formulation as a contribution to the general theory of communication processes, of course. In the psychoanalytic tradition, it may be regarded as within the realm of ego psychology. The same may be said, by the way, for a number of constructs I shall introduce from the system of psychology devised by Kurt Lewin and his followers. Practically all of Lewin's Field Theory deals with varied aspects of what in analytic circles is called ego psychology (Lewin, 1951). In describing processes of the ego functioning as a whole, or as a *gestalt,* Lewin had a better developed conceptualization than did the Freudians, and so I prefer to use his terminology when I think it the more helpful. Neither theory has been sufficiently advanced, in my lifetime, to support the ideological battle adherents of each might wish to wage against each other, and I have never experienced qualms in integrating the two.

In presenting my formulations, I shall proceed in terms of their evolution. It simply is not true that research designs or theoretical constructions spring full-blown out of the heads of their progenitors. I think it might be instructive, therefore, if other potential researchers were to have a look at the way in which separable themes can be gradually differentiated within this research area through sustained concentration. While there are no guaranteed roads to discovery, something surely must be said for sheer persistence—or is it obsessiveness?

Accessibility to Treatment

The concern that originally occasioned this research over a decade ago was an applied not a theoretical problem. Studies of family service agencies showed that a rather appalling proportion of cases were being seen for one in-person interview only (Blenkner, 1954; Kogan, 1957). Even after corrections were made for the fact that in some cases service was completed in one interview, and in others the original referral had been inappropriate, a substantial number of persons were still in need of treatment. Although they had come far enough along to present themselves for treatment, they were not being held. One could, of course, make an analysis of clients' limitations and lack of motivation (Ripple, 1957), but regardless, an insufficiency on the part of the social workers involved was still implied. After all, if the client has the strength to ready himself completely for treatment, he might well be able to go all the way and heal himself too. The personality tends to do this with all wounds, more or less well-advisedly. It was our hope, therefore, that a program of research might reveal principles that would serve to guide workers and improve their rate of success in establishing *helping relationships.*

Studies were conducted, in collaboration with Jacob Kounin and some of our students. In scouting the problem area for promising leads to what is more significant in relationship-formation with *professionally helpful people,* we reviewed characteristics of workers who were known to have noteworthy success in holding clients. A trait repeatedly ascribed to such practitioners was *warmth.* Warmth is hardly a refined term around which to hinge a program of research. Asch (1946), for example, has shown the centrality of the "warm-cold variable" in a well-known study of interpersonal perception, and Kelley has followed him in a subsequent study (1950). However, both Asch and Kelley were interested in perceived warmth only in relation to other preoccupations; neither investigated the phenomenon itself in any depth. I have found repeatedly that it is worthwhile to attend to such terms in clinical usage. With all their imprecisions, they often point to phenomena of key importance.

From interviews with clients who had recently had first contacts with potentially helpful persons, we tried to extract what they found most important (Polansky and Kounin, 1956). We concluded, as have others, that a trait in another person derives its significance to the perceiver because of what there is in it for him (this truism is nowadays couched more pseudo-mathematically in social science). The significant thing about warmth lay in the promise it held for the client: it implied high motivation to help or *benevolence of intent*. As anticipated, however, clients were too canny to base their anticipations solely on motivation. As with perceived motivation, relationship-formation in the helping situation also requires perceived *power to help*. We had expected the client to be carried along by a halo-effect from warmth; instead, we found the two judgments were made quite differentially, a finding confirmed also in experimental studies (Kounin *et al.*, 1956).

Both findings were eminently reasonable. The only advantage of our tedious empirical work over *a priori* analysis lay in the demonstration that many clients are also reasonable creatures. But, they are more, and we had other results that cautioned us against overrationalistic theorizing about the "instrumental value" of the interview. First, the average client consciously intended the interview to be merely a means to a more distant end, but it did not remain so. The initial interview has potentials for satisfaction as well. A variety of "relationship needs" are uncovered. Much of the significance attached to the interviewer's warmth lies in the fact that many needs receive immediate satisfaction during the interview. A client who is consciously aware that he is going to the family agency because he wants them to value him as a person, and reports this, would be ominously odd; one who does not experience such needs once contact is under way may be equally so.

The other finding was to me quite unexpected. From his talks with clients, Kounin, in particular, was impressed by the number who commented on the *communication* sector of the interview. It was at his urging, therefore—and against my reluctance to clutter our research—that we included a number of measures having to do with feelings about communication. Because of this skepticism, I was the more impressed at results of a cluster analysis done on a series of structured *postinterviews* with over a hundred clients. There was only one index (group of rated statements) which correlated significantly with all the other dimensions of interview-satisfaction, and it was *not* benevolence of intent. Rather, it was the set of statements we had rationally grouped into a measure we called *Experienced Freedom to Communicate Feelings.*

Why this should be such a pivotal dimension became more visible in the experimental work. For the client to feel uninhibited in this crucial way reflects skill and integrity on the part of the interviewer; also, certain clients who appear more secure and related also expect to be more open. Hence, it was soon evident that the *freedom in communication experienced by the client is a product of both his readiness and the skill with which he is met,* and this is probably why it constitutes so sensitive an index of the net success of the encounter.

A number of attempts were made to specify the skills (interview acts) necessary to the communication of "warmth." These studies included one on the expected behavior of potentially helpful persons (Thomas *et al.,* 1955), later extended to an American adolescent population by Worby (1955), and replicated in Holland by Kadushin and Wieringa (1960). There was support for the notion that everyman is his own psychologist: that subjects had rather consistent ways of drawing inferences from interviewers' behaviors to assessment of their motives. Moreover, where there was perceived benevolence of intent, greater freedom to communicate was also anticipated.

Concern with the unreachable client continued, and two years later the locale of the research was Bellefaire, an institution for emotionally disturbed children in Cleveland, Ohio. By now the problem was being stated as one of *accessibility to treatment.* A major reason for residential treatment of many youngsters has been their lack of response as outpatients. However, in many instances the question of whether the child could be successfully treated had never arisen. One had not been able to bring him far enough along to *involve* him in treatment. The residential center, therefore, must be peculiarly geared to help the inaccessible child open up. Our goal was to discover principles to guide the rational design of the treatment milieu so that it would offer maximal support for this critical process. Specifically, we hoped to find how to facilitate movement of the child toward accessibility in interview treatment through action of social pressures in the living situation. At this point, the intent was a study of the social psychology in the institution, with emphasis on the social. The hope was that individual differences, while present, could be ignored.

Because the *target dependent variable* was accessibility to individual treatment, we devoted energy to specifying this concept. The question was: After a child had been seeing a caseworker for some time, how would we decide how accessible he was showing himself? Or to what extent was he involved in treatment? With help from some of the Bellefaire staff, and stimulating consultation with Selma Fraiberg, the following were listed as elements of the concept:

1. Valence of the caseworker—or attraction to the caseworker
2. Capacity for self-observation
3. Motivation for change

4. A global measure of "trust and investment" in the relationship
5. Freedom to communicate feelings verbally in interviews.

In subsequent studies, the children were rated on each of these dimensions. From these ratings, which were of course reflections in part of how things go together for the caseworkers, we found all the elements significantly intercorrelated, save one. The exception was the Valence of the Caseworker, which appears to fluctuate much more than do the other aspects of interview behavior, as the transference shifts from positive to negative. There was additional support for the idea that Freedom to Communicate Feelings was highly relevant to the process of treatment and to accessibility.

At this point, we began to refer to the dimension of *verbal accessibility* and to regard it as the key variable. The need to clarify the notion conceptually also became more urgent.

Conceptual Definition

Verbal accessibility may be defined as the degree of readiness of the client (or patient) to communicate in speech, and to participate in talking about, his determinant attitudes. A few terms in this definition warrant explication.

Early in our work, we began to think of this dimension not so much as a variable, in the usual sense, as an example of a *quasi-stationary equilibrium*. The model of the quasi-stationary equilibrium was given first by Lewin (1947); it has been later applied with rewarding effect by Coch and French in studying influences on production rates in a factory (1948). Essentially, our notion was that verbal accessibility is relative between persons and within a given person. Hence, it can be seen as responsive to the field of forces at the present moment in time—one set pushing for greater VA, the other inhibiting it. This model is intrinsic to our conceptualization, but it is a graphic paradigm, of course, rather than a formulation from which hypotheses can be strictly derived. Nevertheless, it has proven helpful in ordering the forces involved in so complex a situation. "Readiness," then, is understood to refer to the resultant of the force-field on the dimension of interest.

Our next question: What is the meaningful unit of communication? In interviewing, it is obvious that we are never simply concerned either with "facts" or with "feelings" divorced from images. Every unit of speech, like all human action, has its conative, affective, and cognitive aspects. One can abstract among these to concentrate on the cognitive aspect, but only at risk. There are no facts in the patient's history, as he gives it. Every description is both true and untrue: it is as he wishes to recount it, as he believes he recalls it, as he hopes it happened. Hence, we never really listen for "history," but for a sense of the patient. We attend to a set of attitudes that characterizes him.

By *attitude* I refer to a drive or drive-derivative with an object and with an associated affect (in short, an internalized object). Although the term attitude is used in social *and* clinical psychology, it is really the same in both. There is no gain, therefore, in inventing a new term, or taking refuge in militarisms like "bit" to unitize speech. As used here, attitudes are affected by one's social situation, but they also serve internal purposes—including the maintenance of defense. The aim of all therapies, in my opinion, is the production of change in attitudes, regardless of the ideology within which the therapist thinks he is working.

Measuring VA requires that the attitudes being verbalized be assigned weights. Surely it makes a difference which attitudes the patient is willing to discuss. An idea that came to mind was that VA be coordinated to the *depth* of communication. But what is meant by depth? It is instructive to examine the meanings invested in this term by other investigators of the interview process.

Bordin offers this definition of depth of interpretation:

Any behavior on the part of the therapist that is an expression of his view of the patient's emotions and motivations—either wholly or in part—is considered an interpretation. A patient has varying degrees of awareness of his motivations and emotions. Depth of interpretation is a description of the relationship between the view expressed by the therapist and the patient's awareness. The *greater the disparity* between the view expressed by the therapist and the patient's own awareness of these emotions and motivations, the *deeper the interpretation* (1959, p. 238; italics added).

One supposes the issue is whether or not unconscious material is brought suddenly into consciousness for the patient, but the definition does not state this explicitly. Neither do Bordin and his associates discriminate, apparently, between *clarification* (at the conscious and preconscious level) and true interpretation (at the unconscious level). Following their definition, a great disparity between the therapist's interpretation and the patient's awareness can exist because the therapist is dead wrong. At least, this has happened at times to me, and when it does, I am likely to get the kind of jamming of communication reported by Speisman (1959) in an oft-cited study. On the other hand, where the interpretation is correct, it may lead to some momentary rumination on the part of the patient, but it has seldom resulted in strong reduction of communication. Bordin's analysis of depth is not deep enough to be of much help.

Truax (1963) has reported a Depth of Intra-Personal Exploration Scale (DX) which was "developed to quantify the degree and depth of client self-disclosure, self-exploration or transparency occurring in the psychotherapeutic encounter." This scale appears to encompass in one rating elements we had described separately as VA and Capacity for Self-observation, along with some nuances of trust and investment in the therapeutic relationship. It raises the question whether a client or patient who is not very complex, and who operates on a preverbal level, is or is not transparent if he fails to show ability to make sense of his own behavior, no matter how frankly he states his feelings. The scale seems best suited to the slightly obsessive-compulsive student counselees from good family for whom the Rogerian method is at its most effective.

It is difficult to pin down what "depth" really signifies. There is a strong implication that the deep attitudes are unconscious, but we also know that myriads of trivia are dragged under into repression by association with critical experiences, and we do not mean these. Similarly, we expect "depth" to refer to intense affect, but an affect may be used as a screen against quite another emotion, as in the histrionics of the hysterical adolescent. Some insight seems upon us when we contemplate differences among people, with respect to their apparent depth. "Depth" is somehow associated with the notion of having had self-doubts and conflicts that others may not have felt—until we read Kafka and recognize that a real obsessive is often visibly scarred from the wounds of old moral battle, all of which were skin-deep. Let us now leave this issue, therefore, with recognition that, since each of these ideas has a germ of truth, depth must be a complex subject.

Kurt Lewin had to face the same problem in his famous paper on differences between American and German character (1935). He described the American as surprisingly open on short acquaintance, but with a secret reserve, while the German is reserved on acquaintance, but very open once friendship is established. In searching for concepts to express what he observed, he identified accessibility with peripherality. Thus, "One will have to ascribe to the more peripheral regions the field of open, common, 'public' life of the individual, to the more central regions the field of private life of the individual." Rickers-Ovsiankina, who has made important contributions to the study of what she terms *social* accessibility, employed the same conception in one of her early papers (1956). Unfortunately, the definition is simply circular labeling, rendering it impossible to test whether the relationships stated really exist in nature.

While such phrases come naturally to students of Lewin, they are misleading. Lewin's article was written prior to some work in which he specified relationships among chains of regions and, of course, before Bavelas (1948) and others had introduced gleanings from the newer geometries and algebras. The dimension "inner-outer" is not the same as "central-peripheral" in topology. Moreover, in my attempts to make derivations from these conceptions I discovered, again, that one gets nothing from purely positional constructs without additional postulates. In a recent study that puts Lewin's description of the difference between German and American character types to empirical test, Plog (1963) refers to Lewin's concentric circles as a "schematic representation," which is how they may best be viewed.

In considering differences among attitudes, it finally became clear that a way of expressing asymmetrical interdependence was needed. That is to say, a small change in attitude A leads to a large change in attitude B, but it takes a large change in B to cause a small change in A. This is exactly the experience one has in psychotherapy. It is not that talking about current, ephemeral realities has no effect on underlying problems, but merely that it is often less efficient than getting down to where things originally went wrong. I found that the relationship I wanted to express had been dealt with by Zajonc (1954) in a study of certain problems in perceptual organization. The weightier side of the interdependence he called *determinant;* the other, *dependent.* Hence, *determinant attitudes* are those whose change seems most likely to bring about strong changes in other related attitudes. Clinically, we would say they result in far-reaching alterations of personality structure.

With these formulations we arrive temporarily at a satisfactory conceptual definition of VA but we are left with severe puzzles about operational definition. It is of passing interest, therefore, that the most prolific investigators in this burgeoning field have not been slowed by scruples of theory. Kanfer (1961) has concentrated purely on the volume of verbal flow in an interview. Even Jourard, who has done major work in his concept of *self-revelation*, relies on an operational definition in which his concept is coordinated to the sheer number of areas which the subject reports himself willing to discuss with X number of potential communicatees (1963).

It appears by simple chance that the more a subject is willing to discuss, the more likely he is to expose determinant attitudes; therefore, I have borrowed the technique of Jourard and Rickers-Ovsiankina for some of our studies of VA. A drawback of their technique is the reliance on self-reports by subjects. While we have obtained encouraging evidence regarding the validity of such data (Blum and Polansky, 1961; Appelberg, 1964), they contain a variety of distortions which must lower their precision.

The Clinical Significance of Verbal Accessibility

Theories of psychotherapy are famous for the ease with which they incorporate what is known, once it is, and the difficulty they have in predicting the unknown. With this in mind, it is fun to review the misgivings with which we were faced prior to the actual collection of data on VA. One set was much in line with the typical dubious reaction of clinicians to detailed research on the processes of treatment. I was told a concept like VA was far too elusive for measurement.

A more telling question was: Even if one could successfully measure VA, what would it *mean?* It was pointed out that youngsters can emote endlessly, and this does not lead to progress in their treatment. Neither did we have any reason to suppose that a child's VA promised anything about his "treatability." Although I, at least, believed that capacity for verbalization was almost a prerequisite for insight therapy, I found I was unable to prove it by appeal to either established theoretical principles or empirical work. We were reminded repeatedly that *nonverbal* communication is not to be underrated, that many children receive their prime help in residential treatment by primary mothering, habit-training, and the like, even without open discussion of what is going on. Under the impact of all this, I find myself asserting plaintively in a paper written about that time, "When *diagnosis* is uppermost in one's mind, the ability of the client to present his attitudes openly is, if nothing else, a considerable convenience . . ."! (Polansky, Weiss, and Blum, 1961, p. 155.)

There were arguments on the other side as well. There is general agreement that in the treatment of aggressive children the switch of drive discharge from purely action to verbal channels is to be desired. It is also used as a sign that impulse-mastery, trust and growth are starting to take place. Thus, Redl and Wineman list "Increased ability to use verbal modes of communication . . ." high in priority among the therapeutic gains of their boys in Pioneer House (1952). Hellmuth Kaiser indicated that, as far as he could see, the chief criterion of a correct maneuver in psychotherapy was whatever would facilitate directness of expression of determinant attitudes (Enelow, 1960; p. 158, n. 6). In one of his few published papers in this country, Kaiser noted that it is characteristic of a large proportion of neurotics of all types to be unable "to stand behind one's words" (1955). But his was an extreme position.

A review of psychoanalytic writings yielded a mixed impression. Despite the overwhelmingly verbal nature of the technique of free association, there is ambivalence about being so dependent on the spoken word. Some therapists are evidently embarrassed to find themselves involved with a method of helping that has proven patently inappropriate to clientele in poorer neighborhoods. One can find references glamorizing *non*verbal communication. It is as if gestures, grimaces, and grunts possess magical qualities and depth of preverbal impact which discount the much greater probability of error in decoding than one has with spoken English.

In his Introduction to a set of papers on "The Silent

Patient," Rudolph M. Loewenstein has summarized his view of the significance for treatment of what I would term VA.

> Speech in the analytic process serves as a means of discharge and a binding of affects; it adds to thoughts and memories a degree of perceptual and social reality; it leads to an objectification of inner processes; it permits the differentiation of past and present, the testing of psychic realities, and makes psychoanalytic insight possible. It promotes the integrative processes to which we ascribe the major part of the therapeutic effectiveness of psychoanalysis (1961, pp. 4f).

Perpaps the strongest arguments for the potential curative value of promoting VA as such are to be found in David Rapaport.

> It seems justifiable to make these formulations: (1) Communication enriches the store of experiences and thereby counteracts ego-limitation; (2) Psychic life is not a one-way avenue in which defenses limit communications: communications may also combat the deleterious effects of defenses.... (6) It provides new percepts and resuscitates old ones; thus it also makes for an integration of isolated experiences and further integration into broader or new units.... Communication enhances the "synthetic function of the ego" (1951, pp. 727f).

Verbal Accessibility in Ego Development

Rapaport's remarks are directed at the potentials for *therapeutic* work one might find from increasing the patient's VA. At that time, however, I did not fully appreciate the implications inherent in VA for the *self*-healing processes of the ego. Several times I have remarked on the tendency of the personality to try to heal itself, even if the efforts it makes are misguided—as happens in the case of pathological defenses. Even if the impulse to bind up one's psychic wounds is biologically there, everyone is not equally capable of doing so. It is of course the person whose capacity for self-healing is the less adequate who is the more likely to have to appear in our offices in need of help.

When Rapaport comments that "communications may also combat the deleterious effects of defenses" he is pointing to this phenomenon of self-healing. One can go further. There is now reason to believe that to the extent a child grows up with a high level of VA, his whole capacity for problem-solving and thinking logically may be affected. These ego functions are not only necessary to acting as one's own therapist but also intrinsic and extremely significant parts of generalized ego strength or, speaking more technically, *ego integration.* The person whose writings have seemed to me most important with respect to this generalization is Lev Semenovich Vygotsky. He worked in Russia, mostly under Stalin, and he died young. But he left a manuscript that has since been edited and translated by Hanfmann and Vakar (Vygotsky, 1962). His work provides the theoretical underpinning for many of the poverty programs now in America, which are dedicated to helping poor youngsters function more effectively by increasing their language skills.

Vygotsky deals with the ontogenesis of meaningful speech. Although his theory contains gaps, what he did work out is certainly very stimulating. He quotes William Stern (1914) as having posited three roots of speech: an expressive, a social, and an "intentional" (aiming to communicate objective meanings) tendency. Vygotsky accepts that the first two are in fact found among animals and infants and therefore may be regarded as equivalent to instinctual givens. But he objects to regarding *intentionality* as one of the roots, as it is a trait of quite advanced or mature speech. Rather than being accepted as a source, it must be seen as the product of long development.

His image of the psychogenesis is as follows: (1) We begin with a primitive or "natural stage." (2) Next, there is a beginning of the use of experience, the budding of the child's practical intelligence. In speech development, the child learns the correct use of grammar, for example, before he understands the logic it implies. "He masters syntax of speech before syntax of thought." (3) After accumulation of experience, the child enters a third stage "distinguished by external signs, external operations that are used as aids in the solution of internal problems. This is the stage when the child counts on his fingers, resorts to mnemonic aids, and so on. In speech development it is characterized by egocentric speech." That is to say, *the child, in trying to think through an activity, uses the external aid of talking to himself while he is carrying it on.* (4) According to Vygotsky, this talking to oneself *aloud* becomes less and less and disappears about the time the child enters school. Hence, he is now in the fourth stage, or "ingrowth stage" of *inner speech,* carried on soundlessly. Talking to oneself aloud is to Vygotsky a critical step in the course of mastering the external signs which, transformed as inner speech, constitute *intentional thought* (1962, pp. 46f).

Inner speech became for Vygotsky an important object of investigation. Indeed, it is the process that bridges thought and language, but in an unexpected direction.

Here, too, we considered several hypotheses, and we came to the conclusion that inner speech develops through a slow accumulation of functional and structural changes, that it branches off from the child's external speech simultaneously with the differentiation of the social and egocentric functions of speech, and finally that the speech structures mastered by the child become the basic structures of his thinking. Hence, . . . thought development is determined by language. . . . The child's intellectual growth is contingent on his mastering the social means of thought, that is, language (pp. 50f).

It is commonplace to recognize that in social communication we try to put our thoughts into language. Vygotsky forcibly reminds us that we also put our language into thought. In an adult, the two have become interdependent: the quality of thought determines the quality of his language; but the quality of language may set upper limits on the development of thought.

Vygotsky's ideas have obvious implications for those engaged in research on the effects of unstimulating, limited environment (cultural deprivation), and they have already been so employed by John and Goldstein (1964). It is worthy of note, however, that his notions also are relevant to children who undergo the equivalent of cultural deprivation on an emotional basis within an otherwise middle-class home, and who end as schizoid—not only withdrawn, but rigid, concrete-minded, limited.

We may infer that anything which interferes with the verbalization of early determinant attitudes is likely also to deter the development of thought. The mother who discourages communication of feeling, by either rejecting or engulfing her child, is also discouraging his intellectual maturation. Because intentional speech is differentiated out of earlier roots in speech with expressive and social *(getting close)* aims, a psychological environment that makes it impossible for the child to move along these more primitive channels and to outgrow them will impair his movement into more advanced speech. As a consequence, insofar as speech is useful for internalizing logical, abstract thinking, emotional or "dynamic" deterrents will eventuate in structural deficit. Through deterring language acquisition, infantile emotional fixations defeat intellectual growth as well.

Given such a failure of development, further processes are set in motion. For example, the inability to abstract hampers synthesis. How, then, can the patient "stand behind his words," when he cannot come to one mind about what his conflicting attitudes add up to? Similarly, if there is a lack of sensitive differentiation of affects, so that the patient cannot distinguish between irritation and murderous rage, either in words or in his thoughts, how can he say this to the therapist without feeling like a fool? How to express tenderness, without feeling like a big baby? In other words, deficits in ability to differentiate and to organize lead to deterrents against talking at all.

Vygotsky's work has relevance in accounting for the existence of a chronic *low need* to communicate verbally. It recalls to us that models of ontogenesis describe what *can* occur, not an inevitable sequence. A large proportion of the population operates, even in adulthood, on a level of thinking that is not very rational or objective and with speech that has remained preintellectual. They have never felt the need to pass beyond the egocentric phase of speech development, in Piaget's sense (1962). That is to say, they speak from their own point of view because they have never questioned whether it is the same as their hearers'. Speech, then, may be used for drive expression; it may or may not be used for *social* ends—that is, showing affection and influencing others. But the attempt to use it for *problem solution* is quite unfamiliar.

Again and again, with schizoid patients, I have been impressed with the relatively few questions they put in interviews where, presumably, they have come for help with their problems. As Khan (1960) notes, they *exhibit* their mental processes but they do not discuss, and they have no conception of a process by which two persons, talking about a puzzle, might come up with a solution superior to that achievable by either one. The nearest they can come, when this problem is pointed out to them, is dutifully to ask approval of their remarks or try to get the therapist to "tell me what to do." It is of passing interest that part of their difficulty stems from their families where, quite regularly, we find exhortation but not discussion—or, even worse, the use of words to manipulate the child so that his whole idea of human converse is linked with notions of parental intrusiveness and slyness.

The low need to communicate determinant attitudes

verbally in *treatment* has at its root failure to mature, or regression. Under such circumstances, in a talking treatment we may advisedly utilize the patient's willingness to verbalize in the service of affect-expression, sociability and defense, and gradually help him *learn* to talk in rational, abstract, and problem-solving ways. With skill and luck, out of the experience to which he is helped in the interview, the client internalizes some of the same capacity, first as inner speech and later into the warp and woof of his thought processes. Here, finally, is the explanation of why just offering a sympathetic ear can be so powerful a tool in our casework or psychotherapy.

Verbal Accessibility: Cause or Effect?

The theorizing of Vygotsky, Kaiser, and Rapaport offers persuasive support for the significance of VA. It would be nice to be able to record that I knew this all along; but it would not be true. Vygotsky's book was not published in this country until several years after our research was under way, and I did not read it until long after the original studies had been published. The most complete statement of Kaiser's theory available was not published until eight years after our research began (Fierman, 1965). The fact is that the barrage of criticism leveled at my conception by the then consulting analyst at Bellefaire and his casework staff unsettled me. I had overlooked the fact that while it is the job of experienced, expert practitioners to be the more knowledgeable, it is the job of the expert investigator to be the more penetrating.

Nevertheless, I went ahead partly out of overcommitment to a course of action which circumstances would not permit me to alter, and even more out of stubbornness. If a scientist is stubborn in the face of clamor, and proves to have been right, he is regarded as morally courageous, or even heroic—like Freud. If he is stubborn, and proves to have been wrong, he is said to be pigheaded and, typically, neither he nor his persistence is recorded in the history of science at all. In this instance, I insisted we were dealing with an issue that could not be resolved on *a priori* grounds, for it involved empirical questions, and I would let nature decide who was right. Although each of us must recognize natural laws, they do not appear something we can establish by popular referendum, even if the electors have all been analyzed or are otherwise substantial property holders.

I overlooked the antiquated form of scientific logic in terms of which we were trying to clarify our differences. Basically the question was being raised: Is a higher level of verbal accessibility able to be the *cause* of improved ego integration? Or, as seemed more likely, is VA simply an *effect,* a reflection of the better level of ego integration that already exists? Put another way, one might argue that children in treatment who are already healthier will show more VA; but it is unlikely that simply by increasing their VA they will become healthier.

The argument was phrased analogously to whether symptomatic treatment is worthwhile. After all, if the symptom is merely an effect of underlying conflict and anxiety, it makes more sense to try to deal with the conflict than to work on the symptom. Otherwise, one may simply remove the symptom, but the anxiety will remain, and so another symptom might take its place (Reid and Shyne, 1969). This is a logically defensible position. Doubts about purely symptomatic improvement stem not only from this logic but also from the experiences of most of us who do psychotherapy and are honest observers of our own effectiveness. Nonetheless, this issue, too, presumes a one-way cause-effect relationship between the variables involved. And this is not the way the mind seems to be organized. Rather, *the various elements of the mind constitute a total, mutually interdependent field.*

The parts of the personality constitute a *gestalt*. This is what makes all psychotherapy possible in the first place, as I shall later demonstrate. The fact that the ego is a field made up of interdependent parts is the sole salvation of all the bad therapists in our midst. It renders their imprecise lunges more therapeutically potent than they deserve to be. For if you exert pressure on the wrong psychological lever, but in the right direction, it is apt to show a beneficent effect. In the long run, all the leverage available to all the psychotherapies is interconnected.

This small application of modern *metatheory* to the question of priorities in psychotherapy has some unexpected results. It reminds us that symptom and underlying anxiety are, in actual fact, influencing each other all the time. From this, there is an obvious deduction. Treating a symptom will, if at all effective, concomitantly affect its underlying cause. Now we must be careful. If change in symptom is *linked* to change in associated anxiety, it does not necessarily follow that improving or removing the symptom will *lessen* the anxiety. As the surface behavior is altered, the underlying conflicts and anxiety *may* become worse. This we saw earlier in our discussion of the lady with the aching feet.

It follows naturally that if one wishes to be cautious and maximally efficient in treatment, he will prefer to concentrate on the "basic cause" rather than its surface manifestation. However, it is not always possible to do this, either because we do not know how or—as frequently is the case— because the symptom itself is so dangerous to life it must be dealt with immediately. Alcoholics, who are slowly suiciding via the bottle, must be stopped even if by incarceration; ulcers must be medically treated so as not to hemorrhage. And, as I have said, in most less dramatic instances, removal of a noxious symptom is likely to be accompanied by alleviation of its underlying conflict, even if the full picture of the latter process is as unconscious to the therapist as it is to the patient.

Our small excursion into the dissolving effect of a field theoretical approach on a number of tired issues among clinicians was made with a purpose. We merely wanted to demonstrate that it was in fact plausible that a change in VA could very well lead to a favorable change in the over-all functioning of the personality. To say that something is logically defensible in our thought processes is not to say that it is true in nature. As Kurt Lewin liked to comment, "This is an empirical question," something to be settled by collecting and analyzing data. Our theorizing predicts at a minimum that the general level of ego integration or personal maturity is correlated with the person's VA. In the next chapter, we shall discuss whether we found this correlation and a number of other empirical issues about VA.

Nor is this simply a matter of casual interest for the theory of personality. If it is plausible that one can bring about therapeutic gains by concentrating on helping the patient or client better "to stand behind his words," then this offers a method of therapy communicable at some levels to the beginning caseworker or therapist, while still of interest to the most sophisticated. If VA is found correlated with a number of other important variables about the personality, this is well worth knowing for diagnostic reasons. After all, we have here a characteristic of the person that can be assessed rather well in the course of the first several interviews, simply as a by-product of the interviewing process, "for free." If this variable, heretofore relatively neglected in the clinical literature, should prove highly indicative of what to expect of one's patient, it would be an additional aid to diagnosis of the first magnitude.

References

Appelberg, Esther. "Verbal Accessibility of Adolescents," *Child Welfare, 43,* 1964, 86–90.

Asch, Solomon E. "Forming Impressions of Personality," *Journal of Abnormal and Social Psychology, 41,* 1946, 258–290.

Bavelas, Alex. "A Mathematical Model for Group Structure," *Applied Anthropology, 7,* 1948, 16–30.

Blenkner, Margaret. "Predictive Factors in the Initial Interview in Family Casework," *Social Service Review, 28,* 1954, 65–73.

Blum, Arthur, and Norman A. Polansky. "Effect of Staff Role on Children's Verbal Accessibility," *Social Work, 6,* 1961, 29–37.

Bordin, Edward S. "Inside the Therapeutic Hour," in E. A. Rubinstein and M. B. Parloff, eds., *Research in Psychotherapy.* Washington, D.C.: National Publishing Co., 1959.

Coch, Lester, and John R. P. French, Jr. "Overcoming Resistance to Change," *Human Relations, 1,* 1948, 512–532.

Enelow, Allen J. "The Silent Patient," *Psychiatry, 23,* 1960, 153–158.

Fierman, Louis B., ed. *Effective Psychotherapy: The Contribution of Hellmuth Kaiser.* New York: The Free Press, 1965.

John, Vera P., and L. S. Goldstein. "The Social Context of Language Acquisition," *Merrill-Palmer Quarterly, 10,* 1964, 265–276.

Jourard, Sidney M., and Patricia Richman. "Factors in the Self-Disclosure Inputs of College Students," *Merrill-Palmer Quarterly, 9,* 1963, 111–148.

Kadushin, Alfred, and C. F. Wieringa. "A Comparison: Dutch and American Expectations Regarding Behaviour of the Caseworker," *Social Casework, 41,* 1960, 503–511.

Kaiser, Hellmuth. "The Problem of Responsibility in Psychotherapy," *Psychiatry, 18,* 1955, 207–211.

Kanfer, Frederick H. "Comments on Learning in Psychotherapy," *Psychological Reports* (Monog. Supp. 6-V9), *9,* 1961, 681–699.

Kelley, Harold H. "The Warm-Cold Variable in First Impressions of Persons," *Journal of Personality, 18,* 1950, 431–439.

Khan, M. Masud. "Clinical Aspects of the Schizoid Personality: Affects and Technique," *International Journal of Psycho-Analysis, 41,* 1960, 430–437.

Kogan, Leonard S. "The Short-Term Case in the Family Agency,"*Social Casework, 38,* 1957, in three issues.

Kounin, Jacob, Norman Polansky, Bruce Biddle, Herbert Coburn, and Augustus Fenn. "Experimental Studies of Clients' Reactions to Initial Interviews," *Human Relations, 9,* 1956, 265–293.

Lewin, Kurt. "Some Social-Psychological Differences between the United States and Germany," *Character and Personality, 4,* 1935–36, 265–293.

Lewin, Kurt. "Frontiers in Group Dynamics," *Human Relations, 1,* 1947, 143–153.

Lewin, Kurt. *Field Theory in Social Science.* New York: Harper & Row, 1951.

Loewenstein, Rudolph M. "Introduction," *Journal of the American Psychoanalytic Association, 9,* 1961, 2–6.

Piaget, Jean. Comments on Vygotsky's Critical Remarks. Pamphlet. Cambridge, Mass.: The MIT Press, 1962.

Plog, Stanley C. "The Disclosure of Self in the United States and Germany." Read at Annual Meeting, American Psychological Association, Philadelphia, Penna., 1963.

Polansky, Norman, and Jacob Kounin. "Clients' Reactions to Initial Interviews," *Human Relations, 9,* 1956, 237–264.

Polansky, Norman A., Erwin S. Weiss, and Arthur Blum. "Children's Verbal Accessibility as a Function of Content and Personality," *American Journal of Orthopsychiatry, 31,* 1961, 153–169.

Rapaport, David. *Organization and Pathology of Thought.* New York: Columbia University Press, 1951.

Redl, Fritz, and David Wineman. *Cohtrols From Within.* New York: The Free Press, 1952.

Reid, William, and Ann Shyne. *Brief and Extended Casework.* New York: Columbia University Press, 1969.

Rickers-Ovsiankina, Maria A. "Social Accessibility in Three Age-Groups," *Psychological Reports, 2,* 1956, 283–294.

Ripple, Lillian. "Factors Associated with Continuance in Casework Service," *Social Work, 2,* 1957, 87–94.

Speisman, Joseph C. "Depth of Interpretation and Verbal Resistance in Psychotherapy," *Journal of Consulting Psychology, 23,* 1959, 93–99.

Stern, William. *Psychologie der fruehen Kindzeit.* Leipzig: Quelle and Meyyer, 1914. (Quoted by Vygotsky.)

Thomas, Edwin, Norman Polansky, and Jacob Kounin. "The Expected Behavior of a Potentially Helpful Person," *Human Relations, 8,* 1955, 165–174.

Truax, Charles B., and Robert R. Carkhuff. "Client and Therapist Transparency in the Psychotherapeutic Encounter." Read at Annual Meeting of American Psychological Association, Philadelphia, Penna., 1963.

Vygotsky, Lev Semenovich. *Thought and Language.* Cambridge, Mass.: The MIT Press, 1962.

Worby, Marsha. "The Adolescent's Expectations of how the Potentially Helpful Person will Act," *Smith College Studies in Social Work, 26,* 1955, 19–59.

Zajonc, Robert B. Cognitive Structure and Cognitive Tuning. Unpublished Ph.D. dissertation, University of Michigan, 1954.

Chapter 9

Verbal Accessibility and Character Structure

OUR STUDIES IN THE CHILDREN'S INSTITUTION BEGAN WITH the intention of emphasizing the determinants of VA that derive from the social context. We hoped to avoid becoming entangled in knotty problems of individual differences. Unfortunately, it was not possible to maintain this stance and still do justice to our evolving knowledge. It became evident early that individual differences among the children were too pronounced to be disregarded. It was then that I began to think of VA together with the model of a quasi-stationary equilibrium: change in reaction to fluctuations in the momentary situation, but with a long-range constant level to which the individual returns. Rickers-Ovsiankina and Kusmin had arrived independently at the same formulation (1958). Thus, VA might be regarded both as a variable reflecting forces in the social situation *and* as a meaningful attribute of personality or character. How meaningful I could not yet know, but it began to appear that this aspect of personality was highly indicative of much of the rest of functioning.

207

To regard VA as a stable and "significant" attribute required demonstrating a number of things: (a) Stability in time; (b) Stability in varying social situations or contexts; (c) Predictability, on the basis of other knowledge about the personality; (d) Fruitfulness for making forecasts, in turn, about the person.

Stability in Time

The first set of measurements we made at Bellefaire was related specifically to VA as evidenced in casework treatment. To estimate this, we utilized the records dictated by the workers. At that stage of the agency's history, records were in the form of "summary dictation"—that is, summaries of contacts were dictated three months after the child's admission and at intervals of six months thereafter. Using methods previously described (Polansky, Weiss, and Blum, 1961), we were able to assign each child a position on a partially-ordered scale. We then compared the children with respect to their relative ratings after three months of treatment, as compared with fifteen months. Our analysis showed a relationship significant at .02 by chi-square test and we reported it as such. In a subsequent study, however, Ruth Weber (1963) had occasion to re-examine the same data. It appeared that there had been errors in computation, and with these corrected the relationship was no longer significant, although it still showed a trend toward relative stability of position on VA.

The main evidence for such temporal stability comes from the study by Rickers-Ovsiankina and Kusmin (1958). Using a scale of self-reported *social accessibility,* they found a correlation of .52 among a group of college women retested after four years, and .69 for a group of both sexes, retested after eighteen months. These are the only confirmatory results available, thus far, although the predictive studies below certainly lend further support to the probability of constancy of the attribute.

Stability in Varying Social Situations

The next issue was whether VA fluctuates so with changes in immediate situation that there would be no correlation across varying social contexts. We have several studies on which to draw. One study was done with Blum at Bellefaire, and is also reported in our joint paper with Weiss (Polansky, Weiss, and Blum, 1961). In each cottage in which the children lived, there were four staff persons with whom a child might communicate—a group worker and three cottage counselors. Each adult was asked to rank the children in terms of how free they were in talking with him, personally. Kendall's W tested degree of similarity of such rankings among the four: the higher the W, the more constant was the child's behavior. For five cottages and rankings of VA on six scales of content, all but two W's were significant, most beyond .01. In other words, the child's VA was seen as similar among all four communicatees, in each cottage, on each attitudinal dimension.

Ratings by cottage personnel could then be combined into a single score of *openness to adults* in that situation. This index was then correlated with the caseworker's rating of the child's VA in *casework*. Relationship between the two was significant at .02, by chi-square test. Two years later, Appelberg did a study that involved a replication of these measurements, but with an altered sample of both children and adults, of course. Her results confirmed ours (Appelberg, 1961).

In the course of getting these measures, we also asked the children to report their own VA. Our results indicate that the children who say they are higher on VA are rated so by both caseworkers and cottage staff, a finding also confirmed by Appelberg. Hence, there is support for the validity of self-reports, although this hardly seems needed in view of the numerous indications of construct validity in the studies done by Jourard and his colleagues (see references).

In Nooney's experiment (1960), we wanted a measure

of VA that would be obtained with its objective masked from the subject. We had noticed that the varying VA displayed in sentence-completion tests is often as noteworthy as the content expressed. Accordingly, Nooney developed a reliable method of scoring such completions for VA and extracted two matched forms, or sets of stems. One set was given to subjects in the classroom, with the understanding they were to be read by the investigator and then used in arranging the groups for a later experiment. The second set was given after an experiment in which there was induction to perceive fellow-subjects as more or less similar to one's self as people. The sentence-completion stems were now to be filled out, ostensibly to be read by one fellow-subject or another (depending on the experimental condition involved). Nooney found a test-retest correlation of .28 (P < .02), across the changed circumstances and altered communicatee. Correlations ranged as high as .90 in some conditions (Nooney and Polansky, 1962). He concluded that where there was inhibition of VA, it operated uniformly, but where there was an experimentally induced increase in forces impelling communication, individual variations in response were such as greatly to reduce test-retest reliability.

Evidence of constancy across situations (i.e., to differing target persons) could probably be adduced from self-report data in our own and others' studies, but it would be impossible to decipher it from response-set. The studies cited have the advantage that the findings involve independence of ratings. Once again, there is the indication from moderate, but statistically significant, correlations of stability of the personality attribute.

Predictability from Other Knowledge of the Person

Another basis on which one might conclude he had an attribute of the person that was both stable and meaningful would be whether he could successfully make judgments about this variable without it being directly in view. Behavior that cannot be predicted in this way may of course be beyond the reach of our current technology. But it is possible that the dimension involved is too ephemeral and superficial to permit such assessments. Gordon Allport (1937, p. 443), for example, spoke of the "open" versus the enigmatic" personality, the difference based largely on the likelihood one could predict responses. We must note, however, that predictability of patterns, as well as persons, varies with how situation-bound they are.

For present purposes, prediction may take either of two forms. One is to be able to make a true prediction, future in time. This is the most convincing demonstration, for a number of reasons. There is also what Allport called *condiction* —the ability to estimate status on a given variable from knowledge of other (presumably somewhat independent) features of the person in the present. The assumption made is that only if VA is a meaningful feature of character will condiction be probable.

Our first attempt at a prediction study was at Bellefaire. We hired a caseworker to code the children's histories, each of which had been submitted prior to the child's admission to the institution. Partly in order to add interest to her task, we asked the worker, Naomi Glaser, to try to predict where each child would stand on VA after he had been in treatment for fifteen months. She assigned the youngsters "high," "medium," and "low" categories without knowledge, of course, of how their eventual VA had been judged by another team of case readers. Much to her own surprise, her accuracy in classifying the children surpassed chance at the .001 level. Our consulting psychiatrist had given up the same task in dismay over the supposed sparsity of information in the records, so we were of course curious about the criterion in Mrs. Glaser's prediction. All she could report was that she had based her assessment on "ego strength" of the child as it seemed to come through in the history.

With this much encouragement, we tried more ambitious studies. Psychometric evaluations had been done on nearly all the children shortly after admission to the institution. Dr. Melvin Allerhand, who had done most of the evaluations, reviewed his records with us, checking Rorschach and WISC factors against the child's VA in casework as rated from summaries at fifteen months (more than a year later). Eleven Rorschach factors were found that had discriminating power, most having to do with over-all goodness of functioning. We also found that in this setting low IQ did not necessarily predict poor VA, but high average or superior IQ predicted high VA (Polansky and Weiss, 1959). The number of factors found significant exceeded chance expectancy, of course. One of the most striking was this: if the child responded to aspects of the Rorschach cards which usually evoke anxiety responses, he was high on VA; if he did not respond (denial?), he proved low after fifteen months. These results, again, were tentative, but further supportive of the conclusion that was emerging from our work.

Perhaps the most striking evidence of the predictability of VA was in Ganter's study (Ganter and Polansky, 1964). Children seen in two child guidance clinics were given four sessions each in a *diagnostic group* as part of work-up. The group workers made a series of ten ratings on the child's behavior in the group. Less than half these children subsequently entered individual treatment. Three months after therapy was under way, ratings of VA were obtained from the therapists, using modified versions of the indices employed at Bellefaire. Half the measurements that had been made in the group were significantly related to the child's subsequent VA in therapy.

The five factors found successfully to predict VA in individual treatment were next winnowed by testing the number of "false positives" or "false negatives" obtained by including one or more in a pattern used for predicting. Several were found to add nothing to precision in predicting. The two most significant we labeled: (a) the child's organizational unity, and (b) the child's capacity for self-observation. Organizational unity, a term taken from Kurt Lewin, implies an adequate degree of differentiation, along with competent psychic apparatuses for coordinating disparate drives, etc.

We inferred that VA was an aspect of ego functioning, interlocking with and dependent upon organizational unity and the capacity for self-observation. We concluded that if this were so, then a course of treatment aimed at modifying just these functions should also result in increased VA in individual treatment.

Thanks to the support of their clinic, and the skill and dedication of Grace Ganter and her colleague, Margaret Yeakel, we now have a field test of such a proposition. Nearly fifty youngsters were seen in a project they headed in a specially designed group treatment program. This program was regarded as *intermediary,* in that it aimed at readying the inaccessible child for office interview treatment. The encouraging results of this program have been presented in a recent monograph (Ganter, Yeakel, and Polansky, 1967). It appears that we are beginning to understand accessibility in general and VA in particular sufficiently well to be able to change them in a fair proportion of cases.

Finally, one of the most effective items for predicting eventual VA among boys admitted to Bellefaire could be taken rapidly from the face sheet: age at admission! There was an asymmetrical relation, such that those older when admitted (over thirteen) were extremely likely to be rated high on VA, whereas preadolescents showed more spread. The probable reasons for this we will discuss later, but one hypothesis we held was that the younger children were "sicker" or they would not have required residential care so early. We made blind ratings of the symptoms, abstracted onto check-lists, ranking the boys on their "pervasiveness and intensity." There was a trend, which was not significant, for the younger boys to be more disturbed.

With the exception of the work with Ganter and Yeakel,

we had little success in trying to isolate a particular mechanism or syndrome as "basic" to VA. Rather, there are a number of instances in which factors indicative of ego defect or dysfunctioning are shown to be negatively related. Contrariwise, VA seems positively related to that quality of the personality so generalized it could best be expressed as "organizational unity."

There are a number of demonstrations that condiction of VA is possible. We were of course not the first to identify verbal inaccessibility in treatment with the neglected, predelinquent children of the slums. Redl and Wineman (1951) geared much of their program to an assumption that the children they treated could not be reached very well by a "talking treatment." In a recent paper, Eisenberg (1962) has reviewed 140 cases of children in foster care in the vicinity of Baltimore who were referred for psychiatric consultation. He felt it possible to list certain clinical features as prevalent, even though the children fit no single diagnostic category. The first noted was: "*They are relatively inarticulate. This is more than a matter of limited vocabulary. Their reluctance to verbalize and their lack of verbal facility reflects a subculture in which feelings are expressed in doing rather than talking.*"

Jaffee and Polansky (1962) designed a survey to test the impression among clinicians that there is an inverse relation between VA and delinquency-proneness. VA was operationalized via three instruments: a measure of attitude toward revealing intimate feelings; actual patterns of communication to significant objects, as reported; and responses on a semi-projective device calculated to "pull" affective expressions. Samples were obtained of three populations: low-income black, low-income white, and middle-income white. The boys in each sample were separated into two subgroups: one called High Delinquent (i.e., high on Gough's So scale, as combined with local court records and teacher ratings), and one called Nondelinquent. There were statistically significant differences in the direction postulated on the scale measuring attitude about intimacy of communication. The projective device demonstrated a readiness to *act* on feelings rather than to express them verbally, as consistently present in the High Delinquent subgroups. Differences on self-reported VA were not so sharp, but again they were in the direction hypothesized. An interesting sidelight came from the High Delinquent low-income black boys. In contrast to their general tendency to clam up, they reported a willingness to "tell bad things about my father" to their best boyfriends at a level found in no other group. Jaffee's research also showed that the Delinquency-Prone, low-income black boys came from the more disorganized, poorer, and neglected families (Jaffee, 1960).

Jourard (1961) has published a brief report of a study relating his measure of self-revelation to results of projective testing. Forty-five students in a graduate education class were administered the self-disclosure questionnaire; at a later class meeting the Rorschach was administered. There was a low but significant correlation between extent of self-disclosure (as reported) and productivity of Rorschach responses. Nevertheless, we must note that in the research at Bellefaire, with individual administration of the Rorschach and a far more independent measure of VA, Allerhand and Weiss did *not* find sheer number of responses significantly related. It was natural to wonder whether the youngsters in treatment at Bellefaire differed in their VA from a comparable group not identified as emotionally troubled. This became the major aim of Appelberg's (1961) study. Since Bellefaire served nearly entirely Jewish clientele, a comparison group was recruited from the membership of the B'nai B'rith Youth Organization. The test of VA was by self-report. The boys in treatment were found to score lower on VA than did those "outside," but there was no significant difference between the samples of girls.

An interesting demonstration of the condictability of VA is found in Tucker's research (1961), also part of the interrelated series we were conducting at that time. Tucker undertook an experiment on the reactions of paranoid schizophrenics to two styles of interviewing. We felt they were an extreme group whose responses should be most revealing for our theory. In the course of his study, he distinguished two types of paranoids: (1) A *tractable* group—patients who had only begun to elaborate their delusional system, continued to experience anxiety, make some effort to reach out to people, etc. (2) An *intractable* group—patients having elaborated a firm, well-articulated delusional system, rigid, lacking insight, hostile, argumentative, etc. With the use of an ingeniously devised rating system, ward attendants were able to categorize patients on this dimension with satisfactory inter-observer reliability. These judgments were based, of course, on behavior on the ward.

In Tucker's study, VA was measured by an adaptation of Osgood's semantic differential technique. The key issue, actually, was whether the patient, in rating a series of words on various scales, would or would not be willing to make *commitments* in the form of extreme ratings. (We had noticed, as have others, that psychotics are likely to prefer the medium, noncommittal ratings in attitude scaling. See Polansky, White, and Miller, 1957.) VA was here operationalized as "standing behind one's words," one might say. It was postulated that despite their apparent bluster and stubbornness the intractable group would be the less willing to make extreme ratings. Results indicated an obtained difference in line with the hypothesis, significant at .005. Using this veiled but objectively scorable measure, we find that VA was less for patients more advanced in the paranoid stance. Tucker's results at first glance seem at odds with the apparent bravado regarding the distortions and delusions with which such patients may recite them—until we recall that the attitudes they are spilling forth serve largely defensive, evasive purposes. It is our experience that much as they try to appear self-assured, such patients do not stand behind their paranoid outbursts, for they have not integrated into them an unconscious knowledge of the reality which they deny but cannot wholly avoid.

Verbal Accessibility Among Low-Income Rural Mothers

As so often happens in research, it was some years before I found an opportunity to continue organized research into VA. The next large-scale investigation occurred in connection with a study of five-year-olds and their mothers from a group of poor families living in rural Southern Appalachia. Each of the sixty-five children was enrolled in an experimental Headstart nursery school program.

The general intent of our research program was to improve child welfare services. The most important problem seemed to be how we could help mothers whose children were receiving the less adequate lifestyle or, as we called it, a lower *Childhood Level of Living*. We directed a diagnostic study of the problems involved in identifying the personality features differentiating mothers whose children were living better from those whose children were the worse off.

I knew from the studies reported above that VA could be measured sufficiently validly and reliably to permit correlations with other features of the personality. Hence, the doubting clinicians by whom I had been upset in starting our studies had been proven wrong, empirically. The question now was whether some of the generalizations that seemed to be emerging from research on clinical populations in the North would generalize to the women from the Southern mountains, hardly any of whom had ever been in any sort of treatment.

Our data were gathered in several ways. Research caseworkers held a series of interviews with each woman, during which standard social histories were collected. From these contacts the social worker rated each woman on her VA, using a composite index of some forty items. Despite the nature of our sampling, which guaranteed a restricted range on most variables since in many respects the women were a highly homogeneous group, we found a surprising number of statistically significant correlations.

One general trend from the previous data on emotionally disturbed children seemed to indicate that VA was associated with better ego integration, or what we have loosely termed generalized ego strength. This seemed immediately visible in the results of some psychological testing in which our mothers participated. The mother's VA, as rated by the caseworker, correlated with her IQ as measured by our psychologist—naturally without knowledge of the social worker's results—at .32. The correlation with Verbal Intelligence was even higher, with r = .40, significant at the one per cent level of confidence. Each mother had also participated in a standardized interview, which had been taperecorded, and her verbalizations were coded on several dimensions. I said earlier that I did not equate VA with sheer verbosity (Cope, 1969). It is of interest, therefore, that we found no relationship between the woman's volume of speech on the taperecorded interview and the caseworker's over-all rating of her VA, based on a number of contacts in her home and elsewhere. But her VA did correlate with the extent to which she differentiated her feelings and organized them, in the standardized interview, and with the extent to which she revealed abstract thinking in what she said.

The VA of a child, even after fifteen months in casework treatment in an institution, could be predicted beyond chance expectancy on the basis of estimates of his ego strength prior to admission. That VA is similarly predictable in the mothers here studied was also demonstrable in this study. Based on objective information from history regarding her educational achievement, dating and occupational adjustment, each mother could be given a rating of her apparent ego strength in late adolescence. The association between this retrospective assessment and her current VA was significant at beyond the 2 per cent level of confidence. In short, her degree of openness about expressing her feelings could be predicted at beyond chance from a knowledge of how competent she was as a youngster.

In this study, too, there were a number of demonstrations that condiction of VA is possible. For example,

Rorschach protocols could be scored for evidences of maturity of the personality. Those mothers rated higher on VA by our caseworkers gave more Functional Integration responses on the Rorschach, which is usually taken to indicate greater maturity in the personality (Phillips, 1968). Borgman also devised some ingenious new ways of handling protocols from the Thematic Apperception Test (which always interests clinical psychologists but generally yields only vague, impressionistic data in any study where it is subjected to more rigorous examination). One index he devised was a measure of "loneliness" which, from the theory of object relations, indicates a continuing needful, childlike level of functioning when it is strongly present in an adult. The less the expressed loneliness on the TAT, the greater the VA of the mother. This association, too, is in the direction of identifying higher VA with greater personal maturity.

Fruitfulness of Verbal Accessibility for Prediction

If VA is a sufficiently stable and "central" feature of character to permit prediction, one might expect that it would be a determinant, in turn, of other features. With the mounting evidence from our own studies and encouraging reports from Jourard, the meaningfulness of VA became more and more apparent. A key question in the Bellefaire series of studies, and one asked repeatedly at professional meetings, was: "What does VA have to do with treatability?" The answer was slow in coming, because cases had to accumulate on whom we had comparable measures of VA, and who finished their treatment, before we could relate VA to treatability.

The study needed was eventually completed by Weber (1963) with revealing results. Weber compared VA as measured after three months of treatment with ratings of a child's status at the time he was discharged from Bellefaire.

Outcome at discharge was assessed on the basis of the child's fulfillment of various expectable demands of his age and sex role, insofar as these are germane to life in a treatment center. She found that children rated higher on VA three months after admission were adjudged better adapted on role-fulfillment at the time therapy was terminated— often three or more years later. In other words, in that setting VA was an efficient predictor of the outcome of treatment. One might have inferred that those higher on VA were better off to begin with, but in Weber's sample those low on VA (in casework) were as well adjusted in the living situation as those high, at the time of admission. In other words, those with higher VA seemed to make more progress and to be better able to use the treatment situation.

On closer scrutiny it appeared that there were, indeed, areas in which relatively nonverbal children showed equivalent gains—chiefly in handling their assigned chores, managing impulses, etc. The major difference between the groups, in fact, lay in the greater ability of youngsters who were initially high in VA to relate to adults.

The only other study of which I am aware in which the variable VA, or something like it, has been tested for ability to predict outcome of therapy is one reported by Truax and Carkhuff (1963). They found a positive, significant correlation between a measure of "patient depth of self-exploration or transparency in the second interview" and judgment of the final constructive change in the patient. This is said to be true of hospitalized adult mental patients seen in individual treatment and also of another sample seen in group therapy. However, they report a reversal of these results when dealing with the group therapy of institutionalized adolescent delinquents.

Although there are few relevant studies about the final outcome of cases, we do have one involving whether they stay in treatment. Florence Hollis (1966) analyzed communications of clients in several family service agencies during their first interviews, including women who came for help with marital problems. She found that, contrary to her own expectations, women who devoted the greater part of the first interview to describing their situation while ventilating feelings (description-ventilation) about it were the more likely to continue in treatment. This result is reminiscent of the study done by Kounin and Polansky in which we found that those clients who reported themselves freer to communicate were generally the more satisfied with their first interviews in every way.

Blum and I did a small, informal study at Western Reserve University, testing the efficacy of VA for predicting interpersonal competence. Briefly, we hypothesized that those students beginning training in social work who showed higher VA would do better in field work, at least in the initial stages. The test used was the incomplete sentences technique developed with Nooney (1960), administered in a class situation, with its true purpose masked. We found that those scoring in the *lowest quartile* on VA did make poorer grades in field work at the end of their first year of training, and that these extreme scores also efficiently identified those who were either counseled out or dropped out of school.

Regarding the prediction of students' abilities, we have another study in the series by Jourard (1961d). He reported a correlation of .79 between the total self-disclosure scores of twenty-three sophomore students in a nursing college and their final grade-point average taken through their junior and senior years. Also, students who rated as "good" in relating to patients had obtained significantly higher total disclosure scores on a questionnaire administered a year earlier than did students rated "poor."

In our study of rural mothers, we also found support for the notion that VA can be used to predict other facets of a woman's functioning. The quality of mothering is, of course, extremely hard to define. I have already referred to our use of a Childhood Level of Living Scale as one means by which this can be scored. This scale is completed on the basis both of direct observation of the child's home and life circumstances and from talks with his mother about how he is handled, what he gets fed, and the like. The scale may then be scored either as a total or in two broad components —one dealing with sheer Physical Care, the other with Cognitive/Emotional Care. It was found that the correlation of the maternal VA with the over-all level of care being received by a child was .47 (P < .01), a substantial correlation in view of the fact that all these mothers were from low-income families in the same mountain county. As one might have expected, however, the correlation with Cognitive/Emotional Care received by the child was .58, which was considerably higher than that with his Physical Care score. One might wonder whether these results were simply a function of the fact that the more intelligent mothers also score higher on VA. Nevertheless, with Verbal IQ "partialed out" statistically, the correlation between VA and the Childhood Level of Living was still .33, and significant. Moreover, the child himself shows the effects of this greater competence in his mother. Mothers with higher VA had more intelligent children, a relationship again significant at beyond the one per cent level of confidence.

Recapitulation

The results available regarding the fruitfulness of VA for prediction lend further support to the propositions advanced. We have certainly caught hold of a facet of personality that was sufficiently stable not only to permit being predicted *to* but also to warrant prediction *from*. Therefore, it must either determine central aspects of personality functioning, itself, or be closely connected to other important dynamics which do so—as we theorized in the preceding chapter.

VA has been found to be "flexibly stable" across time and changing social situations; it can be predicted from history, using a crude criterion of ego strength; it can be predicted and condicted from psychometric data with a similar conception of relative psychological maturity in mind. It was predicted from observations in a diagnostic group for emotionally disturbed children; it showed a striking relationship to age at admission to a children's institution; it was predictable in young mothers from an appraisal of their role-achievements in late adolescence. It has been observed to be negatively related to delinquency-proneness in pre-adolescent boys; and possibly to defensiveness in taking a Rorschach. Boys with identified emotional disturbance were found lower on VA; even among hospitalized paranoid schizophrenics a distinction on this variable could be related to depth and fixedness of pathology. VA has been found predictive of treatability in a residential setting of disturbed children and adults; it has shown some usefulness in selecting interpersonal competence among students in two helping professions: nursing and social work; it distinguishes those mothers whose children are enjoying the better care. Finally, although not shown specifically in any of these studies, there is the observed negative relation of VA with familial and "cultural" deprivation, reported by many clinicians. I turn next to this problem.

Cultural Differences in Verbal Accessibility

Variations in VA with cultural background may be treated as an extension of the study of personality characteristics, as we are here speaking of modal personality. Considering how small the research literature is about VA, there are already a surprising number of studies of cultural differences.

One of the earliest reports was a study of Negro-white differences in the South by Jourard and Lasakow (1958). They found that white college students reported more self-disclosure than did Negroes. In a subsequent study, Jourard (1961a) compared members of different religious faiths on the campus of the University of Florida, using his self-disclosure questionnaire. Jewish males were higher total disclosers ($P < .01$) than were members of other denomina-

tions. Jourard (1961b) also compared self-disclosure patterns between British and American college females,
comparing twenty-five undergraduates from the University
of Florida with a like number, matched in sex and social
class, etc., from the University of Nottingham, England.
He found a significant difference, in favor of the American
youngsters.

The famous paper by Lewin on differences between the
American and German character was referred to earlier. In
his research, Plog (1963) raised the question of whether
these differences would still be found more than twenty-five
years later. A self-disclosure questionnaire was developed
with American students, and carefully translated into German. Students were selected from four varied American
colleges and universities and a similar number in Germany.
A difference in favor of the American group was found significant at .001. In contrast to these demonstrations, we
have reports of negative findings. Rickers-Ovsiankina
(1961) tested the same Lewinian hypothesis as did Plog,
but extended her study to eight universities, representing a
total of seven cultures, including the American. She found
no consistent differences regarding who talked most, to
whom, about what (p. 872). In our study with Jaffee (1962),
we had groups from three contrasting American subcultures. We found no obvious differences among the three
with respect to VA, as we measured it in that study. At that
point I concluded that the studies of purported cultural
differences in VA thus far must be regarded as more in the
realm of specimen-collecting than organized attempts at
building a theory. Even when significant and credible differences were found, they were not able to be explained by
reference to any more general theory or social variable.
However, promising results do seem to be emerging with
respect to social class differences.

Mayer (1966), for example, investigated whether middle
class housewives were more or less open than were lower
class women in disclosing their marital problems and negative feelings about their husbands. He found that the middle

class women revealed a greater number of their marital concerns to others and did so at greater depth than did the working class. Both groups were most likely to confide such feelings to their husbands, if anybody; but there was a trend to keep such thoughts within the family (i.e., only among relatives) among the lower class, if they talked to others at all.

Mayer's findings were reminiscent of some reported by Basil Bernstein (1962), in England, regarding the relationship between what he called the "restricted language code" and social class. Briefly, Bernstein found that whereas middle class Englishmen seemed to have available both an *elaborated*, universal language, suitable for communicating with strangers, and a *restricted* language appropriate only among intimates who understand its limited vocabulary and usages in the same way, the lower class person was confined to a restricted code. A characteristic of this restricted code, incidentally, is its oversimplified syntax which itself tends to limit the complexity and logical precision of what is to be expressed or thought!

Although Bernstein noted the relationship of speech-style to social class (as had George Bernard Shaw before him), he offered no satisfactory explanation for its existence. It is not enough to say that lower class people talk the way they do because that is what they have been taught by their cultures. This is the same as saying, "Culture acculturates." What else is new? Rather the problem is trying to understand *why* a particular subculture becomes so organized that it militates against permitting development of complex language codes or, put another way, it actively inhibits the development in its youngsters of an *elaborated* style of speech.

That some subcultures do this, I have no doubt. Some politicians are known deliberately to speak ungrammatically to rural audiences lest they be classified as "too big for their breeches." A young man who goes to college is under careful scrutiny when he comes home that he not betray any sign in his manner or speech of having been influenced by his education, if he comes from a poor family "back in the coves." The challenge to theory was to understand not why culture acculturates but rather why it resists development of an elaborated, differentiated language code. An exciting explanation can be developed by extending the propositions of Hellmuth Kaiser.

Individual and Group Determinants of Verbal Inaccessibility

The adaptation of Kaiser's theory will be presented as a series of propositions. Some statements may appear rather distant from the concerns already stated, but their relevance will become evident as we proceed.

a. We approach the problem of VA in terms of forces inhibiting people from explicit verbal revelation of their more important attitudes. The major inhibiting force is anxiety; to be verbally *in*accessible is a defense against this anxiety.

b. It is postulated that the form of anxiety most significantly at issue is *separation anxiety,* which many regard as *the* primordial anxiety (Bowlby, 1960).

c. Separation anxiety may be countered in various ways. Probably the healthiest resolution is to establish communication between two mature persons—a situation of intimacy without loss of identity. However, as Kaiser has emphasized, the most typical neurotic defense against this anxiety is the *delusion of fusion.* The person seeks to bolster the fantasy that he and some significant other are one and the same. The fusion fantasy is reminiscent of the infant's feelings about his mother. If exploited later in life, it is to be seen as a regressive defense.

d. The person with a strong need for the fusion fantasy will seek to evoke experiences in his "real world" that tend to validate it. Support may come from such derivative mechanisms as:

1. Maintenance of a close, clinging proximity to the significant other (often called anaclitic dependency).

2. Motivated helplessness, making it impossible to function "on one's own." (Another form of dependency.)

3. Avoidance of actions that heighten the sense of being an independent entity. One prevalent form is reluctance to make conscious choices or decisions, preferring to *feel forced* by circumstances.

4. Various modes of denial of the existence of distinctions among people. These include such derivative mechanisms as (a) shunning persons perceptibly unlike oneself; (b) stereotyping people, so that they become *meaningless—* as objects for empathy or for comparison with oneself; (c) maintaining solidarity in one's group around a strong demand for uniformity, and rejection of deviance; (d) *limiting or derailing the explicit verbalization of important attitudes, since the effort to be understood reminds one of his separateness from the listener;* (e) *constricting development in the ego of cognitive apparatuses which facilitate the recognition of interpersonal differences and nuances of feeling.*

We have italicized the subsidiary defensive maneuvers that play the more important roles in the present theoretical discussion; namely, in limiting verbal accessibility. However, the other patterns will probably be found compresent where the need to protect the fusion fantasy is very great, and so they are presented as context.

e. As a derivation of the above, it is hypothesized that among persons for whom the need to maintain the fusion fantasy is greater, there will be a preference for a *restricted language code.* Such a device, as Bernstein pointed out, makes individuated response less possible. In other words, the restricted code is seen as operating in the service of the fusion fantasy by limiting cognitive abilities.

f. It is similarly derived that among those to whom the fusion fantasy is strongly needed, there will be inhibition against the explicit verbal communication of intensely experienced, individualized feelings (cf. d.4(d) above).

g. There is evidence from earlier research in clinical settings that VA is less when the emotional disorder is the more pervasive. It is postulated that reliance on the fusion fantasy as a regressive defense is greater the more the person finds himself unable to cope with environmental stresses or internal impulses. The classic example, of course, is the tendency of "green" troops to stay together under fire, but there are also numerous illustrations from research on formation of group norms under conditions of stress or uncertainty.

h. On the level of group process, it is postulated that any defensive maneuver prevalent among the members of a group will be given a positive connotation and incorporated into the values of the group. It follows that in groups containing a substantial proportion of persons who experience a beleaguered existence, the fusion fantasy and its derivative mechanisms will become normative. Use of these defenses will be supported by group consensus and will be inculcated in the young. Included in the phenomena likely to be compresent are heightened pressures toward uniformity, especially in the realms of attitude and feelings; use of a restricted linguistic code; and relative verbal inaccessibility.

i. It is hypothesized that because of the effects of their life situations on the processes indicated above, evidence of reliance on the delusion of fusion in the service of defense is more likely to be found in the lower socioeconomic group, in this country, and in particular subcultures characterized by hardship and isolation.

The impact of social stratification is seen, in this formulation, as mediated by defenses likely to be supported by a given position in the social structure. Although this analysis is more complicated than the view of people responding directly to the "opportunity structure," we believe it may prove more parsimonious in synthesizing a wider range of phenomena and in suggesting nonobvious relationships. For example, the theory predicts that, contrary to older opinion in the field, the demand for adherence to standards of their *own* group is greater in the lower socioeconomic group than in the middle; and that, in addition to the sense of hopelessness, there will be *counterachievement* pressure exerted on children by their parents and others.

An empirical test of this proposition was conducted with Sara Brown (Polansky and Brown, 1967), in a county in Appalachia. As predicted, we found that youngsters of lower socioeconomic status attending an isolated school "back in the coves" were in fact less verbally accessible than were youngsters from more middle class families living in an industrialized town in the same county but more in the mainstream of American life. Although the theory expressed above can by no means be regarded as having been subjected to rigorous testing, it remains the broadest integration I have achieved to explain inhibition on language development in at least some cultures. It further explicates why some individuals resist developing a form of language that would make them too aware of their own individuality. This theory demonstrates the potential power of Kaiser's conception of the *delusion of fusion* as a parsimonious formulation in social as well as in clinical theory. Among other things, it throws new light on such phenomena as *behavioral contagion* and imitation (see Chapter 11), and the application of ego psychology to psychodrama.

Familial Differences in Verbal Accessibility

If differences between cultures or subcultures are verified, we shall have to assume that they are transmitted through the family. I have long had the impression that the relative VA of a patient is likely to reflect the atmosphere in his family. Some families seem more likely to permit or facilitate free self-examination and expression of feelings. This is true, by the way, even within the same culture. For example, some youngsters from the "back coves" of Appalachia show surprising ease in communicating feelings, in contrast to the reticence of most.

Jean Haring (1965) reported a study that bears on the issue of family patterns of VA. In her position as intake worker at a social agency serving adolescents in Cleveland, she interviewed the youngster, the mother, and—in the majority of cases—the father. Her study is of special interest in that she succeeded in getting the clients to complete necessary research instruments bearing upon VA, in addition to the usual intake interview necessary for responsible service. Hence, we have data collected under real-life conditions. Ratings were made of relative spontaneity in the intake interview of adolescent girls, boys, fathers and mothers. When tested for resemblance, the ratings showed a similarity between girls and their mothers that was statistically significant at beyond .001. On the other hand, boys did not resemble their mothers and their behavior actually was rated as the *opposite* of their fathers', on the same scale! In another phase of the study, Haring examined whether there are family differences concerning topics regarded as permissible to discuss. She found a close similarity between attitudes of girls and their mothers, and—to a lesser extent—boys and their mothers. Fathers did not appear too influential in establishing what is and what is not available to discussion. The suggestion is, therefore, that insofar as the family may be thought to influence the VA of troubled youngsters, it is likely to find girls more affected, and the mother as the parent who "sets the tone." In Haring's study as in most others, mothers far outstrip fathers as preferred targets of communication.

No opportunity presented itself for confirming Haring's results until recent research with mother-child pairs in Appalachia (Polansky, Borgman, DeSaix, and Smith, 1969). In this study we had independent ratings of the VA of the mother and her child, which was one advance over Haring's data. The VA of the child was judged on a six-point global scale by the nursery school teacher; that of the mother was taken from the index used by the research social workers. The association was significant at beyond the 5 per cent level of confidence. In other words, five-year-olds who were more verbally open were likely to have mothers who were also verbally open. This effect is produced, I have no doubt, by a combination of identification with one's mother, a total home atmosphere in which attitudes are—or are not—permitted expression, and something more pervasive about the total conditions of the child's life. For example, as one might expect, the child's VA was also significantly associated with his over-all standard of living.

The relation of familial patterns of communication to illness in the child has of course been much studied, especially in respect to the etiology of schizophrenia (Singer and Wynne, 1965). Kovacs (1966) has demonstrated the usefulness of studying the disorders of attention revealed in parental speech in understanding the child's confusions.

Sex Differences in Verbal Accessibility

I am happy to say that I would hate to classify sex differences as merely, or even primarily, a matter of culture. Yet we must now report about research on this variable. Jourard (1961a) refers to a "frequently demonstrated fact" that women are higher self-disclosers. Haring had ratings of the relative VA of all four family members in her study, and she found her adolescent girls who were in difficulties showed far more VA than did their male counterparts.

Plog, on the other hand, did not find a sex difference in his study; Rickers-Ovsiankina and Kusmin (1958) describe a complex relationship to other variables, but no clear-cut superiority of women over men in their study of college students. I conducted a study involving six samples of ninth- and tenth-grade students in Southern Appalachia. These samples included an isolated mountain group; a rural county in the Georgia "flatlands"; middle and lower class whites from a small town; upper lower and lower lower class blacks from another mountain county (Polansky, 1969). VA was measured in this survey-type study by self-reports, attitude scaling, and projective techniques. There is considerable variation within each sex group, but taken over-all, and on all three measures, the adolescent girls were significantly superior to the boys. This finding is consistent in nearly every sample studied.

If future research should continue to show the weight of the evidence in favor of higher VA among girls than boys, this will of course have important general implications for interview treatment. It does not imply that boys cannot be treated by interview techniques. But it will require specialized interviewing skills to help them become accessible to this form of treatment.

There is a great deal more that can be said about verbal accessibility. Our analysis has dealt with which people show more or less VA. There are related issues, also worthy of study. For instance, we once did research on the person likely to be chosen as a confidant—a question involving the personality it takes to be a favored *target* of clinical communication (Blum and Polansky, 1961; Jourard and Landsman, 1960). Other research has been conducted on which attitudes are the more likely to be openly communicated in this culture. Some of us have found surprising consistency in the *rank ordering* of which content will be revealed or held back, even if two groups of subjects differ in their over-all openness. That is, if the person will talk at all, he is the more likely to talk about things "everyone" finds it permissible to discuss (Jourard, 1961b; Plog, 1963; Appelberg, 1961; Jaffee and Polansky, 1962). Sometimes, of course, this leads to somewhat laughable observations. In several Jewish family agencies, my colleagues and I noted that while our middle class Jewish clientele might tell us quite a bit about their sex lives, it was nearly impossible to find out precisely what their incomes were! Well, to each his own.

We have today no general theory to account for the differences in contents which are or are not likely to be verbalized. Taylor and Altman (1966) have brought together a list of nearly 500 conceivable conversational topics graded in terms of their "intimacy." Anyone proposing a study in this general area would do well to study their materials.

Let me sum up the three goals of the discussion. First, I have fleshed with more detailed propositions the skeletal statement that verbal communication can be viewed usefully in terms of ego psychology, specifically ego structure. Second, I have shown that at least some of the hypotheses encountered in ego psychology lead to testable and interesting issues for empirical research, just as they have important implications for clinical work. Third, by means of a specific variable, VA, I have shown that there is no real conflict between social and personality approaches to theorizing. In the explanation of subcultural variations in VA, I have meshed the two levels of discourse in a fashion that does justice to both and yet does not simply state a truism.

Although we dealt with the general topic of VA, the more typical clinical challenge is its opposite: verbal *in*-accessibility. The general theoretical issue is "Why do people talk?" but the problem we face daily is more often "Why will this particular fellow not talk?" Or, if he talks much, "Why does he say so little?" In a general way, this chapter has dealt with restraints against VA deriving from the person's character and from his long-range cultural background. These deterrents represent a combination of inadequacy and unwillingness, inability and certain general, fixed attitudes that are an integral part of the personality. This chapter, then, has concerned itself with *structural* inhibiting factors affecting VA. It is more fun and, in practical work, often more to the point to look at the *dynamics* at work in the client and in the interview situation. For a further illustration of the application of ego psychology to clinical communication, let us turn next to duplicity in the interview.

References

Allport, Gordon W. *Personality.* New York: Holt, 1937.

Appelberg, Esther. Verbal Accessibility of Adolescents. Unpublished DSW dissertation, Western Reserve University, 1961.

Bernstein, Basil. "Social Class, Linguistic Codes and Grammatical Elements," *Language and Speech, 5,* 1962, 221–240.

Blum, Arthur. "Peer-group Structure and a Child's Verbal Accessibility in a Treatment Institution," *Social Service Review, 36,* 1962, 385–395.

Blum, Arthur, and Norman A. Polansky. "Effect of Staff Role on Children's Verbal Accessibility," *Social Work, 6,* 1961, 29–37.

Bowlby, John. "Separation Anxiety," *International Journal of Psycho-Analysis, 41,* 1960, 89–113.

Cohen, Arthur R. "Upward Communication in Experimentally Created Hierarchies," *Human Relations, 11,* 1958, 41–53.

Cope, Corrine S. "Linguistic Structure and Personality Development," *Journal of Counseling Psychology Monograph, 16* (No. 5, part 2), 1969.

Deutsch, Martin. "The Role of Social Class in Language Development and Cognition," *American Journal of Orthopsychiatry, 25,* 1965, 78–88.

Eisenberg, Leon. "The Sins of the Fathers: Urban Decay and Social Pathology," *American Journal of Orthopsychiatry, 32,* 1962, 5–17.

Fairbairn, W. Ronald D. "Schizoid Factors in the Personality," in *Psychoanalytic Studies of the Personality.* London: Tavistock, 1940.

French, John R. P., Jr. "The Disruption and Cohesion of Groups," *Journal of Abnormal and Social Psychology, 36,* 1941, 361–377.

Ganter, Grace, and Norman A. Polansky. "Predicting a Child's Accessibility to Individual Treatment from Diagnostic Groups," *Social Work, 9,* 1964, 56–63.

Ganter, Grace, Margaret Yeakel, and Norman A. Polansky. *Re-*

trieval from Limbo. New York: Child Welfare League of America, 1967.

Haring, Jean. Freedom of Communication between Parents and Adolescents with Problems. Unpublished DSW dissertation, Western Reserve University, 1965.

Hollis, Florence. Development of a Casework Treatment Typology. Unpublished research report, The Columbia University School of Social Work, 1966.

Hollis, Florence. "A Profile of Early Interviews in Marital Counseling," *Social Casework, 49,* 1968, 35–43.

Jaffee, Lester D. Delinquency and Impulse Control. Unpublished DSW dissertation, Western Reserve University, 1960.

Jaffee, Lester D., and Norman A. Polansky. "Verbal Inaccessibility in Young Adolescents Showing Delinquent Trends," *Journal of Health and Human Behavior, 3,* 1962, 105–111.

Johnson, Wendell. *People in Quandaries.* New York: Harper & Row, 1946.

Jourard, Sidney M. "Self-Disclosure and Other-Cathexis," *Journal of Abnormal and Social Psychology, 59,* 1959, 428–431.

Jourard, Sidney M. "Religious Denomination and Self-Disclosure," *Psychological Reports, 8,* 1961a, 446.

Jourard, Sidney M. "Self-Disclosure Patterns in British and American College Females," *Journal of Social Psychology, 54,* 1961b, 315–320.

Jourard, Sidney M. "Self-Disclosure and Rorschach Productivity," *Perceptual and Motor Skills, 12,* 1961c, 232.

Jourard, Sidney M. "Age Trends in Self-Disclosure," *Merrill-Palmer Quarterly, 7,* 1961d, 191–197.

Jourard, Sidney M., and M. J. Landsman. "Cognition, Cathexis and the 'Dyadic Effect' in Men's Self-Disclosing Behavior," *Merrill-Palmer Quarterly, 6,* 1960, 178–186.

Jourard, Sidney M., and P. Lasakow. "Some Factors in Self-Disclosure," *Journal of Abnormal and Social Psychology, 56,* 1958, 91–98.

Kovacs, Margaret E. "Attention Patterns of Parents with a Schizophrenic Offspring," *Smith College Studies in Social Work, 37,* 1966, 1–23.

Mayer, John E. *The Disclosure of Marital Problems.* New York: Institute of Welfare Research of the Community Service Society, 1966.

Nooney, James B. Verbal Accessibility as Determined by Perceived Similarity and Personality. Unpublished Ph.D. dissertation, Western Reserve University, 1960.

Nooney, James B., and Norman Polansky. "The Influence of Perceived Similarity and Personality on Verbal Accessibility," *Merrill-Palmer Quarterly, 8,* 1962, 33–40.

Pepitone, Albert, and George Reichling. "Group Cohesiveness and the Expression of Hostility," *Human Relations, 8,* 1955, 327–338.

Phillips, Leslie. *Human Adaptation and its Failures.* New York: Academic Press, 1968.

Plog, Stanley C. "The Disclosure of Self in the United States and Germany." Read at Annual Meeting, American Psychological Association, Philadelphia, Penna., 1963.

Polansky, Norman A. "Small Group Theory: Implications for Casework Research," in Leonard S. Kogan, ed., *Social Science Theory and Social Work Research.* New York: National Association of Social Workers, 1959.

Polansky, Norman A. "Powerlessness among Rural Appalachian Youth," *Rural Sociology, 34,* 1969, 219–222.

Polansky, Norman A., and Sara Q. Brown. "Verbal Accessibility and Fusion Fantasy in a Mountain County," *American Journal of Orthopsychiatry, 37,* 1967, 651–660.

Polansky, Norman A., and Erwin S. Weiss. "Determinants of Accessibility to Treatment in a Children's Institution," *Journal of Jewish Communal Service, 36,* 1959, 130–137.

Polansky, Norman A., Erwin S. Weiss, and Arthur Blum. "Children's Verbal Accessibility as a Function of Content and Personality," *American Journal of Orthopsychiatry, 31,* 1961, 153–169.

Polansky, Norman A., Robert B. White, and Stuart C. Miller. "Determinants of the Role-Image of the Patient in a Psychiatric Hospital," in M. Greenblatt, D. Levinson, and R. H. Williams, eds., *The Patient and the Mental Hospital.* New York: The Free Press, 1957, 380–401.

Polansky, Norman A., Robert D. Borgman, Christine DeSaix, and Betty Jane Smith. "Verbal Accessibility of the Appalachian Mother: A Casework Challenge." *Social Work Practice, 1969.* New York: Columbia University Press, 1969.

Redl, Fritz, and David Wineman. *Children Who Hate.* New York: The Free Press, 1951.

Rickers-Ovsiankina, Maria. "Cross-Cultural Study of Social Accessibility," *Acta Psychologica, 19,* 1961, 872.

Rickers-Ovsiankina, Maria, and Arnold A. Kusmin. "Individual Differences in Social Accessibility," *Psychological Reports, 4,* 1958, 391–406.

Schanck, Richard L. "A Study of a Community and its Groups and Institutions Conceived of as Behavior of Individuals," *Psychological Monographs, 42,* 1932, Whole No. 195.

Singer, Margaret T., and Lyman C. Wynne. "Thought Disorder and Family Relations of Schizophrenics: IV. Results and Implications," *Archives of General Psychiatry, 12,* 1965, 187–200.

Taylor, Dalmas A., and Irwin Altman. "Intimacy-scaled Stimuli for Use in Studies of Interpersonal Relations," *Psychological Reports, 19,* 1966, 729–730.

Truax, Charles B., and Robert R. Carkhuff. "Client and Therapist Transparency in the Psychotherapeutic Encounter." Read at Annual Meeting of American Psychological Association, Philadelphia, Penna., 1963.

Tucker, Gregory E. A Study of Verbal Accessibility in Hospitalized Paranoid Schizophrenics in Response to Two Styles of Interviewing. Unpublished Ph.D. dissertation, Western Reserve University, 1961.

Weber, Ruth. Children's Verbal Accessibility as a Predictor of Treatment Outcome. Unpublished DSW dissertation, Western Reserve University, 1963.

Weisman, Avery D. "Silence and Psychotherapy," *Psychiatry, 18,* 1955, 241–260.

Zeligs, Meyer A. "The Psychology of Silence: Its Role in Transference, Countertransference and the Psychoanalytic Process," *Journal of the American Psychoanalytic Association, 9,* 1961, 7–43.

Chapter 10

On Duplicity in the Interview

WE CAN DISTINGUISH BETWEEN TWO BROAD TYPES OF formulations in social casework and psychotherapy. On the one hand, there are ideas relevant to over-all management of the case—the strategy of treatment. On the other, there are notions about details of the procedure—treatment tactics. In this chapter we will discuss the latter level of theorizing as well as illustrate the way ego psychology is used in daily practice.

Because it is the major milieu of our professional helping, the face-to-face interview remains the most important area for tactical skill. Proficiency in the art of interviewing is a *sine qua non* of expert casework or therapy. One would therefore expect a host of publications on the theory and technique of casework interviewing, but there is no such collection. Perhaps it is difficult to write about such things, and we are here dealing with a skill and set of guiding principles best imparted and learned in relation to concrete experiences. The obverse is that broad generalizations about "how to interview" are ludicrous. They teeter on the knife-edge that divides the high-minded from the simple-minded. After years in practice, it is a bit discouraging to reread an essay touted to the pious as a classic admonition in our field. How profound was the advice to the earnest student, "start where the client is!" Was there a choice?

Another reason for trepidation about writing on interviewing is the opinion of one's friends. Much of what a worker has learned over the years is property owned jointly with his peers. Who shall have the temerity to act as synthesizer for us all? Yet I have been encouraged by responses in institutes with graduate social workers to set down some of these thoughts. Not final answers, they may serve to stimulate useful dialogue toward further clarification.

The theoretical context for the present analysis has been given in earlier chapters. I dealt with the phenomenon of verbal accessibility as a structural variable, an enduring facet of the client's personality. Now we move on to view the client's verbal accessibility more dynamically, as it fluctuates in the immediate interaction of the interview. Our interest will be on forces *restraining* or *inhibiting* direct, spontaneous communication in the interview. In order to lay bare some of these complex motivations, I shall concentrate on speech by clients that represents blocked, or partially-blocked, communication. Following Kaiser (Fierman, 1965, pp. 54ff), I have characterized such speech as representing "duplicity" in the interview.

Silence usually represents an extreme of blocked communication, but we will not discuss it here. Silence in the interview is of less practical concern to most caseworkers than to psychoanalysts, for example (Zeligs, 1961). For one thing, we are not often in a relationship likely to survive massive resistances. Indeed, there is a question whether it is advisable to continue a casework relationship if it seems to represent so powerful a threat as to invoke stubborn refusals to talk.

Duplicity in the Interview

Kaiser does not explicitly define duplicity. He prefers to illustrate what he has in mind through examples, parables, the device of the dialogue. This form of European *Gemütlichkeit* may be the only way to convey a conception rich in apperceptive mass, but some American professionals find this style discombobulating (Higgins, 1966). Therefore, I shall submit my own definition.

There are two related features of verbal communications that we call duplicity. First, the same words are made to serve two purposes, even as they are being spoken—purposes that are often at right angles to each other, or even directly conradictory. Thus, the client's overt intention is to describe his situation to the caseworker. But the clarity of what he offers is substantially dissipated because he is preoccupied with the need to evoke a particular feeling-response, even as he gives "facts."

The second aspect of duplicity derives from Kaiser's comment that the speaker does not appear to "stand behind his words." The speaker does not seem all of a piece. A psychiatrically naive client once commented that he felt "fragmented," and this was certainly reflected in the convolutions of his speech. Often, after one points out to a client the manner in which he has presented himself, he will say, more in relief than rancor, "I have long felt myself a phony."

I am very well aware that some of the examples of duplicity I shall give have usually been put in other contexts. Speaking in an illogical or seemingly irrational manner may be ascribed to a structural defect, such as "looseness" or "scatter"— which can represent organic damage, among other things. It is by no means my intention to imply that such interpretations are always incorrect. However, I have often found a mode of speaking that seemed at first to reflect an essential thought disturbance was *actually within the control of the ego* and being used defensively.

Two main defensive functions are likely to be subserved by duplicity in communication. They may be labeled *maneuvers to evade responsibility* and *maneuvers to retain control.*

Maneuvers to Evade Responsibility

The main task of the client in the casework situation is to contribute his share to a purposive conversation. Any leading themes there may be in his motivations or defensive needs are likely to become noteworthy in the way he goes about speaking. I am indebted to the paper by Enelow (1960) for recognizing that the client's problem in assuming responsibility will show itself as a desire to evade responsibility *for his own words!* But why should he wish to do this?

Enelow summarizes concisely what the stakes are for the client. In order to "stand behind his words," the person must have evolved an image of himself as an independent entity, expressing what *he believes.* But the assumption of an explicit identity implies the acceptance of his *aloneness,* an experience that is basic for everyone, but which continues to be frightening to some of us throughout life. To cope with this awareness-of-separation anxiety, Kaiser postulated that neurotics entertain a *delusion of fusion.* The client who cannot bear his separateness will maneuver to create this illusion in real life. In the interview, this will come through as an attempt to create a situation as if the client, and the worker, were somehow blended into a larger whole. He will imply that he is moved not by his own motivations but somehow as an extension of the caseworker, or of someone else. Indeed, so strong may be the fusion-fantasy that the client may prefer to see himself as "forced," so long as this means someone else is taking responsibility, even if his response to this, in turn, is to feel put upon, and therefore indignant! Below are some illustrations of how this type of duplicity is visible in action; several were drawn from Enelow, the rest are from my observations in interviewing.

1. Creating a situation in which one is *asked to speak.* The client begins an account of some happening that presumably is relevant to what he is doing with the caseworker. Unaccountably, he trails off into silence in the middle of the tale, until the worker says, "So?" or "You were saying?"

2. Being *unable to speak first.* The client is silent, needing the worker to "Make it easier" for him to talk. Easing his way usually consists simply in the worker's saying something, thereby taking responsibility for the conversation's beginning. Related to this decision reluctance is inability to choose a topic—e.g., "Tell me what I should talk about."

3. Offering *conversational bait.* This consists in beginning a story, proceeding to a critical point, and then asking, "Guess what happened?" Beyond the dramatics, the aim also is to get the worker to say "Tell me."

4. *Surfing on someone else's conversational wave.* The same client who at first finds it difficult to choose a topic on his own may yet finish the worker's sentences, from the middle.

5. Administering a *conversational* Rorschach. The prime example is the client who mumbles in an inaudible voice. He appears to be speaking, but he does not wish to commit himself by enunciating clearly. It is as if he were saying, "I offer you some clues. Interpret them as you will, and then respond to what you think I said."

6. Skulking behind the *declamatory question.* "So he made me mad. Wouldn't anyone be angry?" In this claim to universality, the client announces that he does not want his reaction questioned or discussed. Why does he not simply say so?

7. The *optional pass play.* This client demonstrates a kind of verbal doing and undoing such as the worker last encountered in the writings of classical philosophers—except that our offices seem not quite the place for Kant. He uses the device mentioned earlier, "I'm a man of firm convictions, one on each side of the issue." Greedily retaining all options through his indecisiveness, he plays it safe. The worker is then enticed either to clarify for the client or at

least to be the one to insist that he clarify where he stands.

8. Coming on *pilgrimage to the oracle*. The client watches the worker's face with an expectancy that hovers between the worship of a Beatle fan and the deathwatch of a hopeful heir. He has an intense desire to find agreement or support for what he is saying; indeed, he will cheerfully reverse the *words* he is using to achieve this. But of course he will not ask for this outright. "If you really loved me, you would know what I need."

9. Putting *one's foot in another's mouth*. The client offers a selected quote from uncollected thoughts. "My husband said you're not fit to sleep with pigs, but I plead your case." By adroit tactlessness, the client lets the worker have the bad news, while simultaneously setting up friction with a third party.

10. Taking the *loyalty oath*. This client, evidently without any sense of doing something unusual, consistently refers his opinions to some outsider. "My father always said. . . ." "My husband told me. . . ." More sophisticated, somehow, is the version, "I was brought up to believe . . . , which leaves open the question of who now does the believing for the speaker. Manly, and felt as suitable, but completely analogous is the statement, "Where I come from, they say. . . ."

I have described these operations as if they were consciously thought out and devised as traps for the unwary caseworker. In my experience, the client who employs these devices usually is selectively inattentive to them and quite unaware that they play a role in his interview behavior. Not only the intent but even the style of the maneuver may be unconscious.

Maneuvers to Retain Control

We are all familiar with the client who has to take over the interview process, lest we fumble it. Yet, when one asks colleagues why clients do this, the ideas about it are rather vague. The client is said to be a "controlling" person, or he expresses an infantile will-to-power, as if these were fundamental givens in the personality, with further analysis unnecessary. The strong desire to control the interview also serves defensive purposes, in most instances. What are some typical dynamics?

One reason a client may constantly have to structure¹ every relationship into a power hierarchy, with constant jockeying for position, is the associations he has to the issue, "Who is the stronger?" After some help, it may become evident to client and worker that the former is *contemptuous* of weakness, in a rigid, merciless way which derives, I imagine, from the scrupulous distinction he makes between the "good mother-bad mother" images. But recognizing his contempt may come easier for him than registering his *fear* of being weak. For to be weak is to be vulnerable, according to the formula, "If you are the stronger, you will be able to walk away and leave me." Hence, there may be a need to dominate (as to infantilize) those in his environment, in order to escape the ultimate catastrophe of being left alone.

Another reason he struggles to control the interview is that, in his way of living, he is constantly *comparing*—himself with others, others with others. With this client, one will sooner or later come to a recognition of a deep sense of inadequacy, but this is not to be mistaken for the core of the disturbance. The question is why the client has not come to terms with what he has to work with, in himself, so that he can go about the business of getting what he can out of life. To tell such a person he has to "love yourself before you can love others" is to talk nonsense, for he is already quite adequately engrossed with himself. Rather than saying he is in love with himself, it would be more accurate to say that he is in love with an *image for* himself. Indeed, he is addicted to polishing the image.

In many such persons, we find a history of having felt *detached,* as a result of the mother-child relationship. The child, perplexed by this, feels he is somehow odd, not as others, even not quite human. Therefore he takes the only way out he can think of: if he acts like others, he gradually should become one with them. Although this home remedy is understandable, as life works out it is ill-advised, for the problem of detachment persists. In the struggle to be human, rather than a piece of waste, a "nothing," there is an intense intolerance of criticism, along with other symptoms, such as preoccupation with matters of *shame* and *blame*. This concern with "Have I dirtied myself?" is confused occasionally with guilt, by younger workers. The client will welcome such mislabeling of his preconscious feelings, for defensive reasons, even though he has not internalized others' standards to a degree that would make guilt meaningful in his case. But with fear lest something unexpected come out—which he hopes for, but dreads— the need to maintain control of the situation is of course heightened.

These dynamics will usually be found in constellations, overdetermining the inability of the client to conceive of a relationship between equals, and one in which neither is in danger of being absorbed by the other. The attention and motivated cunning he devotes to one-upmanship in the interview signals us regarding the concealed anxiety.

With such general background regarding the impulse to control, let us turn next to some typical, by no means mutually exclusive, examples of how this pattern may play itself out in the interview.

1. *Circumstantiality*. This hardly needs discussion as a method by which clients succeed in dominating the interview. Talking at length, with tedious attention to emotionally neutral details of the environment or events, the client keeps the conversation in his own mouth. He avoids having to face questions he would not like to consider, effectively shuts off comments he would not like to hear, and so forth. A frequently cited characteristic of the voluble client is that he engulfs the hearer, surrounding him with amoeba-like pseudopodia. The connection with living out the fusion-fantasy is obvious.

2. *Planned adolescence*. Sometimes related to compul-

sive talking is a flightiness that makes it hard for us to catch what the client is trying to get at. If the worker feels confused, it is always possible this was the client's intention, and the main thing to be understood from his talk. Perhaps the client cannot afford to be too logical; if he were to think in a straight line, he would find himself drawing conclusions in areas he would rather not face. Similar comments apply to the related tactic of presenting oneself as a "good little girl" but incapable of sustained thought.

3. Speaking in *pronouncements*. Another maneuver, similar to circumstantiality but less markedly controlling, is for the client to conduct his side of the conversation as if the worker were an audience. Although he presumably came for help, even after a few interviews the client still almost never asks a question! A typical reason for not asking is that the client is not sure he will like the answer. Hence, he may go as far as to comment, "Now I know what you'd say. . . ." With others, the avoidance of questions is related to the obsession with perfection. There is fear (unconscious of course), or hating to have to ask, for this is an admission there is something one does not already know. I frequently have found that this pattern was already established during the school years, and it partly accounted for the client's unwillingness to raise his hand in class when he did not understand.

4. Turning in *homework*. The lecture to the caseworker may go better if the speaker has his notes in hand. Many clients think about what they want to discuss (or talk about?) in advance of their next appointment, some to the extent of preparing written memoranda. This step presents problems for handling, because after all the carryover into life outside the office-hour is a desired indication of the penetration of the casework. However, we must bear very much in mind that preliminary work usually includes preparation for what is *not* to be said, as well. Because I believe in the importance of helping the client to express himself directly, I am most reluctant to deal with written communications. The practice (to save time!) of having the

client *write* his autobiography also seems potentially destructive to an active treatment.

5. *Escape into love.* This maneuver does not require much commentary, except to emphasize that "transference" does not begin to describe the way such feelings can be used. The extreme form, in which a client actually seduces a therapist (the latter usually thinks it was his idea!) is typified by: "How can you ask me to talk about all this unpleasantness in myself, when you're a boy and I'm a girl?" Another version, less sexualized, is: "I did not tell you, because I did not want to hurt you." Escape into love is used for defensive control as well as to cover the hostile phase of the transference.

6. *Escape into hate.* This gambit has been reported less often than escape into love, but it certainly is used. With great difficulty, for instance, we get the client—who has been dropping pretty broad hints—to say, "I guess I don't really like you." As we indicated in Chapter 6, there are a variety of reasons for this feeling which, I must emphasize, is experienced as quite real. In the present connection, however, I want merely to point to its use as a lever. The implication is that the caseworker should now watch his step and try to get into the client's good graces. This is similar to the schizoid adolescent's remark: "I don't trust you." It is not possible to meet the demand for a guarantee of course, nor is it conducive to the youngster's reality testing to imply that trust is gained from discussing it intellectually. So long as we are being as straightforward and dependable as we can be, we should guard against giving up our own independence of action. To do this will destroy "trust" on a deeper level, for the client will recognize it as either weakness or a cheap attempt to seduce him for obscure purposes. With a bit of exploration, it usually comes out, anyway, that such a youngster feels unable to trust anybody—and this is the real problem.

7. Invidious *comparisons with one's predecessor.* There are a number of functions served by discussing one's relation to a previous worker. The one I want to emphasize is

the use of such a description as an indirect way of prescribing one's own treatment. In telling us what he did and did not like about the former treatment, the client also lets us know what he prefers. Of course he may have a point when he obliquely criticizes us in this way, but why not bring it out openly?

8. *Passive resistance.* In addition to the desire to evade responsibility, the use of passive control is another good reason to employ the "tell me what to talk about . . ." routine.

9. *Coercive tears.* Some tears are sad, and some are mad, and the fundamental mission of anger is to move the environment into line with one's needs. It is sometimes terribly hard to distinguish what lies behind a client's tears, but there is no doubt they often interrupt a painful line of thought, distract both worker and client, make us feel unaccountably guilty, and so forth.

10. The *hard sell.* This is another mode of relating, familiar to us all. And it is the client at his most dramatic and convincing moments. Except that a little voice within us complains, "Methinks thou doth protest too much." Super-salesmanship is identified with the ill-defined group we call hysterical personalities (of both sexes). However, as in escape into love, it is easy to overlook the defensive controllingness that lies behind the dramatics as behind the sexiness.

11. The great *debate.* Litigiousness is pervasive in the patterns of many people, although they will argue whether this is really true of their behavior. The function it serves, for some at least, is to counteract the sense of emptiness and nothingness; in "standing against" they feel suddenly more sure of themselves, and more of a piece. A person with such needs will manipulate the caseworker by arguing, to argue.

12. *Mea culpa.* The extreme form of this self-recrimination is often found in an agitated depression that has reached hospitalizable proportions. My caricature of the sequence is: The client acts as prosecutor and files a list of

complaints; he sits as a judge at the trial, ruling on admissibility of evidence; as jury, he hears the case in hostile silence; finally, as defendant, he pleads guilty—to the wrong charge! Nothing bossy about all this; nobody mad at being crossed by life.

13. *Self-derogation.* We could devote an entire chapter to the various functions of "running oneself into the ground." The client may be making himself out as a mess, to spite one of his parents, or both; indeed, he may be caricaturing one of them, as in male homosexual "camping." "Look what a ridiculous thing you are, and have produced." He may be warding off demands for achievement (which he exaggerates). "From whom little has been given, little can be expected." Frequently he is wincing against expected bad news about himself by keeping the process of breaking it in his own hands. Or he may exaggerate his defects because he does not want clarity or self-definition. The non-committed outline he maintains (for he does not believe the bad things he says of himself) is, in turn, useful for two other purposes: he can maintain a secretly vaunted opinion of what he would be like if he ever *tried;* and the indefiniteness of his self-image facilitates the process of losing himself in some other—the fantasy of fusion. Obviously, the last thing the worker can afford is to let himself be provoked into sympathetic reassurance, in the face of all this complexity!

14. The *structured use of time.* I am convinced that long before the Rankians decided to use the time-dimension in structuring casework treatment, clients did (Taft, 1933). Think how the end of the hour can be used. Painful material may be delayed until then so that not much can come of it. Important decisions, which the client wants to make a gesture of having "discussed," but does not really want to, will be introduced with the remark, "I did mean to ask you today what you think I ought to do about. . . ." The other possibility, of course, is that this "material" is offered as an enticement to delay the ending of the hour, which the patient finds painful, as he does any separation experience.

Out of the same concern, by the way, he may break off the hour prematurely, unable to stand having separation imposed ("You can't fire me, I quit."). This type of reaction is noteworthy, as it may well signal the way the client precipitates other endings in his life. So fearful is he of its possible ending that he cannot take getting involved in a relationship. This familiar dynamic reflects itself in the interview.

All clinicians in their own practices can make a list similar to this one. The patterns are labeled "maneuvers." At this point, it does not yet matter which we see the more frequently. We are still at the stage of specimen-collecting in which to be able to say that a given pattern *did* occur, and to begin to ascribe its function, is quite enough. Quantitative issues may be relevant later. Hardly any of the maneuvers cited here will be found to be used *only* in the service of a defensive need to control. But our task was to select those patterns for which this is at least one of the motivations. Finally, there is the obvious question whether the list would not profit by further grouping, or extending, in terms of a deeper grasp of ego functions involved, semantic clarification. I believe this will prove true, but at this stage of work on the theory of interviewing we should be wary of a premature lumping to conclusions.

Handling

We have seen a variety of ways in which duplicity is displayed. At one time or other, each of us undoubtedly uses one or more of these maneuvers, for reasons similar to our clients'. The dread of loneliness is a universal anxiety, and the delusion of fusion a position to which any one of us might fall back, more or less persistently. The question that naturally follows, therefore, is: What should the worker do when faced with these maneuvers in an interview?

We have to judge whether, after unveiling the fears being concealed, a less crippling way of dealing with them is likely to be found. How necessary is his defense to the client, at this point? Will our relationship bear strain? While one might routinely note the peculiar forms of duplicity being employed, as part of continuing diagnosis in all contacts with clients, in a good many instances noting them may be all we can do. Nevertheless, a serious reading of the theory involved encourages an activist stance. For a client, or anyone else, to cling to an illusion of one-ness is a poor substitute for true closeness to fellow humans on a more mature basis. It neither heals nor satisfies. Kaiser postulated that whatever would make it more possible for the client to talk directly and honestly in the interview would be a step in the direction of better emotional functioning, and this is certainly true in our experience. Rather than recounting the contraindications to intervention, let us list some situations in which a caseworker might find it worthwhile to try to penetrate duplicity.

The most obvious is one in which the client has come for help with a problem he sees as in his own functioning, or in an important interpersonal relationship that is marred by how he operates as a person. The worker may have to try to dissolve such patterns in seeking to establish, or re-establish, communication within a family. Distortions or blocks in communication are frequently stepped around in contacts concerned mainly with "environmental manipulation." Yet, from work with prison inmates and transient men, for example, many of us have long concluded it may well be all the more important to get down "to tacks" as quickly as possible in such cases. So long as the client is keeping us, and himself, in the dark about his real wishes, and his chances, our conversations toward joint planning will be farcical. Often, until we can get the other person to stop his double-talk, at least momentarily, it is well-nigh impossible to get any case history on a relative. We must also confront the fact that there are instances in which the caseworker's willingness to accept the client's indirection is a potentially noxious side effect of his "tact." Even in routine calls on recipients of AFDC, for example, acceptance of evasion in place of honest talk can only contribute to an image of weakness and insincerity. At some point, collusion in evasive conversation becomes corrupting.

Assuming, then, that we want to do something about breaking through the duplicity, what do we do? Kaiser gives us only a very general picture of the principles he found useful, and I do not believe they are a quite accurate image of his own *modus operandi* (Fierman, 1965, pp. 158f). Here are my own, therefore, which are perhaps still not much of an improvement. I begin with a few general principles and go on to some specific techniques.

1. Because much duplicity reflects the client's fear of experiencing his own separate identity, anything that helps the resolution of the confusion or noncommitment will be a step toward greater verbal accessibility. The obverse is also true: one can treat identity diffusion in part by trying to help the client commit himself about what he means.

2. The worker should try to watch for duplicity in his own talk with clients. While we may not find it strategic to verbalize everything we happen to be thinking, we should try to be sure we can stand behind what we do say. This kind of behavior by the worker offers the client a role model out of which he may incorporate greater directness of speech. There also appears to be what Jourard and Landsman (1960) termed a *dyadic effect*. It is harder to maintain duplicity with someone who does not play this game (e.g., a literal ten-year-old).

3. Insofar as possible, the caseworker should aim for plain English, regardless of the social and intellectual status of his client, and expect it in return. This means the cliches of the slums are quite as open to the comment "I don't get you" as is the argot of the professions. While it is not really necessary, as Heywood Broun once commented, to "call a spade a dirty, lousy spade," verbal shock is not routinely to be avoided, despite its dangers.

4. In common with Enelow (1960), I have found that an easy way to get through several forms of duplicity in clinical interviews is simply to ask the client to fill you in with con-

crete details and specific facts, especially when these seem to be evaded.

5. Requesting clarification works very well with perhaps a voting majority of clients, and often it leads to greater commitment on the part of the client. For example, I do not believe it useful to say to the client who makes opposing statements about the same thing, "I see you feel two ways about. . . ." Rather, one might recall with him the statements, ask him which one he means—or does he mean both? For the worker to label his ambivalence for him provides no challenge to the client's synthesizing ability. By the way, I find very few instances in which a client will lie outright to me, and in pushing for clarification, it is sometimes helpful to say openly that this is not what one has in mind.

6. In a large number of cases, the inability of the client to be verbally accessible derives from his intolerance of imperfection in himself. If he misrepresents his feelings, it may be hard for him to "take it back"; instead, he may waste effort on repairing the old statement. There are many rigid persons who *over*value the spoken word, for they see it as a product of themselves. They may feel it necessary to act upon whatever they have found themselves saying even if it was only part of what they felt. (This represents a danger in the technique we are describing.) Hence, the issue of being able to admit error is often worth reviewing. It seems quite appropriate for the worker to comment at times that what he has said does not fit what he meant to say—something that will come hard to the know-it-alls of our mental health professions.

I am aware that these remarks sound as if I do not believe that slips often—perhaps, usually—directly reflect the unconscious. I do, of course. Once again, however, I would urge that there may be other motivations in addition to the one revealed in a slip, and that to "stand behind one's words" one must take them *all* into account. To assume routinely that the "slip always represents the true feeling" is both oversimplified and pedantic.

7. The need to aim for precision of expression has been mentioned. How can it be implemented? A client often deals with an issue that is chronic and repetitive. If the worker has to keep pointing out the same thing, he must try to do so in a different way in successive interviews. The aim is to avoid getting trapped in one's own word-ruts, whose sounds gradually lose impact for client *and* worker. A second device is to substitute figures of speech for abstractions. The best example which comes to my mind is to contrast the color of the direct translation from the Hebrew of a pastoral people, in our services, with the generalities in the sermon of a recent divinity school product. "The Lord is my rock . . ." vs. "Are we dedicating our lives to the eternal verities?"—meaning, some people in this congregation will steal from the poor. Interpretation by parable also works well in most cases, but requires ingenuity.

Finally, there is the question of using examples from one's own life. Here the dangers are that one will either imply that "to do as I do is to be normal, healthy, and virtuous" or reveal too-intimate facts that will deeply color the relationship. I often find it useful to comment on how I am feeling *at the moment,* in the interview, as a way of "reflecting back" effects on me of the client's behavior. Occasionally vignettes from one's own more outside life may be useful, but they have to be used with discretion. However, freedom to reveal one's feelings *in the present interaction* may serve a role-model function for the client, as it does for the group in group therapy. Obviously I take a dim view of trying to exploit the "dyadic effect" (Jourard and Landsman, 1960) by talking much about oneself in casework treatment. The dangers from one's own exhibitionism far outweigh the presumed gains: the whole maneuver is clinically too sloppy, as I see it.

8. Euphemisms are frequently as revealing, and filled with duplicity, as are cliches. "I have this little problem with weight" may mean, "I'm a greedy slob." Depending on the timing in the relationship, and whether the client has *yet* shown visible signs of a sense of humor (most do, as they

improve), the self-serving function of wood-pussy language often can be depicted simply by echoing it, with a slightly questioning tone. To join the client in euphemisms, after a certain point, is not helpful. Worse, it can prove unnerving, since the client (who has some sense of what he is doing) may wonder how dangerous or disgusting is the symptom that the worker, too, must circumvent discussing it.

I could add to this list, but it grows long. Besides, the more criteria one lays down about how to be verbally accessible, the more impossible it becomes to say anything at all —a fact worth bearing in mind. After all, an obsession with being "honest," such as adolescent clients proudly wave at us, can become as inhibiting of freedom of speech as it is of assembly. I like to say that the older I get, the more I will settle for at least a decent hypocrisy in my fellow man. Does not our hypocrisy have the right of spontaneous expression, too?

This chapter has dealt with a single aspect of client behavior as it is experienced in the casework interview. A form of blocked, or partially defended, communication has been identified which, following Kaiser, we have termed *duplicity*. In the present context, this is seen as a pattern, which is postulated as ultimately a defense against the fear of experiencing one's aloneness. Two categories of maneuvers have evolved—maneuvers to escape responsibility and maneuvers to retain control—and examples of each were given. Finally, some suggestions were made regarding modes of operation by the caseworker that may prove useful in helping the client overcome his tendency to use these defenses, momentarily or as part of a more pervasive life pattern.

We offer this as a contribution to the conceptual formalization of casework technique, on the molecular level of skill in the interview. It relies heavily on the insights of Hellmuth Kaiser in psychotherapy, but seeks to specify them and relate them to the casework process. In so doing we have tried to make vivid for the reader an arena in which the various concepts of ego psychology find intensive and fruitful application.

References

Enelow, A. J. "The Silent Patient," *Psychiatry, 23,* 1960, 153–158.

Fierman, L. B., ed. *Effective Psychotherapy: The Contribution of Hellmuth Kaiser.* New York: The Free Press, 1965.

Higgins, J. W. "Review of Fierman," *American Journal of Psychiatry, 122,* 1966, 1194.

Jourard, S. M., and M. J. Landsman. "Cognition, Cathexis and the 'Dyadic Effect' in Men's Self-Disclosing Behavior," *Merrill-Palmer Quarterly, 7,* 1960, 178–186.

Polansky, N. A. "The Concept of Verbal Accessibility," *Smith College Studies in Social Work, 36,* 1965, 1–48.

Taft, Jessie. *The Dynamics of Therapy in a Controlled Relationship.* New York: Macmillan, 1933.

Zeligs, M. A. "The Psychology of Silence; Its Role in Transference, Countertransference and the Psychoanalytic Process," *Journal of the American Psychoanalytic Association, 9,* 1961, 7–43.

Chapter 11

Ego Functions in Psychodrama

IT IS TYPICAL OF NEARLY ALL TRAINEES IN CASEWORK OR psychotherapy that they can tolerate receptivity for only so long. Sooner, rather than later, they break in with "This is all well and good, but what do I do?" At that point, I tell them what I was told in my time. "In order to do, one must first understand. If you fully understand, the question of what to do is easy." Of course that is not completely true, and they know it, and I know it. The jump from analysis of what is wrong to deductions about how to repair it does not happen automatically. Besides, the learner can understand only so much at any one sitting before he feels the urge to try some of it out on somebody, if only to retaliate against the instructor for telling him things about himself that are hard to swallow. Perhaps it is as well that this is true of those destined to be practitioners rather than simply knowers in our fields. If their defenses were so organized as to permit endless immobility and analysis, it might not be safe for their clients and patients. Art is long, and science is eternal but, as Lord Keynes reminded us, "In the long run, we shall all be dead." Certainly, it is important to move as rapidly as possible from knowing to doing. The question is, "How rapidly?"

This is not a "how-to" book, nor was it intended to be. Nevertheless, despite deliberate limits in this introductory book, it has seemed useful at times to mention treatment techniques, as I did regarding the management of duplicity. Techniques serve to illustrate how the ego operates; much of what I know came originally from my own attempts at treatment. For these reasons I think it appropriate to introduce a few examples of ways to apply what we know about the ego.

The last chapter offered an application of ego psychology to the process of the interview. It would be profitable, next, to show how the theory works in some form of group treatment. But which group treatment? Today everyone is doing something to groups, and there is an endless literature on group therapy, group dynamics, human relations, subhuman sub-relations. I decided it might be more interesting to the reader to use as illustration a form of treatment of which he will have heard, but which has become less in vogue as wilder forms of mutual psychological undressing are being indulged in by the current refugees from young people's church groups.

Our topic will be psychodrama and the ego mechanisms and functions that become most visible when treating emotionally ill people. We shall see, again, the varied ways in which *communication*—verbal and nonverbal—can take place, how it may be used in the service of defense, or harnessed to the service of therapy. We shall also comment on the *self-observing functions of the ego,* varieties of *identification,* including some which are unwanted, and deliberately *induced regressions* whose aim is the furtherance of treatment. The material in this chapter has been revised from a paper written with Elizabeth B. Harkins.

Psychodrama is a powerful modality in the psychotherapies which has not had the widespread application its potentialities warrant. Few prestigious psychiatric facilities maintain ongoing programs. Although many mental health professionals have had at least some exposure to the technique, it is treated as if it were expected to be a passing interest. One is embarrassed in some circles to confess to a fascination with psychodrama extending over a period of years.

One seldom finds psychodrama approached with the combination of hopeful curiosity and scientific skepticism that has served to develop social casework and psychotherapy to their present stages. Our view is that the method is neither a panacea nor a nullity. It is a mode of treatment that can be helpful to a good proportion of patients a fair proportion of the time—which is about all one can say about any of the psychotherapies.

We arrived at this appraisal despite considerable initial dubiousness. There are, understandably, a number of reasons why the method has not gained more popularity. Most of us prefer our method of treatment to be grounded on a well-developed general theory of personality, such as the psychoanalytic. Psychodrama as a movement seems fixated at the curious professional phase in which a promising technique has yielded new insights into human personality and its enthusiasts then try to erect a whole theoretical metropolis along these few avenues of vision. "Psychodrama's scientific roots are buried deep in Moreno's philosophies of spontaneity, creativity, the moment, and theories of role and interaction" (Yablonsky and Enneis, 1956, p. 149). It is not necessary to accept all of Moreno's metatheory in order to avail one's patients of the benefits of the technique which he and his co-workers have done so much to develop.

Other factors have inhibited the spread of psychodrama. For one thing, its demands are incompatible with the character defenses of many fine individual therapists, thus violating their preferences even more than does group therapy. It requires interpersonal energy, moment-to-moment inventiveness, and occasional controlled flamboyance in a measure not all of us have. Because of the spontaneity necessarily involved, the therapists are open to intensive group scrutiny. Even the intensity of nonverbal communication released in the group is uncomfortable for therapists who like to hide behind abstractions.

The psychodrama situation involves a focal patient (the *protagonist*) embedded in a group situation. At its best, it is lively and complex. Only a megalomaniac would presume to have all strands of the individual and group process under observation, much less precise control. It is necessary to take calculated risks, again and again. Finally, psychodrama is a technique that can drain the worker; he grows tired, and resistant to conducting sessions after six or more months of continual working, especially with hospitalized psychotics and character disorders.

Despite these drawbacks, we persisted with this mode of treatment, trying to improve our skills in its use and to understand better its rationale. We were mature practitioners at the time, more impressed by new results than new formulations. Our persistence came from the knowledge that from time to time exciting results were achieved with some patients who otherwise were left untouched.

An example occurred early in our experience. I had in inpatient treatment a twenty-year-old young man who had been admitted after having been found in the basement of his home in a confused state, and with blood streaming from his forehead, which he had lacerated by beating his head against the basement wall. In the hospital, the confusion cleared rapidly, but he settled into an extremely passive, superficially amenable young fellow with a firm, schizoid grasp on futility and no recollection of the events preceding his admission. He described his mother as extremely hostile and hypercritical verbally; her indifference toward him and her general self-centeredness also evidenced amply during his stay. A marked characteristic was his massive affect-inhibition. He was taken into psychodrama with the hope that this would stir something in him, but here, as elsewhere, he continued his plan of sitting life out.

One day we proposed he enact a scene. He suggested nothing specific, of course, but accepted the idea that it might be useful to show how he related to his mother. He told the group about her verbal temper tantrums and assaults, and proudly announced that he had developed a method of simply not hearing her. Mrs. Harkins assumed the role of the mother, and began a tirade, to which the patient showed no reaction, at first, but he finally admitted some unease. We continued, nevertheless, and I fell into the role of "doubling" (i.e., speaking out what I imagined might be the patient's thoughts) from behind him. Because his individual therapist was speaking, the meaning to the patient was all the stronger. As the scene continued, it suddenly occurred to me that the picture of stubborn resentment of the mother which had been expressed in individual treatment did not fully account for the patient's discomfiture. Still *verbalizing for the patient,* I asked, "How can you be so mean to me when I love you so much?"

The impact on the patient was startling to all of us. He pitched forward from his chair, sobbing like a small child in a blend of anger and despair, and *beating his forehead against the floor!* Concerned lest he harm himself, it was all I could do to wrest his glasses from his face, and then gradually hold him and quiet him, reminding him that he *was* in a hospital, I was there, and no harm would come to him.

Naturally the group was upset, and several other patients were also crying, but we resisted our impulse to isolate the protagonist at this point. Taking him away would be even more frightening to the group. Then and there, we had a brief discussion when he felt better. For the first time he recalled that: (a) he had severe temper tantrums throughout his early childhood; (b) there was a favorite place on the dining room baseboard where he had butted his head at such times; (c) he would sob to the point that he had "asthmatic attacks." None of this had come out in the history given by the patient or by his parents. Neither had he been willing to know that what made his hatred of his mother so upsetting was the fact that he also loved her. Of course the episode he had just completed was a replica of the scene with his mother which led to his hospitalization in the first place.

This excerpt from a long treatment process illustrates what can possibly occur in psychodrama: communication at the level of action and imagery; massive ventilation but also clarification for both therapist and patient; regression in the service of the ego for therapeutic change; and ultimately, rather sudden emergence of repressed images and feelings. We were impressed by the continuity of psychodrama with other forms of analytically-oriented psychotherapy—this is apparent in the varied therapeutic functions performed as well as in the common conceptual formulations applicable.

The peculiar features of this modality which we will emphasize here are: (1) If one views communication on a developmental continuum moving more or less from action, through concrete imagery, to abstract symbols, psychodrama is characterized by the unusually broad spectrum it can employ in the course of a single session. (2) Psychodrama makes possible communication in rich detail; this facilitates maximum reintegration of ideas and affects by the focal patient as well as the emergence of new clarifications and insights not otherwise reached. From this detail and breadth—including the primitiveness—of communication flow the special advantages and dangers in the use of this method.

In carrying out our intent, we first note a similarity of psychodrama to all the other psychotherapies. Provided one has some talent for it, psychodrama is easier to do than to teach; and it is easier to teach than it is to analyze.

Structure of Psychodrama in Our Hospital

Highland Hospital is a private, general psychiatric hospital of about 120 beds. The professional staff consists of eight psychiatrists, one clinical psychologist, and seven social workers. Our hospital has a tradition of a strong activities department, which makes it suitable for patients requiring longer stays and for young patients. Median length of stay fluctuated around four months.

Historically, psychodrama was initiated in 1962 at the behest of the former Clinical Director, Dr. John D. Patton. The program has been staffed over the years almost entirely by members of the Social Service Department, although this has been more a matter of interest than an exclusive policy. By now, psychodrama is a generally accepted part of the hospital's armamentarium of treatment, no more or less glamorous than other services.

Most of those currently in psychodrama are inpatients. However, we do have a number who, following discharge, continue to attend sessions as outpatients. We have never established any strict criteria about which patients to include, other than in the opinion of the individual's psychiatrist he was likely to "get something out of it," and was currently in reasonable contact. We continue to accept patients with a highly experimental attitude about selection. It would be fair to consider the treatment population a typical inpatient group who are not currently severely disturbed.

The format of our conduct of a session follows rather closely that described in the fundamental papers by Moreno (1958) and Yablonsky and Enneis (1956). To quote the latter, "Psychodramatic therapy has five essential components: the group, the subject or *protagonist*, the psychodramatist or *director*, his therapeutic aides or *auxiliary egos*, and a system of methods and techniques adaptable to the requirements of the situation" (p. 150). We did not feel committed to their structure from the start. Rather, we have found no good reason for major shifts from their sound design. We have always operated in ordinary large rooms, with the patients seated either in a half-circle or in the round. Props have been adapted from the objects in the room—with card tables, folding chairs, ashtrays, and a couch perhaps offering the greatest flexibility in imaginary uses to which they can be put. From experience, we believe we would be uncomfortable using a raised "stage." As to specific techniques used, we have either followed many methods cited in the literature or created new ones, sometimes out of ignorance of other's work. However, several features in our situation appear to differ from the main trends in published reports.

First, we do not believe that psychodrama can, by itself, effect a "cure" of a seriously neurotic or disturbed patient. All our patients are simultaneously in individual psychotherapy. We try to have events in the psychodrama coordinate with and feed back into the individual work, where they can be dealt with more intensively under circumstances of greater therapeutic precision and control. Second, our patients are simultaneously receiving a variety of other treatments, including group therapy, the protection of the hospital environment, participation in organized activities to promote resocialization, and often chemotherapy. Therefore, we feel it desirable to be specific about what we try to do in psychodrama which adds something different from the other therapies.

One consequence of this appraisal of the technique as frankly *ancillary* has been our view of verbalization. We do not favor providing the focal patient, or protagonist, with still another setting in which just to *talk* about his problems. Rather, psychodrama is seen as the place one begins by *externalizing* one's feelings and images, with acting and in action. We make practically no use of the device Moreno called the "soliloquy," in which the patient stands before the audience and holds forth about his feelings. Even during the "warm-up" phase of the session, we are constantly on the alert against the patient who seems to want to "talk the thing to death." This is despite the fact that we *do* accept as a major goal in psychodrama as in other psychotherapies helping some patients switch to more verbal-conceptual modes of expression.

One highly intelligent (and exceedingly verbal) woman had managed to "talk herself out of treatment" with her individual therapist for several months. Naturally she tried the same method in psychodrama which had worked so well for her in other settings. We learned, almost by accident, that if we could stop the flood of words and return to the thought she had mentioned *first,* before she began to "undo" it by her usual flooding, the episode that was portrayed in psychodrama was meaningful for her and was then available for her use with her individual therapist.

The tendency to talk in abstractions rather than to come to grips with one's feelings is a facet of what is often called *intellectualizing* in treatment. It is of interest, therefore, that intellectuals seem to take so well to psychodrama. Perhaps this is because of the phenomenon pinpointed by Malcolm Muggeridge: "As Cervantees showed so splendidly centuries ago, the intellectual longs for the excitement of action as eunuchs do for the excitement of sex" (1969, p. 76). In any case, we have not typically had much difficulty in explaining the usefulness of the technique to patients who were, otherwise, quite verbal and intelligent people.

Particularly with younger patients who make a fetish of their pervasively doubting attitude, we proffer the program in prosaic, nonevangelistic terms. Frank discussion of how psychodrama works can be helpful in "loosening" the group and focusing their interest. We do this when new members are assigned; the repetition also serves as a review for ongoing members. We often acknowledge with the group that a particular episode or scene seems to have accomplished nothing more for the protagonist than that he has tried to do something before a group. We remind them that this is indeed *drama,* and we must take a half playful attitude toward it. Such a reminder lightens the mood of the group and helps free them to experiment.

We prefer to have about twenty patients assigned to a group, expecting to average fifteen at any one meeting. From experience, we dread situations in which one staff person must try to handle the entire situation, because of the need to observe significant clues to "audience" responses and the possibility of an upset. On the other hand, a group can be weighed down with too much staff. If active, they reduce the likelihood that patients will have an opportunity to participate. If passive, they encourage the patients to stay on the sidelines, by their example. We prefer three staff members to be present.

Nor are *auxiliary egos* drawn only from staff. Being asked to play the role of another patient's mother or father is often as useful to the patient who is helping as to the protagonist. This is the more possible with groups that operate more continually and over longer periods of time. There is always a cadre of patients with experience who can, should, and do step into auxiliary ego roles. Our groups met weekly, for sessions of one and one-half hours each.

The Aim in Each Session

Regarding the goal of psychodrama, it has been said:

Insight is not seen as the major goal of psychodrama, but rather the ability to become spontaneous, that is, to make new perceptions of old situations, or at least to reorganize old cognitive patterns in such a manner that new and more adequate responses are facilitated (Yablonsky and Enneis, 1956, p. 159).

This seems to us one possible goal of psychodrama. Quite a number are possible with this extremely versatile modality. The goal in each session is a step to the ultimate goal, therapeutic change. What one aims for in a given session may depend on how intact the protagonist is, for example—how ambitious one may be in reaching for true insight, verbalization, or merely role play and communication through gesture. In the remainder of this chapter we will discuss some of the uses to which psychodrama may be put, each desirable with certain patients, at an appropriate phase in treatment.

Psychodrama has something else in common with the other psychotherapies. Each is essentially a beneficent structure in which change has an opportunity to occur. The expertise in therapy consists, then, in exploiting the most promising targets of opportunity which the patients and the group present.

Psychodrama for Affect Discharge

We noticed early in successful sessions the depth and intensity of feelings expressed by the protagonist and others. The discharge involved exceeds what we are able to elicit in the office interview, in both rawness of affect and primitive gestural communication.

A somewhat paranoid young mother sat frozen and silent through a number of sessions. Invited to participate, she finally decided to demonstrate to us what a weak, contemptible person her husband was, and why she could not bear the thought of returning to her marriage with him.

She chose to illustrate his mealy-mouthedness by showing how he acted at a family gathering. This finally came down to a particular incident at dinner at her family's house. From experience, we believe that the impact is likely to be the greater if we help the patient recreate the situation in as real a way as possible. Therefore, I asked a number of questions about who would sit where, at table, how each family member behaved toward her, and the like. The patient portrayed her father as a dictatorial, pompous, self-made man, who ordered his construction workers around in a roaring voice, and carried this over to his home life.

Although the episode was to have shown her husband's style, the patient instead became engrossed in a verbal battle with her father, which became so intense she seized a knife as if to stab him—an actual gesture she had not recalled until that moment. From observations, it appeared that this family battle was partly engendered by rivalrous feelings toward a sister who knew better how to handle the father, and was favored by him.

The episode became so unruly that the patient "left" amidst tears and recriminations, which she then turned against her husband in the car driving home, because he "did not come to my rescue." However, after all this discharge, the patient seemed less rigid, if more openly anxious. She was softer in manner and more open to discussion.

In the subsequent group discussion, three themes were stressed: that she equated hardheadedness and bellicosity with "strength"; that she felt more secure and integrated in the midst of such an outburst than at most other times; and that she was contemptuous of the man she had chosen originally to be different from the unreasonable father—whom she actually tried to emulate. Of course, we do not know that the real man, her father, was the same as the way she had us depict him, but seeing herself as trying to be like that image left her shaken but elated. Two weeks later, she told the group of a satisfying week end with the husband she had wanted to divorce because he would not give her a decent fight!

This vignette can be used to demonstrate a number of principles. We point first to a few things that seem to *augment the primitivism of the affect* likely to be elicited. First, it is most important to be sensitive to details in the scene the patient envisages. Such elaborate re-creation makes it all the more vivid to the protagonist; it also makes it more possible for the auxiliary egos, staff, and patients to warm up to the situation. Second, the affect discharge frequently is the result of relaxing usual inhibitions. The latter is unquestionably facilitated by a process of *behavioral contagion* from auxiliary egos, who demonstrate less conflict and fear expressing strong feelings before the group than the patient would have felt appropriate. We exploit the dynamics of behavioral contagion, as described by Redl (1949) and Grosser, Polansky, and Lippitt (1951). Finally, expression in action increases reintegration for the patient of the more primitive affects.

So impressive were such episodes that we began to think of psychodrama as perhaps *the* specific for treating affect-inhibition. Yet, as in other psychotherapy, one recognizes that ventilation is not enough, and that feelings expressed are themselves often defensive maneuvers. We also noticed the discharge that occurs most unequivocally and "honestly" overemphasizes one range of feelings—the hostile, spiteful, or embittered ones. For a long time we wondered whether this was due to something in us that was being communicated or to our sampling of patients. After all, severely neurotic people are not sick on love. More recently, however, we came across a passage by Anna Freud which suggests that the limitation in range of affect may be due partly to the treatment situation we create. Discussing the analytic treatment of children she notes:

> While free association seems to liberate in the first instance the sexual fantasies of the patient, free action— even if only comparatively free—acts in a parallel way on the aggressive trends. What children overwhelmingly act out in the transference are therefore their aggressions, or the aggressive side of their pregenitality . . . (1965, p. 30).

Miss Freud does not offer an explanation of why there is a differential impact on content from freedom of speech versus free action, and of course she is contrasting children in play therapy with adult therapy. Nevertheless, it is stimulating to have so related an observation from a person who has been working with a markedly different patient population. Time will demonstrate whether she has suggested the nucleus of a more general law.

There is a group of patients for whom the use of psychodrama as an arena in which to ventilate primarily bitter and angry feelings is most in evidence—the young men and women we see so often with personality disorders and problems in the schizoid spectrum.

One appealing sixteen-year-old had to be hospitalized after developing severe symptoms involving phobias, withdrawal, and a loss of reality testing. Even after she had settled to a point where she was attending classes, once more, she continued to be extremely negative toward her parents, hating to visit with them. She finally asked to enact a scene with them, and did so, decanting a little of the rage and disappointment which poisoned her attitude toward them. Here, as elsewhere, we looked for what was obviously not being expressed, since this could be at least as meaningful as what was. It became apparent that if she only despised her parents, as she claimed, it would be hard to understand the discomfort she felt about them. We surmised that she must also love them much.

To this the patient agreed, with relief. However, what now came out was that she was unable to enact even a fabricated scene in which she expressed any warmth toward them. No wonder they seemed rejecting! Then we learned that the problem was more general—she could not let a boy know she liked him, either, which *was* a problem; she could not even say "Thank you" without feeling hypocritical.

This syndrome was familiar to us from the individual treatment of such youngsters, of course. However, in this setting we handled it by engaging her curiosity and real desire for help. We set up a short series of playful vignettes, in each she was to say something warm to an auxiliary ego, while her fellows in the audience gave her immediate feedback on how she sounded, using role reversal, mirroring, and group discussion. The protagonist alternated between being deadly serious and, fortunately, amused. At the end, I teased her a little, but then sympathized with how hard it is to fear closeness while starving for it. I complimented her on how far she had been able to move against her pattern in one session. Later, as I was getting into my car, she dashed up to me with a determined look on her face and whispered, "I like you." All I could think to say was, "I like you, too," before she was off like a frightened doe. It was one of those unforgettable interchanges which keep us all alive as caseworkers and therapists.

We see enacted here the dilemma about closeness faced by such youngsters, with some resolution occurring. Adolescents often beautifully illustrate that when one exploits the psychodramatic situation to bring about *ventilation,* the feelings they are able to put forward are but the beginning of the unveiling process. Resistances operate here as in all the other psychotherapies. Generally ventilation is not enough, in part because the feelings being expressed with the least equivocation are still at some distance from what is troubling the protagonist most.

Especially because of the phenomenon noted by Anna Freud, we must recognize that the expression of hostility may be *overdetermined.* It may be a response to the potentialities of action freedom, and a favored defense, in which one substitutes anger for the deep sense of loneliness and despair that accompanies admitting one needs others. Conversely, psychodrama has worked well in our experience for constricted, overly moralistic, middle-aged patients who must deny their all too apparent anger because it is not "Christian" or "polite" to acknowledge such feelings. Even when such a patient cannot allow his anger to be examined, there is frequent evidence of "spill over" as he plays an ancillary role or simply as he takes vicarious pleasure in the protagonist's free expression of his anger.

The experienced therapist is already aware of a number of dangers in the use of psychodrama, just because it *can* be so powerful a tool. Obviously, when one encourages ventilation the same cautions against premature uncovering that apply in other therapies are also relevant. I have already commented on the tendency of rigid people to premature closure in their thinking, once they have blurted something out. "If I said it, that must be what I think." The idea of standing behind one's words is not that literal! Because sessions involving ventilation seem so vivid and genuine to all concerned, staff must be especially on guard against accepting what is currently conscious as the whole story. Further exploration of what gets expressed is in order. Protagonist and group may have to be reminded of the need for discussion with their individual therapists of the ideas that come out in psychodrama.

One is advisedly cautious with the patient still shaky after a severe breakdown. The most important protection for the fragile patient is his ability to prevent himself and the others from hitting on the things most troubling to him. But at times the staff may have to guard his defenses against too rapid interpretation from the other members of the group.

On the positive side, the use of psychodrama for affect discharge appears to have the following advantages: (a) it affords the patient an experience of self-disclosure in an accepting, noncriticizing environment; (b) the availability of action channels helps some patients to make a gradual switch to verbal-conceptual expression, meanwhile heightening their verbal accessibility; (c) there is frequently a reduction of tension, during which phase the protagonist is more accessible to clarifications and interpretations; and (d) an episode concentrating primarily on catharsis or ventilation may provide an opportunity to move into new integrations, and the uncovering of the unconscious.

Clarification and Insight

In common with other analytically-oriented practitioners, we use the terms *clarification* and *interpretation* with specific meanings. By *clarification* we refer to the process wherein content that is conscious, or readily available to consciousness, in the patient is brought into a new configuration for him. This may involve relating previously isolated elements, or it may require giving more emphasis to a fact than the patient or client prefers to give it. *Interpretation,* on the other hand, refers to proffering to the patient something we believe to be unconscious. In the office, nearly all interpretation is of course necessarily verbal-conceptual; possibilities are extended in psychodrama. The client or patient may be said to have an *insight* when something previously repressed becomes conscious.

The goal of psychodrama we cited from Yablonsky and Enneis is certainly that of facilitating clarification. And it fits comfortably with a background in social casework, as this is the level at which caseworkers are accustomed to operating. It is not that their clients do not have insights, but rather that they do not make interpretations to try to hasten them. Nearly all experienced psychotherapists expect insights to emerge from a steadfast process of clarification at the conscious level, as a matter of skillful technique.

In Highland Hospital, brief leaves at home are a frequently used therapeutic measure. Many patients anticipate how such leaves will be through preliving them in psychodrama. A once regressed schizophrenic girl who had shown marked improvement was anticipating a ten-day visit at home. Her relationship with her parents had been manipulative, but when they fell into her trap she panicked. In projecting her arrival at home (in three different ways) she found herself trying her same old tricks, and again experiencing the familiar feelings of anger and panic. When her simulated parents remained firm she felt more comfortable. Discussion after these scenes brought out the fact that in all probability her parents would not be firm, as they had had no help in this area. She then decided that if she wished to avoid the old feelings *she* would have to be the one to change her tactics.

Much of the literature of psychodrama deals with various techniques involved in bringing about clarification for the patients involved. It would be redundant to add to it, beyond confirming that we too find the method valuable for this purpose. What we should like to do, however, is mention a few observations we have not found elsewhere.

As must be visible in the vignettes already given, there seems to be a fairly regular sequence in a large proportion of those psychodramatic episodes in which the protagonist has really "caught on." Although the protagonist may say he wants to understand a situation, it is not unusual for him to launch into the scene on a wave of *catharsis*. If we ride along with him, more and more facets of his problems are revealed as he seeks *tension discharge through re-enactment*. During subsequent group discussion there often follows a phase of considerable clarification. Sometimes this is hammered home for the protagonist by another patient's redoing the scene, while he watches from the audience; at other times the protagonist accepts the group's verbal appraisal of what he has been doing. Although he might have sought to avoid knowing what he knows quite well, it is rare that what is discussed up to this point has actually been repressed and is truly unconscious. The session may end at this point, with an attempt either by the focal patient or the psychodramatist to pull things together. Or it may continue into questions of *why* the patient behaves as he does. It is not at all unusual, then, for the process of clarification to be capped with a true insight.

This is a familiar sequence, as we noted, and we have learned something about how to try to bring it about. At the same time, remember that clarification is not the only way in which insight can occur. Very often it issues out of an intensive emotional experience in the course of which some defenses are no longer sustained, or become unnecessary. No interpretation may be involved, in the usual sense, but the auxiliary egos may have pushed through intuitively to a preconscious or an unconscious level—just as I did in telling the mother, "I love you."

An extremely important aspect of the process of clarification is helping the staff obtain a fresh and vivid view of the patient's psychodynamics in a way that may alter a case formulation previously taken for granted. This seems to follow from the greater richness of detail and the concentration made possible by re-evoking a scene and giving full play to the spontaneity of the participants.

The protagonist was a twenty-eight-year-old woman, married, and the mother of four children. She had been hospitalized after a long siege of ill-defined somatic complaints, followed by a period of withdrawal, loss of interest in herself and the children. Her difficulties seemed to revolve around her demanding, childish husband. Her inability to deal with him, in turn, derived from her childhood fear of her father. So she decided to show us how things were "when daddy came home. . . ." The idea was for the father to come storming into the house, while her long-suffering mother and the children cowered and hid to avoid his wrath. As we often do, however, we asked her to show where each sat, what her siblings' reactions were like, what her mother said, and other remembered details.

The first thing to emerge was that *she* was not actually frightened, for somehow her father never picked at her. He reserved his outbursts for her brother. Although she felt guilty, she also felt relieved, and "special" that the latter should bear the brunt of the old man's irritability. The second clarification came when the person playing her mother asked how she was to act. "Oh, you hear him coming in the drive, and you tell us all to be quiet and come into the back room where he won't see us." It became evident that the mother, who had always seemed somewhere between a victim and a nonentity in the patient's descriptions, actually played a significant, manipulative role in the family. She effectually shut the father out of the family circle, making him feel a stranger in his own home. It seemed now more understandable that he should flaunt the mistress for whom he finally left the mother, and leave home every evening, even though he faithfully supported them all!

When the second facet was brought out—in this instance by the Director—the patient offered a third, related clarification. "This is what *I* often do with my own children, when my husband comes home, although he loves the kids, and certainly never abuses them." Neither the *need to be special* nor the extent to which she seemed determined to relive her mother's life tragedy had ever before become so visible to me as in the first ten minutes of this playlet.

It is always possible that this drastically revised vision of events would eventually have emerged in her individual therapy. Our point is that in this instance the psychodramatic situation brought about cognitive restructuring for the therapist rapidly and convincingly, and was a major contribution to the individual work.

Dealing with Unintegrated Internalized Objects

A protagonist in psychodrama frequently becomes aware he has been emulating a person he thought he despised. Psychodrama, in common with the other therapies, can be used to facilitate normal integration and release the patient toward achieving a workable sense of *identity* (Erikson, 1956). This is especially desirable among hospitalized patients, many of whom have markedly schizoid features and represent borderline personality organization (Kernberg, 1967).

Sometimes this lack of awareness that they have been modeling themselves after a person they claim to dislike seems to reflect *splitting* (see Chapter 6). Kernberg formulates this as a primitive operation in which the original inability of the infantile ego to synthesize has in later life become rigidly active in the service of defense (Kernberg, 1966). When splitting is involved, the apparent acceptability to the protagonist of the other person may vacillate wildly from session to session. In one session mama was all good and daddy was all bad; in the next, mama was the bad one.

A somewhat more mature patient reveals another mechanism behind the contradictory behavior in which he acts like someone while declaring that he always wanted to be diametrically different from that person. Complexities have occurred in the processes of introjection and identification. By *introjection* we mean the taking in of an idea or image so that it becomes part of one's self. *Identification* refers to a more elaborate process that is not fully understood or described in a consistent way in analytic circles. Speaking generally, it refers to the sequence in which some personal object, to whom we have been exposed, is made part of our image of ourselves. We seldom completely model ourselves after *all* of the other person—as tiny Sam Shubert is said to have done with the admired actor, David Belasco. Typically, we have *partial identifications,* in which we take on one or several facets of the object's personality and make them part of our own.

For example, the late Gordon Allport was my tutor when I was an undergraduate at Harvard, and I regard him, still, as more or less my intellectual "father." I should have liked to emulate his humaneness, his scholarship, and his breadth—together with the position he so long occupied in our field. But I came to reject his self-proclaimed eclecticism because I have never met a man who was not fanatic about one theory who ever came up with a striking idea. And, of course, the preciousness of his speech and writing at the interval of his life when I was exposed to him now appears to me ludicrous, as eventually it did to him. Which is not to say that I did not, for a long time, lay claim to vestiges of a Harvard accent.

I give this bit of autobiography to illustrate both the degree to which identifications may be piecemeal and the extent to which unwanted fragments of the other person may become part of ourselves along with those we cheerfully choose in our youth and continue to like—in ourselves—in our maturity. The most familiar example of this kind of self-rejected identification in my experience was from mothers who came for help about their children's difficulties. Often a mother would tell me how much she had hated her own mother's controllingness and had determined "to treat my children different." I recall one such mother I saw when I was a young caseworker. Interspersed among her remarks about how important she felt it was to give a child leeway were angry shouts at her son to stop what he was doing, smile at the nice man, and so forth.

Most women are not that obvious; the unconscious identification with their own mothers is masked. The woman determined not to be rigid and controlling may be nondirective with her child. So far does she lean over backwards not to discipline the child, or tell him what to do, that we cannot escape the conclusion she is fighting tremendous impulses to be a managerial, smothering woman. Her misreading of Spock is actually a reaction formation. Otherwise, why be so rigid about it? Why not leave the child alone, at times, and discipline him at other times, depending on the realistic needs of the moment?

The awareness that she is acting the mother she had so much not wanted to be comes as a blow to such a woman. We must point out that her mother was, in fact, the only model she had when she was a baby of what it is to be a woman. Her copying took place when she was so young she could neither be aware she was doing it nor pass mature judgment upon the person she would later choose to be.

In psychodrama we sometimes discover that *unwanted identifications* not only have occurred but also have become *idealized*. A mother's querulousness and petulance are more than picked up: they are invested with the value that that is how women *ought* to be; they are admired; they become ego-syntonic.

Something else should also be made clear about identification. It is basically a defense mechanism. We do not identify simply because we love someone, and they love us. Identification occurs because we love them, and *fear the loss of their love,* or we are trying to keep them as *part of us to prevent the pang of losing them.* If a child is totally indulged, offered unconditional love, he will have no reason to identify, just as if he has never been loved, and has nothing to lose. Similarly, identification occurs out of *fear.* The child at the zoo, frightened by a lion's roar, starts roaring himself during the trip home. He is saying, "If I make the lion part of *me,* I will not have to fear him, because it is I who do the roaring, and I can control it." This is called *identification with the aggressor.*

It is because life's vicissitudes mix in us fragments we want to keep with fragments which, as adults, we no longer can accept that we have *unintegrated internalized objects.* One's *bête noire* is unmasked playing privy councillor to his self-ideal. Psychodrama happens to be peculiarly apt for the exploration of such object relationships. All episodes involve images of significant others who are in the patient's mind. "The dreamer dreams the dream": all these representations are part of the patient. In this sense it may not be too important to know—as we shall never know—whether the father and mother were as they are described. The essential fact is that the idea the patient has of each is, itself, real, even if it may later change.

A middle-aged female patient recalled her mother with abhorrence. Unable fully to communicate why, she finally asked to enact a scene in which she proposed to show us the sort of person her mother was, by taking her role. As the scene progressed, she entered in with great gusto, presumably caricaturing the attitudes and mannerisms in her mother which she found so distasteful. When she had finished, however, a group of women with whom she lived in the hospital burst out with one voice, albeit not unkindly, "But, X, that is you!" The patient had already noticed it.

It is usually not possible within the psychodramatic situation alone to puzzle out the origins of introjections or *why* the patient appears "to struggle against identification" in the particular instance that may have come to light (Greenson, 1954). The aptness of psychodrama, rather, extends primarily to bringing the identification to consciousness through evidence difficult to re-repress. More precise exploration of the leads turned up becomes the task of individual therapy.

We have found two techniques that work well to help in the clarification of such problems. Frequently, while the patient earnestly searches his case history for reasons for his lack of success, the answer lies in patterns and mannerisms right at the surface, of which he is aware but does not want to look at too directly. Hence, we can use direct confrontation or *mirroring* of his mannerisms. It is seldom possible in individual casework or psychotherapy to bring his presenting defenses so vividly to the attention of the patient. Preferably, of course, this should be done in an accepting atmosphere and with a light touch.

The other technique we call "exploiting the ripple effect." The term is from Kounin and Gump (1958) who studied the effect, on other children in a class, of witnessing the teacher's manner in disciplining one of their members. A psychodramatic episode necessarily evolves around the imagery of the protagonist, as our case examples illustrate. However, we regard it as extremely poor technique to permit the postepisode discussion to degenerate into a one-to-one "treatment encounter in the presence of a group." Optimally, the episode portrayed should be discussed generally, first by those directly involved as auxiliary egos, and then by as many as wish to join in. The psychodrama serves as backdrop for a fruitful group therapy session.

An episode's impact on the audience is of major concern. One or more patients in the audience will have identified with the protagonist. Sometimes they volunteer, "This is what happened to me"; more often, a staff member becomes aware of their strong response and draws them into discussion. Their empathy will have shown itself in unconsciously mimicking the focal patient's facial expression; it may also come through in evidence of discomfort. Signs of strong identification with the action often indicate that a patient who has not participated is now ripe; these are clues to timing.

Despite their individualities, patients have much in common. Thus it is often possible to involve several in a single session, each of whom is trying to show us how he experienced his parents, or something that happened in his life which came to mind during the previous episode. When we are lucky, one scene builds upon the previous one, as patients teach each other—and us—dynamics.

It is not unusual to find patients who have a need to "perform" and be on stage center but who are also so well defended that no matter what they do or how hard the therapist may work with them, they always succeed in defeating any real action. One patient managed to frustrate us all, in scenes she had asked to try, by her constant interruption of them and her insistence that we were not playing the scene as it should be done. This she did in spite of her inability or unwillingness to give her fellow actors any real clues about the roles they were trying to help her with. If any suggestion was made as to the significance of a given scene, her stock answer was "Yes, but— " This pattern continued for several months. Then she observed another patient engaged in the same kind of maneuvers. She became irritated with him and suddenly realized she was reacting to her own behavior. She talked about this freely and expressed eagerness to try another scene, herself, to determine whether she could avoid a repetition of her old pattern.

Because motivations leading patients to want to participate are diverse, a proportion of the volunteering simply communicates, "You have been in the center of the stage long enough. Now it's my turn."

One hysterical adolescent greeted a variety of scenes with quiet but somehow ostentatious tears. If staff became too engrossed in the protagonist to pick up on these immediately, she was apt to ask to be excused from the audience. Otherwise, she succeeded in becoming immediately the center of attention in the group, pulling the rug out from under the patient we were presently trying to focus on.

Even if the motivations for vicarious involvement are mixed, useful results come from the ripple effect. A thrilling experience with this technique is a session in which waves of clarification seem to spread outward from the protagonist and auxiliary ego until all but the most obtuse patients somehow have found new integrations from being present in the group. Not all the responses, by the way, involve identification. Sometimes it is recognizing role-complementarity. Thus, following a scene in which a younger patient has shown his disappointment with his parents, a middle-aged woman burst out, "I wonder if that is how my son feels about me?" After years spent in coddling her character neurosis, even this much recognition of her son's needs represented progress. The dynamics involved in the ripple effect are the same in group therapy as in psychodrama. The advantage of psychodrama lies in part in its not being so confined to symbolic communication, but being able to use childlike levels.

Transitory Regressions

Often during an episode the worker has the impression that what the protagonist has been evoking is but one of a series in his life, in accordance with the *repetition compulsion*. Consequently, the psychodramatist may follow by saying, "I believe that what you have just portrayed was not the first time something like this happened to you. Does something similar come to mind from when you were younger?" A fair proportion of the patients will indeed recall an earlier scene whose relevance may not at first be so apparent. Thus, defiance toward mother in the teens recalls the battle of the table as a preschooler. But when the patient tries to demonstrate the earlier event, she finds herself unable. A key reason often lies in an inability to unbend. They fear that if they permit themselves childlike behavior, they will not find the strength to give it up. Given the tenuous hold many have on maturity, their wariness is understandable. Yet, do they really have so much to lose? Their rigidity derives from the fact that they are really *pseudomature*. We feel it might be helpful were they to regress a bit, in a momentary and localized fashion, in order to move forward on a sounder basis.

We arrived at conviction about attempting therapeutic use of transitory regressions from experiences in psychodrama, but the idea is of course familiar among writers representing various schools of thought. Moreno has always recognized this process as a key element in psychodramatic therapy. "The persons play themselves . . . as they did once out of necessity in self-conscious deceit, the same life again . . . they re-experience it, they are master . . ." (1946, p. 28).

Heinz Werner, speaking as a developmental psychologist, points out that "an organism, having attained highly stabilized structures and operations may or may not progress further but if it does, this will be accomplished through partial return to a genetically earlier, less stable level. One has to regress in order to progress" (1957, p. 138).

A more complete and highly provocative statement of the rationale of the analyst's participation in regressions for therapeutic reasons is Winnicott's. He makes a number of cogent distinctions with respect to the types of regression encountered in clinical work and between types of fixation.

> One has to include in one's theory of the development of a human being the idea that it is normal and healthy for the individual to be able to defend the self against specific environmental failure by a *freezing of the failure situation.* Along with this goes an unconscious assumption (which can become a conscious hope) that opportunity will occur at a later date for a renewed experience in which the failure situation will be able to be unfrozen and re-experienced, with the individual in a regressed state, in an environment that is making adequate adaptation (Winnicott, 1954–55, p. 18).

Winnicott's referent is, of course, the psychoanalytic setting. In our experience there are several specific reasons for the deliberate provocation of transitory regression in a psychodramatic session. Its use in a more thorough *abreaction of childhood trauma* is one. We may also wish to help the patient undercut a current character symptom by reverting to an earlier way of relating, before it became so fixed. A rigid, inhibited person may have to discover that he can engage in playfulness without falling apart or being shamed by his associates. And *any experience of controlled regression helps us to integrate the childish remnants in ourselves which otherwise we struggle to hide and isolate at great expense in psychic energy.* This explains the healing power of "spontaneity."

The technical problems, then, are: (1) How to help the patient achieve regression; under (2) conditions which are experienced as within his control—*regression in the service of the ego;* and (3) make it momentary and localized in its impact.

Thus far we have found two useful methods in psychodrama. The first is the successive process to which we have alluded in which the patient, while "tracing the affect back," associates an earlier to a present conflict, and then enacts it. The second maneuver involves exploiting one of the dynamics in behavioral contagion, i.e., the *dominance of the unconflicted personality constellation over the conflicted,* to which Redl refers. The psychodramatist may get down on the floor, forsaking his present group prestige to abandon himself fully to the role of the patient's childhood playmate or sibling. In doing this, he also demonstrates his own freedom from fear of consequences and of ridicule.

As with all other techniques, precautions must be observed. A patient only recently reconstituted from an outright psychotic break hardly wants loosening up. A substantial number of infantile patients unfortunately require no outside assistance to act childish; for them the aim of psychodramatic intervention must be in the opposite direction. For a large proportion of patients, *deliberately evoked regression* under the conditions cited is the treatment of choice. This technique emphasizes the range of possibilities within the psychodramatic situation. Whereas clarification and insight treatment utilize the *secondary process* in therapy, evoked regression may put its emphasis more at the level of the *primary process,* although of course not all regression is to this level.

We have described a program of psychodramatic treatment utilized at one hospital for more than five years. Although we began with a skeptical and experimental attitude, we soon acquired general acceptance and conviction regarding its potentialities. Our program seems to differ from a number of others in that the method is seen as frankly adjunctive to individual psychotherapy and it is embedded in a situation where other therapies are being used simultaneously with the same patient. We also have the impression that the continuity and sheer time in psychodramatic treatment (ranging up to two years or more, for some) are somewhat unusual.

Working independently of Moreno's group, we have nevertheless had occasion to confirm the usefulness of a number of techniques he and his followers have created. This is despite the fact that we have operated consistently in the framework of analytically-oriented psychotherapy which they do not necessarily share. Our conclusion is that the psychodramatic situation may be exploited to bring powerful intrapsychic forces into play. When these can be harnessed, striking results may be achieved with some patients in the direction of eventual cure. We do not see the aim of psychodrama as univocal. The psychodramatic situation is especially characterized by its versatility and range of communication possibilities. A spectrum of psychotherapeutic aims can be pursued, depending on the readiness of the patient and the evolving competence of the staff.

This chapter has illustrated the use of psychodrama in bringing about affect discharge, in the service of clarification and insight therapy, in the exposure of unwanted identifications, and in therapeutic regression. Each of these proximate aims of a psychodramatic session may lead to the ultimate one of *enhancing the verbal accessibility* of the protagonist—and, indeed, that of the other patients involved. For some patients with massive affect inhibition, the expression of feelings through gesture and facial expression may be a required prelude to expression in words. For others, who have come to misuse words defensively, the requirement to act out their feelings psychodramatically while also speaking of them may heal the splits they have made between words and affects.

Albert Camus wrote of the Nazis, "When one has no character, one *has* to apply a method" (1956). Because of its inherent flamboyance and the manner of its proliferation, psychodrama has at times been left to practitioners who work with hardly a method and, certainly, no coherent personality theory. The responsible conduct of psychodrama requires both. Our intention has been to move toward integrating this treatment technique into the theoretical corpus of the other analytically oriented psychotherapies.

References

Camus, Albert. *The Fall*. New York: Alfred A. Knopf, 1956.

Erikson, Erik H. "The Problem of Ego Identity," *Journal of the American Psychoanalytic Association, 4,* 1956, 56–121.

Freud, Anna. *Normality and Pathology in Childhood*. New York: International Universities Press, 1965.

Greenson, Ralph R. "The Struggle Against Identification," *Journal of the American Psychoanalytic Association, 2,* 1954, 200–217.

Grosser, Daniel, Norman Polansky, and Ronald Lippitt. "A Laboratory Study of Behavioral Contagion," *Human Relations, 4,* 1951, 115–142.

Kernberg, Otto. "Structural Derivatives of Object Relationships," *International Journal of Psycho-Analysis, 47,* 1966, 236–253.

Kernberg, Otto. "Borderline Personality Organization," *Journal of the American Psychoanalytic Association, 15,* 1967, 641–685.

Kounin, Jacob S., and Paul V. Gump. "The Ripple Effect in Discipline," *Elementary School Journal, 59,* 1958, 158–162.

Moreno, Jacob L. *Psychodrama,* Vol. I. New York: Beacon House, 1946.

Moreno, Jacob L. "Fundamental Rules and Techniques of Psychodrama," in J. H. Masserman and J. L. Moreno, eds., *Progress in Psychotherapy,* Vol. III. New York: Grune and Stratton, 1958, 86–131.

Muggeridge, Malcolm. "Books," *Esquire, 71,* 1969, 74–84.

Redl, Fritz. "The Phenomenon of Contagion and Shock Effect," in K. Eissler, ed., *Searchlight on Delinquency*. New York: International Universities Press, 1949.

Werner, Heinz. "The Concept of Development from a Comparative and Organismic Point of View," in D. B. Harris, ed. *The Concept of Development*. Minneapolis: The University of Minnesota Press, 1957.

Winnicott, Donald W. "Metapsychological and Clinical Aspects of Regression Within the Psycho-Analytical Set-up," *International Journal of Psycho-Analysis, 35–36,* 1954–55, 16–26.

Yablonsky, Lewis, and James M. Enneis. "Psychodrama Theory and Practice," in F. Fromm-Reichmann and J. L. Moreno, eds., *Progress in Psychotherapy,* Vol. I. New York: Grune and Stratton, 1956.

Chapter 12

Verbal Communication and Healing

IN THIS FINAL CHAPTER I WILL RECAPITULATE THE DOMINANT themes discussed and summarize them according to the order they make for me. Before I begin this synthesis of necessarily abstract theory, I should like to quote a characteristically understated passage from Bertrand Russell.

When we came home, we found Mrs. Whitehead undergoing an unusually severe bout of pain. She seemed cut off from everyone and everything by walls of agony, and the sense of the solitude of each human soul suddenly overwhelmed me. . . . Within five minutes I went through some such reflections as the following: the loneliness of the human soul is unendurable; nothing can penetrate it except the highest intensity of the sort of love that religious preachers have preached; whatever does not spring from this motive is harmful, or at best useless; it follows that war is wrong . . . that the use of force is to be deprecated, and that in human relations one should penetrate to the core of loneliness in each person and speak to that (1951, p. 220).

Russell is describing an event in which his empathy for the suffering of his friend's wife rather suddenly broke through his own defenses. He came face to face with the devastating sense of isolation and potential meaninglessness that lies in wait for each of us as a remnant of our childhood struggle toward selfhood. In confronting this existential anxiety he reacted as a healthy person; he found a prescription for how to live rather than a rationale for why to die. Is not the aim in our work, too, to find ways to bridge the chasm between two people in such manner that the contact is deeply felt and still permits each to preserve his adulthood? One of my aims in this book has been to describe how human speech can be used toward this end.

I shall trace some links between the capacity for communication in words and the general efficiency of the ego. And I shall review why it is that I believe a high degree of verbal accessibility is important to the self-healing of psychic wounds and to using help if offered.

Verbal Inaccessibility Reflects Ego Weakness

Ego strength is a loose but serviceable term to describe the resiliency of a client or patient who is under stress. Ultimately, it derives from several sources. We have seen it in terms of the availability to the person of conflict-free psychological energy and the utility of the mechanisms for coping he has at his disposal.

Whether one refers to this quality in the person as his level of ego integration or his psychological maturity, our data and those of others demonstrate consistent associations to verbal accessibility. We have seen that confused and confusing communications from parent to child probably contribute to childhood psychosis. We have found evidence that a lowered VA is associated with psychological primitiveness in groups as diverse as low-income mothers in our rural mountains, hospitalized paranoid schizophrenic patients in an Ohio institution, children in outpatient treatment in a guidance clinic. In each instance, the people who were better put together were also higher on VA. Why the correlation?

Part of our thesis is that there are seldom simple, one-way causal connections between any two coexisting facets of the human personality. The level of ego integration and VA are undoubtedly interdependent phenomena. Still, in order to understand a *gestalt,* it may be necessary to violate it, to analyze it. Let us begin, therefore, by looking at VA as if it were simply being caused by the person's general level of psychological efficiency. For convenience in exposition, let us look at the person in terms of those features that may most visibly *detract* from his verbal accessibility.

1. *Deficiency in symbolic equipment.* The cognitive-intellectual side of the personality embraces such ego functions as thinking, memory, perceiving, and abstracting. These are the appraising and processing apparatuses of the mind. In my earliest studies of VA, I presumed it to be relatively independent of these facets of the ego. After all, even fairly young children and quite dull adults may find it possible to put their most important feelings into speech. I was inclined to discount even the influence of vocabulary size, the possession of *verbal symbols,* on how accessible a person was. Based on the results of research, however, I now take this issue more seriously. There is evidence that sheer skill with words and, indeed, general intellectual adeptness, affects VA.

A meager store of words may hinder anyone in an attempt to state his attitudes. Beyond this, the lack of machinery for expressing nuances of feeling sometimes makes it impossible to talk at all. Suppose a husband is mildly provoked by his wife. A man with an elaborate speech pattern might ask, "Why are you being annoying?" or "Must you be so irritating?" For a person with a limited, stark repertoire there are problems. He might say he is "mad," but his feeling is not that strong. Perhaps he can say nothing until he gets so angry he slugs her. There are many occasions when a person with a restricted pattern, therfore, can select only an immediate verbal fight or an eventual physical one after he has reached the boiling point, or total silence and withdrawal. It is partly for this reason that, in efforts to open up lines of communication within a troubled family, we find ourselves instinctively teaching first that talk is all right, and then the words through which varieties of feeling can find expression. Summing up, then, we may say that the *degree of differentiation* in verbal equipment influences VA.

Why are some of us underdeveloped in these skills? There are a number of possible reasons, of course. For one thing, words are *symbols;* the use of words in an accurate way implies the capacity to learn abstractions. Limitation in abstracting ability may come from poor native endowment; it may reflect gross damage or other insult to the central nervous system. There is a growing opinion that the sufficiency of proteins in an infant's early diet may affect the size of his brain, and this, in turn, adult intelligence. *Concrete-mindedness* is characteristic of persons with schizophrenia, for example; it is also found in any of us during periods of depression or high anxiety. So, a person's physical and emotional health affects his development of word skills and, in turn, his VA.

2. *Splitting of the ego.* I can make my next point clearer by referring to the theory of the non-Freudian, Kurt Lewin (1936). In describing the course of psychological development, Lewin postulated that the mind moves from a state of relatively indiscriminate response and perception to one of increasing *differentiation.* By this he was referring to the familiar principle that one mark of maturation is improved specificity of response. Rather than kicking, screaming, and howling at all discomforts, we gradually learn to assuage one by asking for food, another by pulling

our hand away, a third by hitting back. But in order to respond more efficiently, we must also perceive more precisely. For this reason Lewin believed that the cognitive map of the child became increasingly rich and that perceptions which had once been vague and global were progressively subdivided into shades and distinctions.

I am sure that something resembling Lewin's conception is to be found currently in all generally accepted theories of development (Hartmann, 1964). The notion, nevertheless, leaves an unanswered question. As the mind, really the ego, becomes increasingly differentiated, what keeps the whole thing coordinated? We all know obsessive persons whose endless ability to draw fine distinctions is one of the reasons they cannot "see the forest for the trees." One advantage of a global response, after all, is that the personality does react as a totality. What keeps the person who has achieved a high degree of differentiation from flying off in all directions?

Obviously, unless the capacity for coordination of subparts of the ego evolves at the same pace as does its degree of differentiation, we shall confront an increasingly exotic but chaotic personality. This coordinating capacity Lewin called *integration;* Freudians express much the same idea by speaking of the *synthetic function* of the ego. If a person is to develop healthily, his ability to integrate and synthesize must advance simultaneously with his becoming more and more differentiated.

That the inability to synthesize complex attitudes interferes with one's VA may be readily illustrated. We noted above how hard it may be to describe one's feelings when they are experienced in gross and primitive terms; it is even harder when they are entangled in conflicts (see Ganter, Yeakel, and Polansky, 1967, pp. 24f). Some attitudes must gain ascendancy over others if a person is to "stand behind his words." The inability to coordinate disparate thoughts makes it difficult for some people to speak to the point. They seem to be seeking some way to have their cake and eat it, too; they want to express one feeling while maintaining their right to keep another. Hence, they speak or write in cryptic or agonizingly obscure phraseologies. In fact, there are whole academic fields in which this kind of writing has become *de rigeur,* as if the frank exposure of the rather simple idea under the mass of words would let every outsider know that, after all, "the emperor has no clothes."

For about a decade of my life, I studied the area of group psychology. In the course of keeping up with the endless flood of literature in this field, I came upon a book by an Ivy League college professor. In the tradition that used to be favored at his great institution, he was well-born, well-bred, formidably articulate, but not so bright as to have ideas that would upset the easy flow of intellectual conversation. At great abstractness, he described a tedious research which, only gradually, I deciphered to be demonstrating one point. People who like each other are more frequently found together. I suppose it was all the more unnerving because I had just finished a small study intended to illustrate this truism, and found it is not necessarily so.

But the difficulty of academics in finding a way to be subtle in their triteness is at a more advanced stage of psychological development, of course, than the obvious confusion in the speech of others. Some folks seemingly have abandoned all effort to synthesize their attitudes; they calmly present us with blatantly contradictory statements, side by side—reminiscent of the politician who insists on local self-determination and responsibility, while avidly grabbing for federal funding of every local project. That *he* is this simple-minded seems doubtful; that his hearers are, is pretty apparent.

Forthrightness requires that the individual has found a way to fuse within himself disparate elements. These include, by the way, a sense of reality and awareness of the social appropriateness of what one is saying. It is for this reason that pathological frankness is not necessarily the same thing as Verbal Accessibility. The patient who resolutely declaims the unmentionable usually is not standing fully behind his words, because he declines to admit into consciousness that he feels he should not be talking about the topic at all.

The most obvious example of what we mean by "splits" within the ego is found, in speech, in the presence of mutually contradictory statements. The speaker usually does not experience them as contradictory; he does not place them in juxtaposition. It is as if the one idea were walled off from the other, in his mind. In one of our field studies, we asked low-income parents what they hoped for their children. "Oh, I would like him to become a doctor or a lawyer." And how far did they want him to go to school. "Well, I reckon it would be good if he got the seventh grade."

This kind of splitting within the egos of schizoid patients, in particular, was emphasized by Fairbairn (1952). More recently, Kernberg (1966) has offered a most cogent discussion of the process as a way in which the mature ego may have been pervasively weakened. He notes that splitting quite probably originates in the typical inability of the young child to hold several ideas in mind at once and to integrate them. But what starts as a normally expectable, developmental incapacity may be turned to *"an active, very powerful defensive operation"* (p. 238). In the form of such defensive maneuvers as *denial,* primitive *dissociation,* and the like, the more that splitting characterizes the ego, the more will its synthetic function by undermined.

We saw one result of this process in Chapter 5, in which we discussed the gross dichotomization made by paranoid characters between bad-mother and good-mother images. Where there has been early difficulty in the child-mother relationship, however, the splitting of personal objects is not all; a tendency toward *all-or-none* reaction may characterize the total personality. Indeed, this quality is found in the speech and thought processes of nearly all extremely childish or infantile clients or patients. It seems a paradox that persons given to such all-or-none response should also be so likely to compartmentalize their attitudes, but they are. Attitudes they hold, and need for defensive reasons, are kept isolated from each other, and certainly beyond correction by external reality. When a fanatic is pushed to think beyond his own narrow logic, he becomes not only confused but also rigid.

We can draw further conclusions from this line of theory, relevant not only to clinical work but also to *real-politik*. For present purposes, however, let us just note that anything which reduces the synthetic ability of the ego also hinders VA, and the mechanisms related to splitting are heavily implicated in weakening the synthetic function.

3. *Separation anxiety and the need for fusion.* As I list the aspects of ego weakness that seem to me to have the most to do with impeding VA, I am again impressed with how much they relate to normal maturation of the personality. Comfort in the use of abstractions with discrimination and ease in integrating complex attitudes and ideas are both ego functions we expect will blossom as the person develops. When they fail to do so, VA is also lowered, and it is no wonder that we find verbal *in*accessibility associated with other evidences of infantilism in the character.

Next, I turn to an interference arising out of another vicissitude of early childhood—severe separation anxiety. By separation anxiety I refer quite literally to acute discomfort experienced in the event, or at the prospect, of being separated from the person to whom one has become attached. That there is such anxiety is now generally accepted, although opinions regarding its nature vary. Bowlby has advanced the view that the child's tie to his mother is conceived best as the outcome of instinctual response systems which are "a part of the inherited behavior repertoire of man; when they are activated and the mother figure is available, attachment behavior results ... when they are activated and the mother figure is temporarily unavailable, separation anxiety and protest behavior follow" (1960, p. 9).

Separation anxiety, then, arises when the tie to the mother is interrupted. As noted earlier, many of us see this feeling as the prototype of all anxiety. Adults can perhaps best imagine it in terms of the sinking feeling we encounter when "the floor drops out from under us" as in a fast elevator or in the overwhelming sensations of our childhood nightmares of plunging through space. It will be recalled that one reason the person with serious, unresolved problems in the schizoid spectrum may fear getting close is that he dreads separation.

One might say that separation anxiety occurs when *dependency* is interfered with—but this is too general. "Dependency" is used to refer to the essentially self-centered, impersonal clutching of the depressed person in terror of being left alone. There is also realistic dependency, in which one accepts a helper for the reason that one cannot do for oneself what one needs done, and therefore has to lean on outside assistance for quite objective reasons (Garrett, 1958). When I speak of separation anxiety, however, I have in mind the kind of primitive dependency experienced by the very young child who, at about six months, is finally able to discriminate among persons, and misses his particular object very much should she disappear.

The rationale for the relationship of separation anxiety to verbal inaccessibility derives from the work of Kaiser. He speaks of the *delusion of fusion* which people erect as a defense against experiencing loneliness. In an earlier chapter, we reviewed a series of maneuvers clients show in the interview in the service of the delusion of fusion, which we termed *duplicity* in communication. In Chapter 9, I related the delusion of fusion to cultural forces actively preventing the emergence of VA. In short, once one assumes the delusion of fusion is operative, a number of interesting propositions follow. We could only touch on a few here.

There are significant gaps in Kaiser's theory. He does not account for why some adults show much evidence of the delusion of fusion, the "universal" defense, while others do not. Nor does he account for why some patients cling to it much more strongly than do others. In my observation, it has seemed that the delusion of fusion is relied on the more pervasively the patient is struggling with separation anxiety. Everyone dislikes loneliness, but some of us are in terror of it. Those in terror tend not to have developed methods for relating to others which are satisfying and reassuring, *and* available to adults. Childlike people, including many schizoid personalities, feel great yearnings to be embraced and to be literally in touch through *physical* means; in most of our relationships this is not permissible and we must achieve closeness through the medium of the spoken word. But pervasive separation anxiety, an unresolved problem of early childhood, may interfere with learning those individualized self-descriptions of feeling that make touching through verbal means possible. The indiscriminate need to cling and to receive unqualified love, as it were, makes it more necessary for a patient to keep up a false front and be overconcerned with what others think of him. Separation anxiety exacerbates the problems of shame and blame that we otherwise think of in connection with the anal phase of development.

The resultant sensitivity further inhibits one's VA. If a person is obsessed with problems of blame and approval, it is very hard to discover himself. Everything he finds within himself is immediately evaluated—everything is either good or bad, nothing just *is*. Because the client or patient has this hypercritical attitude, he assumes everyone else does too; he cannot bear to reveal or to look at himself. We find, then, the clinging behavior that so frequently accompanies separation anxiety inhibits the growth of the *self-observing* function of the ego; it also creates a closed off person. Here is still another instance in which a symptom worsens the underlying problem. And removal of the symptom would be a major part of the cure.

The degree of the need for fusion derives from the severity of separation anxiety and its pervasiveness in the personality. This need for fusion, in turn, deters VA. Separation anxiety is also implicated in the kind of childlike clutching which makes shame and one's reputation so momentous. This, too, prevents the patient from verbalizing feelings.

One reason the concept of *fixation* remains useful despite its vagueness is to be seen in the phenomena pointed to above. So many of the indications of childishness which endure into adult life tend to be found together. The person whose thought is marked by concreteness, by rigid splits within the ego, and who shows results of the delusion of fusion is, indeed, also likely to be verbally inaccessible. Kaiser raised the question, "How can a therapist determine what is a correct move to make in therapy?" and answered it, "Whatever helps the patient better to stand behind his words." At first, this may seem a simplistic and even flip solution to a vastly complicated question. But as we examine the reasons why people are unable to stand behind their words, we recognize that Kaiser was simply emphasizing the same goals we all hold—the growth of the patient's personality and his degree of ego integration. His departure from the orthodox theories of therapy lay, rather, in the degree to which he believed that in attempting to speak in an integrated and independent fashion, the patient consolidates his personality. We turn next to the other side of the interdependency—the ways in which speech can in fact lead to greater integration and strengthen the ego.

Healing Properties of Verbal Communication

I believe that Kaiser was essentially correct. Therefore, I will now discuss some of our reasons for believing that the appropriate use of speech enhances growth. Moreover, a high degree of VA is significant to the healing of psychic wounds, whether this is self-healing or accomplished with professional help. Let us now take up some of the positive aspects of speech for the human personality.

1. *Speech and the need-meeting functions of the ego.* So much of our ego psychology has been devoted to laying bare unconscious conflicts and defenses that it was easy to overlook straightforward adaptive functions of the ego. One such function is the meeting of needs, for which speech is a major instrumentality.

Meerloo has provided a provocative list of the needs that motivate verbalization. He includes the need to express emotions and moods; to make sounds; the need for contact; the desire to inform, to state facts; the urge to formulate ideas; the impulse to take a position opposite the world; the need for individuation; the need to control things; the need to control others; to be controlled by others; to express sexual desire; to use words in the service of defense; to express unconscious motives; the need to refuse contact (1952, pp. 84ff). I doubt that Meerloo's listing is exhaustive; certainly, it is not systematic. It does emphasize the diversity that comes to the mind of any experienced caseworker or therapist if he is asked, "*Why* do your clients talk; what motivates their speaking?"

Like all behavior, and indeed all thinking, speech is found in the service of drives or more specific needs. Some of these are conscious, some are unconscious; some are basic and primitive, some are sophisticated and less directly related to the original drive energy. In each instance, however, insofar as talking is used to fulfill the need involved, we would say that it thereby strengthens the adaptive capacity of the ego.

2. *Binding affects and the neutralization of drives.* Even though the child may first use speech to express emotions, or to reach out for closeness, the act of speaking and the word skills he picks up in its exercise soon come to subserve other ego functions. These include what we call the "binding" of affects or feelings—becoming able to cope with one's emotions. This is not the same as having none, although, as we have noted, many schizoid persons try to feel as little as possible. A person with a reasonably strong ego is able to be aware of his emotions, and to tolerate them and retain a sense that he is in control of his fate under most circumstances. He knows that the emotions he is experiencing are part of him—he does not have to split them off —but they are not *all* of him.

Anna Freud wrote:

The ego of the young child has the developmental task to master on the one hand orientation in the external world and on the other hand the chaotic emotional states which exist within himself. It gains its victories and advances whenever such impressions are grasped, put into thoughts or words, and submitted to the secondary process. . . . (1965, p. 32).

By *secondary process,* Miss Freud is of course referring to the level of thought that is logical, coherent, reality-related, and typically conscious. This level, in analytic theory, is contrasted with *primary process* thinking, which is more at the mercy of internal states, less symbolic, more given to making connections between ideas and images through simple association like spatial or temporal contiguity or the like. The primary process survives in all of us in the primitive facets of our minds. Secondary process thinking is more adaptive, for it involves external reality and a systematic approach to it. Therefore, it seems likely to lead to ways of meeting one's needs that will truly satisfy them over longer periods of time. We are reminded by Miss Freud that insofar as verbal communication assists the development of the secondary process, it promotes more effective mastery over one's world, more reliable meeting of needs, and mastery over one's self.

A related notion is to be found in the writing of Anny Katan (1961), who reported experiences in a treatment program for young children. Many of the children in this program seemed unready for child analysis because they were too lacking in speech to express themselves in treatment. Therefore, she and her colleagues set up a program to give the children what we would now call "enrichment" in this area before formal treatment could be started. It is of interest that, about the same time, and in the same city, Ganter, Yeakel and I (1967) began a group work program to prepare children for therapy in a child guidance clinic with somewhat the same rationale, quite independently of Mrs. Katan's work, and unaware of her agreement. Katan concluded that "verbalization of feelings leads to an increase of mastery by the ego."

> If the child does not learn to name his feelings, a situation may arise in which there develops a discrepancy between the strength and complexity of his feelings on the one hand, and his modes of expression on the other. If the child could verbalize his feelings, he would learn to delay action, but the delaying function is lacking . . . the situation may have pathological consequences.
>
> When the child has later acquired the art of verbalizing, he will still cling to the earlier method of acting upon his feelings instead of mastering them through verbalization. This uninhibited discharge may bring him into conflict with his environment, so that he will form either too great fears about the environment or too early feelings of guilt. . . . In such children the ego becomes weak, for it is repeatedly overwhelmed by affects (1961, p. 186).

By becoming able to put a name to his feelings, the child can substitute a verbal for a physical response. This verbalization makes possible the delaying of drive-discharge so that more intelligent action may eventually take place, and so that the action itself can be modulated and guided by external reality. What did Winston Churchill say— "Jaw-jaw is better than war-war"? Miss Freud quotes a passage written by her father in 1893, "The man who first flung a word of abuse at his enemy instead of a spear was the founder of civilization" (A. Freud, 1965).

The ability of the person to associate his *drives* with words heightens his capacity to restrain them and to cope with them. It is for this reason we believe that the subsystem of the ego which we call the superego is also vastly strengthened by symbolic thought. It is possible to nurture a conscience without words, but superego development is greatly speeded with them.

The person, then, who can recognize his emotions and talk about them has an advantage for healing his psychic hurts over the person who cannot. Similarly, the person who can talk, and think, about his motivations is better able to restrain unwise action and to channel his drive energies into effective measures when action is finally taken. Both are processes that strengthen the self-healing powers inherent in the personality. By the same token, both are uses of speech we may try to teach or encourage in a patient whose self-healing has not been adequate to deal with his problems and who therefore has had to come to us. We note again the role of VA as effect, *but also as cause,* of maturation and emotional health.

A note of caution should perhaps be appended about the role of *abreaction* or *ventilation* in therapy. From what I have just said, you might conclude that the mere act of putting one's feelings into words and expressing them to another would suffice for resolving them. Yet most experienced clinicians are justifiably dubious that this can be counted on. My estimate is that helping the patient verbalize is a significant, and sometimes essential, ingredient of therapeutic change, but it is unlikely to be a sufficient one. Edward Bibring (1954, p. 750) asks:

What, then, is the curative mechanism of abreaction? Various therapeutic principles other than "abreaction" (i.e., discharge of emotional tension) are involved in the process of emotional expression. In verbalizing feelings, thoughts, reactions, impulses, conflicts, etc., one learns to see them more clearly, in a more objective perspective. Emotional expression of painful tendencies, when met with sympathy, results in the gratifying feeling of being "accepted" and "understood," of sharing responsibility, and thus offers reassurance. . . .

In brief, the curative value of emotional expression in the treatment of psychoneuroses is not due to abreaction itself, but to a combination with other principles such as manipulation and clarification. . . .

3. *Abstractions and the synthetic function.* In his writing on the developmental sequences in the mind, Kurt Lewin proposed that integration must burgeon simultaneously with differentiation if the person is to be able to coordinate himself and to operate all of a piece. Lewin found it helpful to distinguish, in this regard, between two principles of integration, and contrasted the *simple unity of the person* with his *organizational unity.* In simple unity, the association among ideas and attitudes rests upon such things as their sounding alike, or having occurred together temporally, or having been perceived in adjacent places. The resemblance of this principle to the connections among ideas found in the *primary process* is evident. Organizational unity, however, involves a larger, more logical perspective. Ideas are connected on the grounds of their functional relations—for example, that one act is a means to another, or that several actions must be geared together to achieve an over-all purpose, as in painting or playing an instrument. And, in organizational unity, ideas are also connected on the basis of their logical coherence. The reader may have learned about desks at one stage of his childhood, sofas at another, Tiffany lamps at yet a third. Still, these are all images that might come to mind if he were asked to make an exhaustive listing of "pieces of furniture." In the latter case, he is subsuming all these ideas under an embracing *abstraction.*

The availability of words gives us tools with which to label our abstractions. With these tools, we can communicate more rapidly and conveniently, if not always more precisely. Words as symbols also permit us to sustain longer chains of logical connection among our ideas. And, because they can relate complex structures among attitudes, and subsume varied phenomena under a single label, possession of abstractions markedly supports the synthetic function of the ego. I will not repeat here the explanation offered by Vygotsky of the manner in which words move from interpersonal communication into the internal thought-apparatus. I would just like to emphasize that while weakness in the synthetic function of the ego may reduce VA, the ownership of words may strengthen the synthetic function. It follows that anything in the early life of the child which severely inhibits his verbalization at that age will act to make him more concrete-minded, less able to synthesize in later life. This is true if his environment is action-oriented and intellectually constricted; it will also be true if his parents prohibit or discourage the verbal expression of feelings and urges he is experiencing. Highly vocal people are likely to end up brighter!

We have become increasingly alert to the role of the early life environment in this kind of ego limitation. An astonishing number of youngsters have been located in preschool programs who barely knew their primary colors, for example, and for whom such distinctions as pink, lavender, and the like are meaningless. They are handicapped by a background that is a combination of the limited subculture in which they exist and of parents who either do not stimulate them very much, or whose own speech is similarly barren. I have written earlier of subcultures which seem antagonistic to the development of the ability to express individualities of feeling, as this would threaten the unity of the group. Of necessity, youngsters from such backgrounds are forced to *act,* rather than to talk, just as they think in images rather than in words.

By the same token, *words* are not typically viewed as useful in solving practical problems. It is for this reason that "casework as a problem-solving process" seems to me to expect too much readiness from folks reared in barren environments (Perlman, 1957).

But the nonuse of speech, and words, in trying to reach one's life goals is not simply a result of coming from a culturally deprived background. We frequently find that a middle class youngster has been exposed to parents who customarily use speech manipulatively with their children. "Having a good talk about it" too often, in his experience, turns into a legalistic session which he always loses. As a consequence, he becomes mistrustful of words as vehicles for honest communication. They become, instead, chessmen in an adult's game. As a result, we may later have an adult patient who uses words but without true meaning; the words do not seem to penetrate to any honest level of feeling within him, and we mistakenly say he is *dissociating* or *intellectualizing*. A similar mistrust of words is engendered by mouthing them in hypocritical fashion as so many of my generation has done to the younger, who are now in revolt. It is no wonder they ask why descriptions of the sexual act are "bad," while expressions like war, annihilation, nuclear attack are matters for dignified oration in the Congress and in our churches and synagogues.

Each generation lets down the one that follows. Nowhere is this more visible than in the misuse of verbal symbols. As a result, we have youngsters from culturally deprived backgrounds who have been taught a painfully meager language. And we have adolescents from smug and venal families who have learned to mistrust such words as God, Country, and Justice. Functionally, both groups develop difficulty with symbolic thinking and a consequent lowered ability to put their most important attitudes into speech. It seems to me no accident, therefore, that both the children of the economic slums of the central city and those of the emotional slums of the suburbs should choose to talk in the same argot which, in our time, is called "hippie." Colorful as the speech may sound, in the last analysis it is concrete, repetitious, vague, and incapable of carrying a freight of complexity in meaning and discrimination of feeling.

What role does the integrative capacity play in healing? Here we must remind ourselves of the limits on any therapist! It is not possible for us, literally, to reach inside another person's mind and influence him, as if we were pressing a lever. Typically, all we can do is bring one of his attitudes into juxtaposition with another, and wait to see what happens. The patient who is depressed because she is angry, who then proves to be angry because she is chronically dissatisfied, and who follows this by recognizing she can never be satisfied because she always "wants more" has now phrased her dilemma for herself. Does she, or does she not, want to change so that she is less pushed about by her greediness? Is the joy of overindulgence worth the pain of depressiveness? We can play up one attitude or the other, using lights and shadows to emphasize the picture she is sketching of her own dilemma, but it is she who puts it all together. In the last analysis, it is *her* recognition of the way she is interfering with her own life which will bring about the change in basic attitudes. This recognition involves confronting the conflict between her own competing urges, plus her own pressure to resolve that conflict. It is the *synthetic tendency* of the ego which presses for resolution; but she must abstract even to recognize she has a conflict.

With such a person, of course, one can try to do "treatment at the level of the primary process," as I like to call it. Rather than confronting her emptiness and greed, the worker might try to "meet her needs." This is a maneuver in treatment which sooner or later is bound to fail, because she is insatiable: her emptiness is beyond assuagement. One could also try some form of reward-punishment handling or "behavior therapy" as it is now being called—as if this were not part of the standard technique of all who do effective treatment—without insight on the part of the client. How much more efficiently we can operate if the patient is capable of keeping several attitudes in her consciousness at once and of confronting the contradictions in her life.

The argument between those of us who struggle toward clarification and insight in therapy and those who use other techniques should not result in an either-or choice between two techniques (Miller, 1963). Rather, *if* the patient is capable of the kind of participation in her own cure that I have outlined, it seems grossly inefficient not to involve her. If her ability to abstract and synthesize is deficient, however, other approaches to treatment obviously have to be tried.

4. *Problem-solving.* We have reiterated that all speech, like all thought, is motivated. But it would be a

gross simplification to infer that speech and thought are therefore dedicated to solving life's problems. As we have seen, speech can be used simply for the discharge of accumulating tensions; in the next section, we will emphasize its function in establishing contact between people. Speech can be used primarily in the service of one or another character defense, as we tried to establish in discussing duplicity in the interview. And thinking, as appears so dramatically in the instance of the obsessive, can also be distracted into the service of a pathological defense. The question, really, is what sort of speech by what kinds of people is likely to be used to contribute to problem solution.

Not everyone believes in the value of "talking things over." It is interesting, in this regard, to observe differences among teams of workmen, especially a craftsman and his helper. Some do discuss the work on which they are engaged. In other instances, the talk is simply manipulative, with the person in charge telling the other what he wants done. Often, you can see two mechanics at work on an auto, puzzling about what is wrong but not speaking about it. They may coordinate their work by nonverbal communication—when each has had a look at the same carburetor, both recognize it needs cleaning so there is nothing to be said; they may communicate in images, pointing things out to each other, rather than trying to put them into words. Often the conversation they conduct has nothing whatever to do with whatever it is they are working on.

This absence of verbal communication, certainly the communication of meanings, is most understandable when the task on which they are engaged is purely routine. But suppose they hit a stumbling point, at which they do not know what next to do? Here, too, there are many work groups who still will not discuss the problem. One will silently "study on it" while his partner waits to see what trial-and-error gesture toward solution he comes up with.

Similar phenomena are observable in families. Among the poorer working-class people in our mountains, it is not uncommon that the earlier part of a marriage, especially, consists of two people who still remain closer to their peers of the same sex than they do to each other. The husband still wants to go hunting with the boys at every opportunity; the wife seeks her main entertainment in talking and laughing with her sisters and other young women with whom she grew up. It is fascinating to an outsider to realize how often family decisions are arrived at without discussion. It is easy, in such instances, to overestimate the nonverbal communication that goes on between the couple. Often, this consists of nothing more elaborate than the woman's determination to treat her husband as head of the household, no matter how inadequate he may be, so that she just waits for his decision. There is no belief that by sitting down and talking it over two people may arrive at a solution superior to what either could achieve by himself.

In such a culture, symbolic thinking for the purpose of mastering difficulties tends similarly to be downgraded. It is as if some experience of interpersonal conversation and belief in it is necessary for a young person to develop the greater talent for intrapersonal exchanges. A number of writers, including Plato, have sought to set down their most cogent ideas in the form of dialogues. It appears that the capacity to carry on an internal dialogue is extremely valuable in solving problems of more than average complexity. The ability to sustain an internal conversation within the reaches of one's thought process is more likely among youngsters reared in an environment in which speech is used to carry objective ideas and meanings between people.

Persons without such background find it more difficult to take talking treatment seriously—whether it be casework, counseling, or psychotherapy. At worst, they do not respond to words at all; more typically, they expect communication to be simply manipulative, attempts at influencing: "Tell me what to do to make things right." They can be persuaded, at times, that in order to advise them, one needs first thoroughly to understand their situation, so the exchange becomes one in which they inform and the therapist prescribes. It is a real advance for them to achieve the notion that if both talk, and influence each other, something will come out in which both participants change and grow. It has been my experience that something exciting happens to the therapy when patients can be helped to achieve this latter step.

It is not just that the patient matures in his ability to hold up his half of the problem-solving sequence. I have noticed that simultaneously the patient is doing more "work" outside the formal conferences, conducting self-observing sessions and dialogues with himself. The fact that one side of the dialogue may be identified with the worker (not always accurately!) is important, but it is not what I want to emphasize here. The main point is that he has started to *internalize the goal-directed conversation* which therapy is supposed to be. We may say, therefore, that learning to talk things over has made the client more ready for therapy; it has also strengthened his ego so that he is generally better able to think through problems, using symbolic thought in logical, communicable sequences. And he can *negotiate* with others rather than take refuge in fight-or-flight.

5. *On loving and being loved.* Speech for the purpose of reaching out and touching the other is regarded as at a more primitive level than intentional speech, dedicated to conveying ideas and abstract meanings. Still, a major life goal for any person is certainly to achieve love and to give it to others. One function of the ego is the maintenance of satisfying relationships with objects, resolving the schizoid dilemma—the pursuit and dread of love.

Among civilized adults, aside from the sexual act the greatest intimacy we are able to achieve is through verbal communication. So important is this, that it is not uncommon in marital counseling to meet a wife who complains, typically, that their sexual relationship is not enough, and that sex, itself, is spoiled by the fact that "He never speaks to me."

Lovers, especially new lovers, are often highly verbally

accessible. They do not just talk about themselves for self-display; it is as if they truly want to be known. Fritz Redl described the dynamic once, "As you know me, I become part of you." Hence, speech subserves a major ego function, that of making possible *closeness,* on a level and in a fashion which adults can wholesomely accept in each other. Speech, then, strengthens the ego for the mature management of object-relations. What can be more important in the effectiveness of the personality than that?

Helping a client or patient express his most important attitudes and feelings in words is both growth-enhancing and curative. Moreover, a high degree of verbal accessibility is significant to the self-healing of psychic wounds. To be unable to communicate verbally is to be like a person with a chronically low white cell count. Invaded by infection, he has less chance of throwing it off spontaneously. Offered outside assistance, he can less readily respond to treatment.

For all these reasons, I believe that effort directed at heightening the patient's verbal accessibility is always to the point in any kind of talking treatment. Why this is, and how to bring it about, is of the essence to all of us who help through the spoken word.

References

Bibring, Edward. "Psychoanalysis and the Dynamic Psychotherapies," *Journal of the American Psychoanalytic Association,*
2, 1954, 745–770.

Bowlby, John. "Grief and Mourning in Infancy and Early Childhood." In *The Psychoanalytic Study of the Child,* Vol. 15.
New York: International Universities Press, 1960, pp. 9–52.

Fairbairn, W. Ronald D. *An Object-Relations Theory of Personality.* New York: Basic Books, 1952.

Freud, Anna. *Normality and Pathology in Childhood.* New York:
International Universities Press, 1965.

Ganter, Grace, Margaret Yeakel, and Norman A. Polansky. *Retrieval from Limbo.* New York: Child Welfare League, 1967.

Garrett, Annette. "Modern Casework," in H. J. Parad, ed., *Ego
Psychology and Dynamic Casework.* New York: Family
Service Association of America, 1958.

Hartmann, Heinz. *Essays on Ego Psychology.* New York: International Universities Press, 1964.

Katan, Anny. "Some Thoughts about the Role of Verbalization in
Early Childhood." In *The Psychoanalytic Study of the Child,*
Vol. 16. New York: International Universities Press, 1961.

Kernberg, Otto. "Structural Derivatives of Object Relationship,"
International Journal of Psycho-Analysis, 47, 1966, 236–253.

Lewin, Kurt. *Principles of Topological Psychology.* New York:
McGraw-Hill, 1936.

Meerloo, Joost A. M. *Conversation and Communication.* New
York: International Universities Press, 1952.

Miller, Roger R. "Prospects and Problems in the Study of Ego
Functions," in H. J. Parad and R. R. Miller, eds., *Ego-Ori-
ented Casework: Problems and Perspectives.* New York:
Family Service Association of America, 1963.

Perlman, Helen Harris. *Social Casework, A Problem-Solving Process.* Chicago: University of Chicago Press, 1957.

Russell, Bertrand. *The Autobiography of Bertrand Russell.* Bos-
ton: Little, Brown, 1951.

Name
Index

315

Subject
Index